# MILITARY
# LEADERSHIP
## FOR TOMORROW

# MILITARY
# LEADERSHIP
## FOR TOMORROW

Air Commodore
## Jasjit Singh
AVSM, VrC, VM (Retd)
Editor

**KWW**
KNOWLEDGE WORLD
KW Publishers Pvt Ltd
New Delhi

*in association with*

Centre for Air Power Studies
New Delhi

First Reprint June 2013

The **Centre for Air Power Studies** is an independent, non-profit, academic research institution established in 2002 under a registered Trust to undertake and promote policy-related research, study and discussion on the trends and developments in defence and military issues, especially air power and the aerospace arena, for civil and military purposes. Its publications seek to expand and deepen the understanding of defence, military power, air power and aerospace issues without necessarily reflecting the views of any institution or individuals except those of the authors.

Jasjit Singh
Director General
Centre for Air Power Studies
P-284, Arjan Path
Subroto Park
New Delhi 110010

Tele: (91-11) 25699131
E-mail: diroffice@aerospaceindia.org

KNOWLEDGE WORLD

ISBN 10: 81-87966-58-0
ISBN 13: 978-81-87966-58-6

Cover Design: Sgt V. K. Venu

# Contents

# Contributors

Dr. **Pushpa M. Bhargava** is Vice Chairman, National Knowledge Commission.

Air Marshal **T.M. Asthana** (Retd) is a former Strategic Forces Commander and was the Deputy Chief of the Air Staff of the Indian Air Force. Currently, he is a Distinguished Fellow at the Centre for Air Power Studies, New Delhi.

Colonel **Dennis M. Drew**, USAF (Retd) is Dean of the College of Aerospace Doctrine, Research and Education at the Air University, USAF, Maxwell.

Air Vice Marshal **M. Matheswaran** is Assistant Chief of Air Staff Operations at Air Headquarters.

Professor **David R. Mets** is a Professor Emeritus at the School of Air and Space Studies at USAF Air University and is a former Editor of *Air University Review*,USAF.

Group Captain **A.S. Bahal** is a member of the Directing Staff, College of Air Warfare, IAF, at Secunderabad.

Wing Commander **K.K. Nair**, is a Research Fellow at the Centre for Air Power Studies, New Delhi, and specialises in space studies.

Air Commodore **Jasjit Singh** (Retd) is Director, Centre for Air Power Studies, New Delhi.

Lt. Col. **R. Joe Baldwin**, USAF, is Commander of the 446th Missile Squadron, USAF, and a distinguished scholar.

Group Captain **Arjun Subramaniam** is a Senior Directing Staff at the Defence Services Staff College, Wellington.

Note: The views expressed by the authors are personal to them and do not reflect the opinions or policies of any organisation.

# Military Leadership: An Introductory Essay

*Jasjit Singh*

The *raison d'etre* of a military force, of course, is to apply sanctioned violence in pursuit of national interests and win the nation's wars for it. Clearly the primary business of the soldier is to fight: and that of his military leaders is to ensure that he fights with maximum capability and effect, with minimum costs. This may appear adequate for a broad understanding of the role of military power, but it falls well short of a reasonable definition necessary to examine the role and nature of military leadership. Many more precise definitions are available. But as a starting point, I would note here a critical dimension of military leadership as "the ability to prepare or get ready to fight, skill in actual fighting, and the will to prevail in combat against a foe." However, even on a cursory reading, it is immediately clear that this would not suffice either in terms of a theoretical construct or as a functional template for building the right type of military leadership.

We, of course, have a series of attributes and characteristics that we repeat in our military training establishments for the guidance of our budding leadership, at officer level as well as for those below the officer ranks. These are correct and necessary. But we must ask the question, is the mere teaching of attributes (or even their evaluation in the annual reports) sufficient for our future military leaders or even provide a true picture of the individual? When in active service, I was always amused — and confused — by the column on integrity while evaluating an officer in the ACR (Annual Confidential Report). First of all, this continuing approach makes no distinction between personal and professional integrity, both being crucial in military service. Second, how does one rate another person's integrity on a 9-points scale? One can raise many more questions; but the idea is not to raise questions on current procedures, but to emphasise the reality that military leadership, which must rely heavily on integrity, needs to be understood in the broader context.

One definition based on the US Army doctrine of the 1980s is worth considering as a starting point of our enquiry. This frames military leadership as the art of direct and indirect influence and the skill of creating the conditions for organisational success to accomplish missions effectively. It also points to the role of leadership at different levels: senior leaders would need to exercise their influence with a combination of direct and indirect methods (through regulations, oversight, standard operating procedures, and so on) while the junior leaders would have to rely on direct influence through personal contact and conduct. One example comprises the Regulations of the Indian Air Force 1964 (issued under the authority of the Government of India) which stand above all departmental orders, though often violated by the latter.

Building skills is comparatively easier even in the age of rapid technology change than building the capacity to influence the fighting men who would, by the nature of the profession, have to be engaged in conditions of absolute violence where the final prize for the coward or the brave may be the same: loss of life and limbs. Clarity and consistency in the means, methods and ways of exercising influence, therefore, become important. This adds the factor of environment into the leadership paradigm where, at one end, is the frontline where junior leaders and soldiers face direct enemy action, while at the other, the senior leaders and commanders are normally far removed from the pressures of direct combat. But they are, nevertheless, subject to the demands of operational strategy, carrying the official and moral burden of success and failure of that strategy and/or performance of the forces under their command which they may have had little to do with in terms of training and equipping them for the prevailing environment. This in itself generates a powerful necessity for leadership to develop and rely on an institutional corporate culture and collegiate accountability. Most systems of higher defence organisation have been based on the principles of war since the time the Germans developed the General Staff system during the 19th century which also created the professional leadership system.

The critical difference in direct (frontline junior leadership) and the indirect-direct exercise of influence of higher level leadership rests in the scope and extent of their vision and aims derived from that vision. Both levels require courage, strength and stamina (both physical, intellectual and conceptual) but their vision would remain different. If the senior leaders and commanders begin to think of narrowing their vision to the level of the junior direct leadership paradigm thinking of how battles should be conducted at company level, or a two-aircraft strike mission, etc., we are bound to see failures at both the higher and  tactical unit levels. Many examples abound of this type of problem and each of us who has been through 3-4 decades of military service would be able to recall many of them. This issue raises two aspects of leadership: (i) the vital need for delegation of power and authority to the junior leaders to enable them to exercise the influence that we expect them to, besides the tactical skills and the will to win; and (ii) the critical need for senior leadership and commanders to progressively broaden their vision and conceptual acumen as they move up the inevitable hierarchical pyramid of the fighting forces.

As regards the first, the changing nature of the technological environment and future wars has, in fact, intensified the need to delegate authority and freedom of decision-making down the line rather than micro-manage large (and small) forces from a distant operations room. Here we are likely to face a major challenge, that of technology induction for network-centric warfare where a mass of information from the (land, naval and air war) frontline would not only dispel a great deal of the proverbial "fog of war" but also inundate higher headquarters and leadership, saturating the historical ways and means for war-fighting. And yet the operational logic and theory would demand that this should be used to allow the war-fighter leaders in a platoon, ship or aircraft greater, relevant and timely information to influence the much smaller battlespace that he or she is responsible to influence more effectively and rapidly.

Given the shrinking of military forces worldwide, the infusion of lethal longer range precision strike weapons, and so on, the value and lethality of a unit of firepower have increased enormously. Today, a flight of four Su-30MKI combat aircraft can achieve far more that four dozen or more fighters in the Battle of Britain. A study in 1984 indicated that a formation of four modern strike aircraft could achieve kinetic effects similar to those achieved by 1,000 bombers on oil refineries in II World War.[1] Except that we need to note that the enemy would also be capable of achieving similar effects—a factor often ignored due to the relativity of military conflict in preference to unilateral absolutism as the basis of assessing operational capabilities. The tipping point, as has been throughout military history, would be the area of force employment rather than only technology and size of forces (both very important in their own rights, but optimised by force employment). Hence, the issue of military leadership and its conceptual capacity to visualise the enemy's strategy choices and preempting them become important. We must remember that the enemy is defeated not by defeating/destroying his military forces but by defeating his strategy for employment of force for achieving his aims.

## Culture and Leadership

As the world started to move away from Euro-Atlantic focus and its Cold War, the role of different cultures as a factor in determining the course of today's complex and interconnected world began to be recognised in military power and its employment. Policy-makers and strategists tend to view situations through their own cultural and strategic "lens" with insufficient consideration and calculation of the "other's" perspective and interests. The focus thus far has been on the importance of culture at the tactical and operational levels. There is also a growing recognition by the national security community that culture is an important factor at the policy and strategy levels, and the ability to understand and appreciate the role and impact of culture on policy and strategy is increasingly seen as a critical strategic thinking skill. Cultural proficiency at the policy and strategic levels means the ability to consider history, values, ideology, politics, religion, and other cultural dimensions and assess their potential effect on policy and strategy. A more useful way to consider the role of culture in security studies than through the levels of war (tactical, operational, and strategic), is a framework that includes the following three dimensions: **cultural considerations at the individual level; cultural considerations in tactical and operational level military operations; and cultural considerations at the political and strategic levels.**

The knowledge base for leadership has to include the development of culture (with military characteristics) suited to all three levels with a view to build personal as well as professional integrity concurrently. This raises another aspect: the absence of recognising culture (though present in real life, shaped in some segments of the armed forces like that of the infantry's regimental ethos and traditions). If we wish to correct this and inculcate a culture that imbibes the larger loyalty to the nation and the armed forces, we would actually be also creating the foundations of jointness as well as corporate responsibility as indeed happens in other professions like the medical seen clearly in the operation theatre when open heart surgery is going on. What is needed is recognition of the need for developing and strengthening a common code and culture and this requires building institutions that promote the development of culture without getting bogged down by regimental loyalties and turf battles.

## Moral and Ethical Military Leadership

Any study of military leadership, especially the problems and solutions related to value-based character in the armed forces must, by definition, examine the issue of moral and ethical values and the related aspects in the military systems. These inevitably cover a vast spectrum, ranging from the issues of just war to the issues of personal morality and professional ethics. Present society tends to separate the issues of personal and professional ethics into separate compartments on the grounds of "realism" and the right to follow more liberal (even promiscuous) personal conduct while being willing to accept norms, rules and practices that limit liberty in professional life. And when we want to look at value-based character in the armed forces, it would be useful to narrow our focus in the context of this examination to the military leadership.

It is axiomatic that the military in any nation would be a reflection of the society outside. Since the theme of our examination relates to "values," we must, therefore, look at some basics closely in relation to the issues involved, both in the society outside and the military itself. This takes us to the issue of the core values of our nation. Do educated, knowledgeable, and responsible people adequately understand the core values of our nation-state? While the basic tenets are all laid down in the Constitution, can we state with any degree of confidence that these tenets (like the central concept that all human beings are equal, hence, "we the people" value liberty, equality, social justice, etc.) and their moral-ethical dimensions have been imbibed by our society six decades after the Constitution was adopted?

## Herein Lies a Serious Problem

There is a broad agreement among thinking people in our country that our values have deteriorated over the decades, if they have not actually been lost. Corruption in all its dimensions, graft, crime, unwillingness to insist on the right values even when they are known and individually respected are now by-words in our society. But few sit down to reflect, leave alone analyse why is that so, and, hence, what remedial measures should be taken beyond expressing the desire for better values and better "governance" When we want to look at the armed forces, the need for such an analysis is obviously greater since military men are in the profession of life and death on which depends the well-being of the society, the integrity and even the survival of the state. The study of the trends in the society at large in terms of morals and ethics, therefore, becomes an essential ingredient of any study of the military leadership.

It is well recognised that moral values and ethics are imbibed by people from the environment in which they grow up, the "teaching" that they receive from the education (formal and informal) process they go through, religion and its interpretations, the example of others, especially those who become their role models, etc. In other words, the family, the school, and the temple/church/mosque are the key places from where our values are propagated and imbibed. Personal convictions — a critical driver in value-based character — develop from family, community, education, religious/spiritual upbringing and peer influence. These convictions form the bedrock of moral character, shaping it long before the individual joins the military profession.

But rapid and extensive changes in the lives of people have been leading to trends that need to be noted:

- India is going through a phenomenal transition in socio-economic terms which is altering the main structures that create the basis of moral values and their practice. While we see the traditional foundations of moral values weakening, the new ones have yet to emerge. The point of concern is that we don't seem to be making sufficient effort to conceptualise and internalise the traditional values required in the new socio-economic milieu.

- Increasing consumerism, rapidly rising expectations and increasing gap between aspirations and realities have triggered a rising sense of relative deprivation, with a strong urge to improve one's own quality of life as quickly as possible, jettisoning moral values and concerns about the common good; there is a growing degree of cynicism in society.

- The family structure and its influence are increasingly under stress. In particular, the joint family systems are dissolving into nuclear families where working parents are able to devote much less time to inculcating moral and ethical values in children.

- School education has been losing its moral punch since it now places heavy emphasis on academic studies and very high percentages of marks are needed for college admissions, with the result that little attention is given to all round character development. Our poor performance in sports, especially team events, is another manifestation of the same trend. Daniel R. Levine noted a decade ago that in the United States, "Honesty and integrity have been replaced in many classrooms by a win-at-any-cost attitude that puts grades, expediency and personal gain above all else."[2]

- Peer influence has been leaning toward greater personal freedom and lower emphasis on doing the right thing under the rubric of "realism;" the general thinking in society today is that "if it does not hurt anyone else, then I can do whatever I wish" or, "what I do in private life is my business."

- Rapidly increasing urbanisation, rising prosperity and concurrent inequities add a host of other factors that have increased the potential and occurrence of turbulence in society; and morals and ethics get buffeted by such turbulence at an early stage itself, leaving many individuals confused and even ignorant of what is critical beyond the glitter of modern consumerist life.

- While religion has assumed greater salience as an emotional anchor, its ritualisation and exploitation for narrow (mostly material) ends has deprived society of the opportunity to use it for strengthening moral values.

## Military Society and Leadership

*In order to be a leader, a man must have followers. And to have followers, a man must have their confidence. Hence, the supreme quality for a leader is unquestionably integrity.*

– Gen Dwight Eisenhower

It is against the above context that we need to look at the issues of value-based character in the armed forces. The profession of arms is unique in that it has to continuously prepare for, be ready for, and engage in, extremes of violent conflict, where the inevitable end-point of both bravery and cowardice for survivors is death. That is why the values that are required in the armed forces are even more demanding than in other civil professions, leave alone normal peace-time civilian life. This is also the reason why most civilians find it difficult to understand the armed forces and their role and ethos. Some of the questions that are relevant may be noted:

- Assuming that we are clear about, and believe in, our national core values (which I do believe), are we clear about the core values of the military and military leadership?
- Where do moral principles and ethics fit into these core values?
- Do we value our core values?

Obviously, moral values must take the central place in the core values of the armed forces since the military man is engaged in the noblest of professions where he willingly gives his today for his people's tomorrow. Almost 2,500 years ago, Alexsander the Great rose to be one of history's greatest warriors and military leader.[3] His mentor, Aristotle, pointed out that moral credit is not automatic when right actions are done, nor is it enough to know what is right or to say what is right. He suggested that we are morally praiseworthy when we perform a right action if we, first of all, *know* that the action is right, not for a personal goal or prize, second, that we choose the act for its own sake because we know it is right; and third, that we perform action from a firm *habit* of performing that kind of action consistently. This can be achieved only on the basis of moral virtues through habit that becomes part of our character — in other words, on the strength of integrity, both personal and professional.

One can go deeper into this and other aspects that lead to the issues of personal and professional integrity in the armed forces. But if we look briefly at the factors affecting the value system in society at large and the armed forces in specific, then it is clear that we need conscious and institutional processes to inculcate the value system in the context of the realities of modern life. In other words, if the family structure is changing, then we need to strengthen the "family" structure of the armed forces further to provide the strength in the moral fibre which otherwise may begin to fray, especially under stress and danger which perhaps is the only constant in the military profession. If consumerism is altering attitudes and beliefs, we need to find alternatives that are appealing. If the traditional insulation between the armed forces and society is fading away, then we need to ensure that the moral and ethical values in the military are reinforced by suitable steps.

In other words, what we need is much greater focus on education in the social sciences and humanities, with focus on knowledge (as Dr Bhargava highlights in his chapter) and moral values and ethics, ranging from the issues of just war to personal and professional integrity. And this process has to start at the earliest stages of the individual's contact with the armed forces. My central point is that our leadership training (there is very little education) needs to be redesigned to include inculcation of moral values and ethics as an important subject. At present, we seem to be appending reference to moral values to general training on leadership and that too on the attributes and qualities of leadership rather than its conceptual foundations.

But equally, if not more, important, is the critical need to institute (professional) education for those in the military who have the potential to go up the command chain. The focus on education should not be seen as a diversion from "professional" training of military leaders, but something that must grow and increase across a wider spectrum of issues and trends.

The world and its events have become far less predictable than the comfort decades of the Cold War. In this process, the role and tasks of military power have been undergoing phenomenal changes due to technological advances, ideological motivation to apply ruthless violence on innocent citizens (as, indeed, the radical *jihadi* organisation are doing), spread of nuclearisation in Asia and the complications it adds to the security and stability equations around the world, and so on. Application of military power and waging of war, which historically had remained the preserve of militaries, has now been opened wide with the phenomenal spread of sophisticated weapons with high lethality. The era when diplomats and soldiers had a clearer division of labour, in that, when the diplomats failed, the soldiers were called out; and when the soldiers failed or succeeded, the diplomats were called out again, is over. This insulated equation passed into history long ago.

## Notes

1.    See Jasjit Singh, *Air Power in Modern Warfare* (New Delhi: Lancer International, 1985), p. 157.
2.    Daniel R. Levine, "Cheating in Our Schools: A National Scandal," *Reader's Digest,* October 1995, p.66
3.    For one of the best interpretation of his life and strategy, see Partha Bose, *Alexander the Great's Art of Strategy* (New Delhi: Penguin-Viking, 2003).

# 1

# Knowledge and Leadership

*Pushpa M. Bhargava*

Knowledge is quaint; it evolves and multiplies when shared. Can you think of any other thing for which this is true? It is this growth of knowledge through accretion, following its sharing and dissemination, that has been at the base of human progress.

But that is not the only attribute of knowledge. It has many others, some of which are mentioned below.

- For a citizen of any country to protect his rights and discharge his responsibilities, he/she needs to have a certain minimum amount of knowledge.

- For anyone to survive gainfully in the wake of ever-increasing competition, and maintain his self-respect and escape exploitation, he will, today, need to be both a specialist and a generalist.

- There is a hierarchy of data, information, knowledge and wisdom. For information, one needs data. For knowledge, one needs information. For conversion of information into knowledge, one needs wisdom. Knowledge requires collation of information from multiple sources and of multiple kinds. Conversion of knowledge into wisdom requires weaving of experience (one's own and also collective) into the fabric of knowledge.

- Ignorance comes as a package, while knowledge comes in bits. Ignorance is thrust on people; knowledge is acquired. Ignorance is like sand; knowledge is like rock.

- Today, knowledge knows to boundaries, and is a continuum. Man compartmentalises knowledge as an alibi for ignorance.

- There is a direct relationship between a knowledge-based society and good governance; neither has any relationship to affluence. As there is no country in the world today that has a truly knowledge-based society, in no country is governance anywhere near ideal.

- The higher we go up in the hierarchy of power, the greater is the demand for knowledge—not of just one discipline but of the whole continuum—but, generally, the lesser is the knowledge-base. This opens up doors for exploitation by self-interest groups operating nationally or internationally.
- It is not enough to be knowledgeable or have access to knowledge: it is more important to use it when required to ensure equity.
- Religious fundamentalism and terrorism, obscurantism, superstition, and irrational practices are a consequence of vested interests that insulate people from knowledge.
- A knowledge-based society is easier to govern, provided the government intends to be honest, fair, transparent and people-oriented. On the other hand, a selfish and/or totalitarian government does not want its people to be truly knowledgeable.
- Today, knowledge dissemination, not only in the developing countries but also in the developed countries, is extremely uneven. This unevenness provides, perhaps, the largest base for exploitation.
- Mechanisms of knowledge generation, dissemination and use around the world are faulty to various degrees, creating a fertile ground for growth of exploitation.
- Knowledge remains stagnant and decays when kept confined.
- Knowledge equity within a country and between countries is essential for world peace. Knowledge inequity is the most important avenue of exploitation and neo-colonialism.
- Globalisation of knowledge equity will lead, in succession, to: globalisation of rights and responsibilities; globalisation of access, of employment, and of facilities; breaking of barriers that divide people arbitrarily; globalisation of peace, and, thus, progress towards one world.

A large number of examples can be given from all periods of history in support of each of the above statements. I shall, however, confine myself in this respect to what I have said above about religious fundamentalism and terrorism. I will make just two statements in this connection:

- I believe that all religious fundamentalism and terrorism, be it Hindu, Islamic, Zionist or Christian—now or in the past—is a consequence of what I have termed elsewhere as the "seven deadly sins of the clergy,"[1] one of which is to keep people insulated from knowledge.

- Prince Ghazi of Jordan, who is the special envoy of His Majesty King Abdullah of Jordan and has a Ph.D from Cambridge, has, in his scholarly book[2] written under the pseudonym of Vincent Oliveti, attributed Islamic fundamentalism and terrorism to a lack of knowledge and deliberate misinterpretation of the teachings of the prophet as documented in the original Quran, by the Wahhabi-Salafi sect of Muslims that is largely controlled by the clergy.

In the world of tomorrow, knowledge will be power and absolute knowledge will be absolute power. It follows that any effective leadership of tomorrow will have to be a knowledge-based leadership. In this context, one could, perhaps, consider the following "Ten Commandments" as the recipe for knowledge-based leadership.

- Be aware of the attributes of knowledge.
- Recognise the hierarchy between data, information, knowledge and wisdom.
- Learn to convert data into information, information into knowledge, and knowledge into wisdom, by collation and experience.
- Attempt to be a reservoir of knowledge and wisdom of a high order.
- Institute a system that will ensure that knowledge relevant to one's responsibilities is kept updated and is always state-of-the-art.
- Respect the knowledge of others.
- Encourage others to acquire knowledge.
- Share, and not monopolise, knowledge.
- Use knowledge widely and in the largest interest of the largest number of people.
- Encourage questioning and institutionalise dissent.

An area where leadership would be of utmost importance is that of national security for which our defence Services are responsible. The country is already proud of its army, air force, and navy, and the quality of leadership in these three Services. I have no doubt whatsoever that in the years to come, this leadership would grow to be a most effective knowledge-based leadership. What I have said above, I hope, may be of some help in this evolution.

## Notes

1.  P.M. Bhargava, "Seven Deadly Sins of the Clergy," *The Tribune*, January 2, 2006.
2.  V. Oliveti, *Terror Source: The Ideology of Wahhabi-Salafism and its Consequences* (Birmingham: Amadeus Books, 2002).

# 2

# Nature of Aerospace Power in the Coming Decades

*T.M. Asthana*

## Introduction

With the launch of the Sputnik on October 4, 1957, we entered the space age. In the early years, the race for excellence in space was a bipolar issue with Neil Armstrong in Apollo 11 landing on the moon on July 21, 1969. The USA has since then virtually maintained the upper hand in supremacy in space. The military potential of space was realised only in the 1970s, which finally led to full-fledged application of space power in Operation Desert Storm in January 1991. Subsequent operations relied more and more on space. Where 50 satellites were utilised in January 1991 for Desert Storm (of which a minimum 18 were on station at all times), for Operation Iraqi Freedom in April 2003, over 100 satellites were pressed into service. Proportionally, the bandwidth utilised also increased from 99 Mbps in 1991 to 3200 Mbps in 2003. Analysts and experts opine that we have seen only the tip of the iceberg. Space has graduated from civilian use in terms of weather forecasts, etc to participation in operations, both civil and military. Recent military operations witnessed by the world give us a glimpse of how economical and precise they can be, if they are supported by space power.

In the 1960s, space power and air power stood blurred. When space power was actually applied first, it was utilised primarily in three distinct areas, viz. decision-making, planning and execution. The contributions of space power are responsible for the theories of **"Five Ring Targetting"** by John Warden and **"Parallel Warfare"** by David Deptulla, which were so effectively employed in Desert Storm. Simultaneous engagement of strategic, operational and tactical target systems restricted the enemy's ability to recoup, realign or offer a counter. From then onwards, it became clear that the integration of air and space powers could provide rich dividends. As the two theories that evolved in Desert Storm provided economical, optimal and telling options with minimal attrition, it was argued that aerospace power had to be unmistakably meshed into one.

Military operations have progressed from land, to land and sea, to land, sea and air, and now, we need to factor in space power, which has demonstrated its immense potential in an incremental manner. Indeed, we will continue to witness increments in land, sea and air power as well. Military operations will be compelled to synergistically employ them to advantage along with space power. Today, India is an established and well recognised nuclear as well as space power. It is important, therefore, for us to absorb the fact that space, or rather, aerospace power to promote military operations, is here to stay.

The subject of air power is well absorbed today. However, I intend to reiterate some salient aspects before I proceed with the rest of the subject matter.

## Air Power

Ever since Giulio Douhet's "Command of the Air (1921)," we have heard that massed effects against an enemy's centres of gravity can lead to bloodless victory. Every war since then has increasingly seen this theory's vigorous application and air power today stands on a pedestal. Certain terminologies have emerged that we need to keep in mind as we progress. Surveillance, reconnaissance and intelligence i.e. ISR are the oldest and essential elements in the planning and execution of missions. ISR has today reached capabilities to achieve near real-time relays of information. The fundamental responsibility of ISR is to provide **objective directed** intelligence to decision-makers at all levels of command. Surveillance is a relatively regular monitoring activity, whereas reconnaissance is a search for specific intelligence, possibly of a more urgent nature. Together, ISR operations provide the key pieces of intelligence information that help the air force achieve information superiority. ISR operations provide the

NATURE OF AEROSPACE POWER IN THE COMING DECADES    7

best possible intelligence to the commander, producing 'actionable' and predictive intelligence information that can be quickly applied to arrive at operational decisions. Operational optimisation of hyper spectral imagery can even identify targets through camouflage.

Three distinct attributes of air operations make it place heavier demands on ISR operations. These are: reduced reaction timeframes, capability to concentrate forces and firepower with little or no warning, and precision attacks. ISR contributes in a telling manner to achieve air, space, and information superiority, and, hence, ISR must be integrated into campaign planning. Over the years, it has been established that air power application demands central planning and decentralised execution. In our case, strategic planning of air operations is achieved at Air Headquarters while operational and tactical level planning of air operations is delegated to commands. Execution in all cases is decentralised.

The air operations of the Kosovo War produced the terminology "effects-based operations or EBO." Knowledge, information, and intelligence are the keys to application of EBO. An EBO approach starts from the (top down) high level systems perspective and explicitly seeks to understand oneself, an adversary, or any other context where elements interrelate, interconnect or otherwise are interdependent. In a sense, EBO is a revisiting of historical wisdom. Sun Tzu, Clausewitz and Machiavelli have referred to this phenomenon and EBO merely formalised the concept. EBO can be seen as a large-scale chess game in which the moves of the enemy are limited systematically. It inflicts paralysis upon an enemy, using multiple simultaneous attacks. In other words, EBO conducts parallel war. The erstwhile strike aircraft packages that were bulky, are losing their tail, with the number of aircraft tasked for a mission reducing, thus, permitting the released aircraft to resort to parallel warfare. An effects-based approach achieves economy of force as well. As technological innovation accelerates, "non-lethal" weapons and cyberwar will also become operative means of EBO. When the central theme of an operation is EBO, and where precision guided munitions are used, the application of air power ensures minimum collateral or unintended damage. It's never going to make wars bloodless but I think the way all the Services are headed, with the air force leading, much can be achieved in this sphere of operations. At the strategic level, the EBO approach is of as much relevance to "winning the peace" as it is to winning wars.

## The Space Power Conundrum

The term aerospace will be copiously used today in this seminar, yet one finds much vacillation at the highest command levels concerning the medium in which the air force operates. Military analysts too vacillate from using the time-honoured appellation "aerospace" to "air and space" (which, it was said, would some day become space and air) and then back again to "aerospace." Such inconstancy highlights the difficulty airmen face when considering mature air power capabilities, the promise of space power, and the nexus between air and space power.

To date, space applications have been restricted to military support operations only. This is perhaps to ensure adherence to the **Outer Space Treaty of 1967,** which was adopted by all contemporary members of the UN. **This treaty prohibits location of weapons of mass destruction (WMD), claims of territorial sovereignty, establishment of military bases, testing of weapons or military manoeuvres in space.** Consequently, facilities available from space-based assets are meteorological, surveillance, reconnaissance, imagery, navigation aids, electronic warfare, search and rescue, geodesy, and communications. Space and space power are subjects of obvious and growing importance, but our consideration of them is hobbled by a dearth of conceptual thinking about the role of space in military operational matters. For much of its history, scientific wizards rather than operational warriors dominated the military-space community. As a result, military space power is still looking for its great theorist. Despite the paucity of general theory, space operations unquestionably have become vitally important to military operations. Command, control, communications, intelligence, weather, reconnaissance, surveillance and mapping are the most obvious areas in which space plays a major role. But even with the growing importance of space operations, how should air force leaders think about space power? Without some overarching theoretical framework, space and space operations remain only a collection of capabilities, albeit very important capabilities. Three sets of fundamental issues must be vetted if we are to understand space power with the kind of clarity with which we now understand air power, and if we are to understand their nexus.

**First**, we must determine whether the essence actually applies to space power, as we assume it to be. Can space power "apply great power quickly to any tangible target on the planet?" Many people would answer "no" to this question because of political restraints on weaponising space. Others would argue for an affirmative answer based on technical, if not political, feasibility. In either case, the questions concerning the applicability of the essence remain assumed but undemonstrated. Or perhaps there exists a space power version of the essence that differs from all other military operations, including air power.

The **second** group of issues concerns the future of space power. What kinds of military operations are likely to migrate to space, and why? Space may become another "battle space," or it may become only a home to military operations focussed on non-lethal activities in support of combat elsewhere. The horizon is wide open on the options and ramifications of these alternative futures. Let us further examine the "Battle for Space" issue. The versatility of the satellite and the increasing dependence on satellite-based inputs have raised it to a level far higher than just a valuable asset; it would now be indispensable, a fact that has put the satellite under threat. The international community has been deadlocked for years in achieving a ban on space weapons. Notwithstanding, a framework policy needs to be worked out which lays down its aims for dominating space in times of conflict. The goal is to maintain the tremendous military advantages that accrue from using satellites. This document should include an outline of the air force's intent to use the means necessary to prevent an adversary from using satellites for purposes like communications relay, intelligence gathering and timing functions in times of war. In fact, the focus on attack probably would have more to do, at least in the near term, with satellite ground stations and the satellite's communications signals rather than the satellite itself. There is a range of alternatives being explored or under consideration, including options for destroying or jamming the links between an adversary's satellite and earth. If we were in a classified session, I could say more, in terms of non-conventional warfare, but I cannot do so now. Conversely, critics contend that this document (doctrine?) and the fledgling offensive counter-space mission represent the intellectual underpinning of a major shift in thinking that, whether intentionally or not, could lead to the global community crossing the threshold of combat in space. Interestingly, these divergent camps agree that satellites have become an integral component of war-fighting and an indispensable component of global economic and scientific progress. Accordingly, each advocates the need to act now to protect the sanctity of these assets in times of conflict as well as in times of peace. The 1972 Anti-Ballistic Missile (ABM) Treaty prohibits the deployment of space-based weapons to shoot down long-range missiles, but it is virtually defunct since 2002 thanks to the USA. The global debate over weaponising of space is not new, but the international community has been ineffectual in reaching consensus on how to ban all weapons from orbit and prevent spacecraft from being targeted. The UN's Conference on Disarmament (CD) has been essentially deadlocked since 1998.

The **third** set of issues has to do with the relationship between space power and air power. The defining characteristic is an operational regime elevated above the earth's surface. Conceptually, space power would seem to be more of the same at a higher elevation, a concept tacitly endorsed by the air force's basic doctrine. The term aerospace echoes this same theme, as do official pronouncements such as "although there are physical differences between the atmosphere and space, there is no absolute boundary between them. The same basic military activities can be performed in each, albeit with different platforms and methods." But in our conceptual thinking, can we so easily ignore the vast differences between operations in the atmosphere and in space? It is difficult to analyse these and many more issues dealing with space without a general, overarching theory of space power. The task is made even more difficult by several other factors such as limited experience base in military-space operations, the tight security classification concerning much of what goes on in space, and the thoroughly sub-divided responsibility for space operations. Thus, we have a conundrum—a jigsaw puzzle that will some day picture how space power fits or does not fit with air power. Solving the puzzle represents a major leadership challenge.

## Space Command

It is obvious, therefore, that the military must guard against having our dependence on space turn into a vulnerability. Protecting our freedom to use space while having the ability to deny an enemy's use of space will grow more important in the future. We know that when the challenge comes, our nation's leadership will turn to us (the military) for answers. There is no doubt in the minds of most military analysts that conflict in space is inevitable, and that, in the not too distant future. The nation will look upon the military to deal with this form of conflict. Although many military leaders have come to appreciate the criticality of space in the future of warfare, they have not yet embraced the full vision of the Space Command. **Space is the military instrument of national power today and tomorrow**.

We also need to be aware of the fact that the nation will some day pursue a ballistic missile defence programme, be it theatre or national missile defence. The military role in space as envisaged today calls for executing four basic missions in space. These are: space support, force enhancement, force application and space control. A brief description of each of these mission areas will help clarify the roles and responsibilities of the military in space.

**Space Support.** This mission area supports space forces. This is carried out by terrestrial-based elements to "sustain, surge, and reconstitute" elements of a military space system or capability. These activities deploy and operate spacecraft and involve launch and satellite operations.

**Force Enhancement.** Force enhancement operations consist of the operations conducted from space with the objective of enabling or supporting terrestrial-based forces. This is the most generally understood of the four military missions and includes navigation, communication, weather, surveillance, reconnaissance and ballistic missile warning.

**Force Application.** The application of force would consist of attacks against terrestrial-based targets carried out by military weapon systems operating in space. There are currently no force application assets operating in space. Such systems would be developed and used only when it is consistent with the national policy. Often, ballistic missile defence systems that would be based in space are referred to as force application weapons. The air force would classify this mission as space control (see below) because such a weapon would not be attacking a target on the earth.

**Space Control.** By far, the mission area that receives the most attention and the most specific direction is space control—which, among other things, must deal with conflict in space. In military terms, space control amounts to "counter-space" and "space defence." Counter-space is the mission carried out to achieve space control. Offensive counter-space operations destroy or neutralise an adversary's space systems through attack on the space, ground, or link segments of these systems. Defensive counter-space consists of active or passive operations to protect our capabilities from attack or interference. Space control need not necessarily include combat operations in space, but the need for some space weapons in order to accomplish the full space control mission seems inevitable. These systems must have lethal and non-lethal capabilities, be able to inflict either temporary or permanent damage, and must be able to destroy, disrupt, delay, degrade, or deny the adversary's space assets.

**Logically, therefore, an organisation such as a Space Command is called for.**

## Merging Air and Space

On June 21, 2004, another first for humanity was achieved when a 62-year-old American called Michael Melville reached an altitude higher than 62 miles and became the first citizen to fly a craft into, what is technically, space. The vehicle he piloted, Space Ship One, was designed to win the US $10 million Ansari X Prize. The concept of hypersonic aircraft seems like an unlikely dream today but research is in progress. Theories suggest that rockets would propel aircraft into, and out of, space. The propulsion in space could be provided by "scramjet," or "supersonic combustion ramjet," which are basically "pulse detonation wave" engines, utilising liquid methane directed onto the hot fuselage. This, in turn, manages the shock waves, contributing to minimising energy losses and it is estimated that this would permit hypersonic aircraft to attain up to Mach 10 at the lower levels of low earth orbit (LEO). These aircraft could be used as weapon platforms, including anti-satellite (ASAT) weapons, as also to deploy satellites. Unarmed aerial vehicles (UAVs) too are making a niche for themselves through miniaturisation and advanced propulsion techniques, enabling them to operate at near LEO levels with enhanced endurance or loiter. It has, therefore, been opined that air and space will merge, and aerospace power will be the norm. In the Gulf War, Lt Gen Michael Moseley, the combined forces air component commander (CFACC) was also designated as the "Space Coordinating Authority" and charged with integrating space related activities for all US Services and intelligence agencies. Perhaps most important, and unique, from a space perspective, is the introduction of the concept of migrating missions from air to space as time and technology allow. The one mission that does not effectively migrate is the mission of space control i.e. the mission of space superiority. But this is a mission that all air force officers understand completely. The first mission of the air force in any conflict is to establish air superiority. Without air superiority, no other military mission is possible without extreme risk. The same is true for space. Operating from space makes more sense, from a military perspective, than operating in the atmosphere alone.

## Aerospace Command

The term "aerospace" was coined in 1958 to encompass the continuous medium, including both air and space. As the second half of the 20th century has matured the air realm, the first half of this next century will mature our aerospace realm. We speak of aerospace power because we no longer view space as a remote place beyond our reach. We should think of the aerospace domain as a seamless volume, in which, and from which, we provide military capabilities in support of national security. This is based on the realistic premise that the air force, in conjunction with the Aerospace Command, will have the capability to deliver precision guided munitions integrated into a system that provides global, high resolution sensing, precision targeting, and responsive command and control. This system would permit destruction of the EBO target with complete surprise, immunity to currently fielded active defences, and a lower prospect of collateral damage. It could equally well conduct photo reconnaissance missions at the most opportune moment, which may go undetected. **If we want all this, an Aerospace Command is a MUST.**

I have no hesitation in accepting the fact that space contributions, indeed, are also of grave concern to the other two Services. In view of the facts that space control missions comprising space counter-measures and space defence are the current vocabulary in air power understanding, manned hypersonic aircraft will be a military instrument, and extended reach at the call of a button (with air-to-air refuelling—AAR) will be the norm for the air force, the dominating presence in any space command structure will be the air force. It is mandatory that complements of the army and navy work alongside the Aerospace Command in a fashion that is mutually arrived at. The United States Air Force (USAF) Doctrine Document 2-2 of 1998 stipulates that the Air Force Space Command contributes 93 per cent of all military personnel and utilises 90 per cent of the military space budget. Each Service i.e. army navy, marines have component Space Commands subordinate to the US Aerospace Command.

## Principles of War

Rather than a summary or conclusion, I intend to attempt redefining the principles of war when aerospace comes of age in warfare. Aerospace forces are inherently offensive—even when defending, they attack. Aggressive defeat of the enemy's aerospace force is the airman's first priority in warfare—it makes all other operations possible. It is my firm belief that as the aerospace concept of operations develops, the Principles of War would need redefining as follows:

- **Unity of Command.** Unity of command is critical to prudent use of aerospace forces. Centralised command and control is the key to fusing the multiple capabilities that produce aerospace power. The momentary misapplication of aerospace forces is more likely to have immediate strategic consequences than is the case with surface forces. Hence, centralised control, with decentralised execution should be the norm.
- **Security.** The lethality of aerospace forces makes the security of friendly forces from enemy air power a paramount concern. Security may require the elimination/degradation of the enemy's aerospace capabilities.
- **Surprise**. Surprise depends on initiative and is made more attainable by the versatility of aerospace power. Where, when, or how an enemy is struck

is relatively independent of where and how aerospace forces are postured. Choice of time and place always rests with the commander of superior aerospace forces. Surprise is aerospace power's strongest advantage.

- **Flexibility/Versatility**. The ability to concentrate force anywhere and attack any facet of the enemy's power is the outstanding strength of aerospace power. It should be fully used and not compromised.

- **Mass and Manoeuvre**. The speed with which forces manoeuvre in three dimensions allows them to achieve mass faster than surface forces. The commander of forces operating in three dimensions does not sacrifice manoeuvre when mass is achieved—mass and manoeuvre can be employed simultaneously. The simultaneous employment of mass and manoeuvre by aerospace forces creates tremendous leverage when applied against surface forces.

- **Simplicity.** Planning, logistics, and administrative support are complex for all types of forces but, generally, less so for aerospace forces compared to surface forces possessing equivalent combat power. The fluid, featureless, boundless nature of the aerospace environment makes the execution of aerospace operations elegantly simple.

- **Economy of Force.** This principle describes precisely the greatest vulnerability of aerospace power. The misuse of aerospace power can reduce its contribution more than enemy action. Because aerospace power is precious, it must be conserved by caring and competent airmen.

- **Concentration.** Aerospace power is most effective when it is focussed in purpose and not needlessly dispersed.

- **Synergy**. Internally, the missions of aerospace power, when applied in comprehensive and mutually supportive air campaigns, produce effects well beyond the proportion of each mission's individual contribution to the campaign. Externally, aerospace missions can be applied in coordinated joint campaigns with surface forces, either to enhance, or be enhanced by, surface forces.

- **Persistence**. Aerospace power should be applied persistently. Resourceful enemies may rebuild destroyed targets. Air commanders should plan for repeat strikes against important targets.

# 3
# The Essence of Aerospace Power: What Leaders Need to Know

*Dennis M. Drew*

The US military became the ultimate victim of its own success following quiet victory in the Cold War and thunderous triumph in the Gulf War. Political decision-makers challenged the need for such a powerful military when there appeared to be no "peer competitors," and the downsizing began in earnest. The US Air Force was not spared, as its operational heart for the previous 45 years was ripped apart and replaced with smaller pieces in unfamiliar patterns. At the same time, a bewildering array of operational requirements began to stretch the reduced force to the limit. In a bitter irony for airmen caught up in the escalating operations tempo, many of these operations probably would not have been necessary during the Cold War. Victory in the Cold War seemed to confirm the old adage that no good deed goes unpunished (*sic*).

The angst and confusion created major leadership challenges, one of which was the need to redefine the air force. But well-intentioned efforts only added more confusion to an already chaotic situation. In a sense, we tried too hard, too often, and in too many ways. Three different air force vision statements appeared in just one decade: "Global Reach, Global Power" in 1990; "Global Engagement" in 1996; and "Global Vigilance, Reach, and Power" in 2000. Adding to the muddle were the newly minted air force "core competencies," the basic areas of expertise the air force brings to any activity."[1] Unfortunately, even these were quickly amended to accommodate items apparently forgotten.

We gratefully acknowledge the permission of *Aerospace Journal* (USAF) to reproduce this article.

The near-chaotic pace of change and the confusion it continues to generate present enormous leadership challenges that will likely remain with us well into the future.[2] The key to success in dealing with these challenges lies in understanding what aerospace power is all about. After a century of experience in the air and over four decades in space, how can we articulate what makes aerospace power unique? This article answers that key question by deriving and examining the "essence of aerospace power," including its absolute requirements and very real limitations. It explains how the essence provides the psychological and operational rationale for an independent air force and looks at conceptual difficulties surrounding the space portion of aerospace power. Finally, the article casts a glance at the future by noting the dilemma facing airmen as they fly into the third millennium.

## Deriving the Essence of Aerospace Power

In trying to understand what airmen are all about, we must ask the critical question: what capabilities make aerospace power unique? The answer is not found in the relative advantages of speed, range, flexibility, and so forth, spawned by operating in the third dimension. Rather, what sets aerospace power apart is the product of those relative advantages, the essence of aerospace power, which holds that only aerospace power can apply great power quickly to any tangible target on the planet.

## Parsing the Essence

Note that aerospace power rather than air force appears in the statement above. The essence of aerospace power has little to do with ownership. It exists whether one speaks of the US Air Force, aviation elements of the other Services, or air power possessed by allies and adversaries. Obviously, not every air force or aviation organisation has the "full-service" force structure that can totally fulfill the essence.

The word quickly defines one of the cardinal advantages of airmen over surface forces. The speed at which modern aerospace forces can travel to any point on the globe is orders of magnitude greater than that of the fastest surface forces. No place on earth is more than a few hours away, and traditional defensive barriers such as the great oceans no longer provide sanctuary. By the beginning of the second half of the 20th century, air power gave every military threat a sense of immediacy, and war became a "come as you are" affair—a situation that intensified with the dawn of space capabilities.

Perhaps the most important, and certainly the most misinterpreted, word in the **essence** is **power**. Traditionally, power has related to explosive ordnance and target destruction, nuclear weapons serving as the ultimate example. But in the post-Cold War world, the "power" most often delivered by airmen has taken the form of humanitarian aid: food, medical supplies, and heavy equipment. Power can also include people—peace-keepers to the latest crisis, technical experts essential to an important foreign air programme, or diplomats trying to avoid war. Shuttle diplomacy is a child of the aerospace age.

Power can also include information. Knowledge is the purest form of power and is the reason that overhead surveillance, reconnaissance, and intelligence-gathering efforts are so important in both war and peace. Information delivered from above can be used to strengthen a friendly regime, discredit an enemy regime, or directly attack the morale of an adversary's frontline troops. In less hostile circumstances, the information might consist of humanitarian warnings about impending natural disasters or news about disaster-relief efforts.

As for the term target, in the traditional military sense of the word, a target can be anything of military value to an adversary. For example, targets might be the sources of enemy military power (e.g. industrial targets), lines of communication through which military power flows (e.g. interdiction targets), or the enemy's fielded forces themselves. With regard to the last, it is worth noting that air power can take direct offensive actions against an adversary's air forces and surface forces. The latter, however, can do nothing other than defend themselves against air attack—only in very unusual circumstances can they take direct offensive actions against air forces.[3] In a less traditional sense, a target can be hunger, disease, ignorance, lawlessness, or myriad other vexing problems.

Notwithstanding the requirements and limitations yet to be discussed, parsing the essence reveals that the options for using air power are virtually unlimited, providing unparalleled flexibility. In truth, the airman's traditional axiom that "flexibility is the key to air power" should be updated and reversed: aerospace power is the key to flexibility.

## Absolute Requirements

Stunning technological progress during the 20th century made the essence of aerospace power a physical reality. However, three fundamental requirements must be met before the physical reality becomes practical and useful. Left unfulfilled, any one of these three requirements is a showstopper.

The first requirement is the most obvious: the availability of appropriate kinds and numbers of air and space assets. One must understand that required air assets go far beyond airframes and munitions. Almost any nation can procure modern, sophisticated aircraft and munitions in the global arms bazaar. Infrastructure—which educates, trains, disciplines, motivates, and cares for airmen and their equipment—separates real aerospace power from high-tech flying clubs.

The second fundamental requirement is access to timely and accurate intelligence. Air power historian Philip Meilinger once claimed that "in essence air power is targeting, targeting is intelligence, and intelligence is analysing the effects of air operations."[4] Meilinger may have engaged in a bit of hyperbole on this point, but not much. The target intelligence required is not just about technical and tactical matters such as location, construction, defences, and so forth. Of equal importance are the strategic—and operational—level requirements to understand if, why, and to what extent operations against potential targets will contribute to the overall military effort and, ultimately, to political objectives. Strategic—and operational—level intelligence informs decisions about what air power should do. Tactical-level intelligence informs decisions about how air power should do it.

Part of the intelligence requirement is the need to accurately assess the results of operations. Assessing actual target damage has been difficult for airmen since the earliest days of military air power.[5] Even with modern sensor capabilities, it remains a vexing problem.[6] The situation is further complicated by the need to assess not only tactical-level damage, but also the operational and strategic-level effects of that damage.[7] Measuring first-order effects of aerospace operations remains a difficult and complex task. Measuring second-and third-order effects is even more problematic.

The third fundamental requirement is the political will to fully exploit the essence. In the eyes of many airmen, political will has been their Achilles' heel. Cold War fears of nuclear escalation restrained the use of aerospace power in Korea and Vietnam. In the post-Cold War era, the fear of inflicting undue civilian casualties and the fear of losing public support have limited political will. In Operation Desert Storm, for example, the destruction of the Al Firdos bunker in Baghdad, killing many civilians hiding there, resulted in tight restrictions on subsequent bombing in the Iraqi capital. During Operation Allied Force, the need to maintain a united front provided every member of the North Atlantic Treaty Organisation (NATO) the ability to virtually veto strikes on Serbian targets, thus, seriously restricting NATO's aerial assault.

## Disabilities, Vulnerabilities, and Limitations

The unparalleled flexibility of aerospace power does not produce unlimited military utility. Most obviously, aerospace power cannot physically seize and hold territory. Under certain circumstances, air power alone may be able to force opposing forces to vacate territory or prevent them from entering territory. To do so, however, one must envision a situation of air superiority or air supremacy, a ground environment in which opposing forces would find concealment difficult, and an opposing force composed of "regular" forces with vulnerable lines of supply. The advent of operations such as Southern Watch and Northern Watch has led to some discussion of "air occupation" as a concept. Both of these operations met at least one of their major objectives—the enforcement of no-fly zones—but that is a far cry from "occupation" of anything other than the air space over Iraq. Even Britain's "air control" concept, used to police portions of its empire in the 1920s and 1930s, and often cited with regard to air occupation, required the coordinated use of ground forces.[8]

The most significant vulnerability of aerospace power occurs whenever aircraft leave their operating environment. On the ground, aircraft are helpless—fragile, unarmoured, and unable to defend themselves.

Unfortunately, combat aircraft—even in high-tempo war-time operations—spend most of their time on the ground. Their vulnerability is such that in a combat zone, one must take near-heroic measures to protect them in hardened shelters or, at a minimum, in revetments. One finds in the Vietnam War the most telling testimony to the vulnerability of aircraft on the ground. During that struggle, Vietcong and North Vietnamese sappers and mortar teams destroyed 43 per cent more US Air Force aircraft on the ground than were lost in air-to-air combat, and they destroyed nearly as many air force aircraft on the ground as were lost to the vaunted North Vietnamese surface-to-air missile system.[9]

In addition to these vulnerabilities, aerospace power also has its limits. Three of the most important are directly related to one another. First, and most importantly, modern aerospace power is very expensive—on the order of tons of millions of dollars per aircraft, with some even costing hundreds of millions of dollars each. Their weapons can be quite pricey as well, particularly precision-guided stand-off munitions.[10] Second, the combination of complexity and cost results in smaller and smaller aircraft inventories. Although modern aircraft are much more capable than their predecessors, their numbers are much more limited—and numbers do count, particularly for a global power wrestling with parallel requirements in the far corners of the globe. An aircraft can be in only one place at a time, doing one thing at a time. Further, smaller inventories magnify the importance of attrition.[11] Third, prudence dictates that expensive and relatively scarce airframes and crews should be put at risk and expensive weapons expended only against lucrative targets. As a result, high-tech precision aerial weapon systems can find themselves at a serious disadvantage when facing adversaries employing strategies and tactics that emphasis dispersion rather than concentration of forces (e.g. insurgent strategies/guerrilla tactics).

## Rationale for an Independent Air Force

Aerospace power's nearly unlimited options and unparalleled flexibility provide the fundamental and compelling rationale for an independent air force. Several of the world's great air forces, including the US Air Force, gained their independence from surface forces in order to more effectively carry out so-called independent missions—the most prominent being strategic attack. Independent missions, particularly after the advent of nuclear weapons (which some believed gave airmen a means to win wars without the aid of surface forces), provided a convenient bureaucratic rationale for an independent US Air Force in 1947. However, more than a half century of additional experience and perspective has shown that the fundamentale rationale for an independent aerospace force is psychological and operational, not bureaucratic. One finds the reason for this in the very different worldviews or mindsets of soldiers, sailors, marines, and airmen.[12] Ground forces traditionally have been most concerned about the immediate problem they confront—an understandable mindset since most often an enemy at relatively close range does the shooting and killing. This mindset has manifested itself in many ways. During World War II, for example, the ground officers who dominated invasion planning for D-Day were much more concerned about the immediate problem of securing a lodgment on the shores of France than they were about the subsequent breakout into the heart of that country. The beaches of Normandy offered favourable conditions for the amphibious assault, but the hedgerow country behind the beaches represented some of the worst imaginable terrain for breakout operations—a fact illustrated in the bloody yard-by-yard struggle through the hedgerows that lasted for nearly two months.[13] Another example found in US Army doctrine during the mid-1970s concentrated on "winning the first battle." The immediate problem, the first battle, was of the most importance.[14] Only in the late 1970s and early 1980s, with the advent of the AirLand Battle doctrine, did the army look up, so to speak, and stress that what happens far beyond the battlefield is often of great importance. But even with a newfound appreciation for the "deep battle," ground-force commanders find their perceptions constrained by lateral confines that tend to channel their attention and interest. Ground commands must exist and operate "cheek by jowl" across an entire theatre of operations. One must maintain clear divisions of command responsibility to prevent fratricide or counter-productive operations along command boundaries. The upshot is that ground commanders, from the corps level down, have strictly defined areas of responsibility (AOR) that generally extend considerably rearward (reflecting rear-area security concerns) and considerably forward (reflecting the new found importance of the deep battle). Laterally, however, ground commands remain tightly constrained by the parallel AORs of their neighbouring commands. This results in the so-called bowling-alley effect—long but relatively narrow AORs that channel attention and interest and, thereby, constrain perceptions.

The view held by airmen, because of the nature of aerospace power, is the antithesis of that held by, or imposed on, ground forces. An airman's—from the most junior pilot to the most senior air commander—AOR is the entire theatre of operations. Airmen realise that, within political constraints, they can spread their operations across the entire theatre or concentrate their operations—perhaps at one end of the theatre in the morning and at the opposite end in the afternoon. Airmen also realise that, depending upon the adversary and the situation, the most important enemy targets—the destruction of which may lead to ultimate victory with the least cost—may not always be the most immediate, most obvious, or closest.

Compared to the views of soldiers, sailors have a much broader and less constrained worldview. But even their view is significantly constrained by physical and psychological realities. In terms of physical realities, a ship simply cannot sail to some places; thus, the naval worldview tends to focus on the high seas and the littorals. Also, some physical characteristic peculiar to ship-borne aircraft impose limits on their capabilities.[15] Psychologically, because naval fighting ships are very expensive and difficult to replace, their protection rightfully has a very high priority, including a high priority in the tasking of naval aircraft. This defensive priority inevitably translates into reduced offensive utilisation. During Desert Storm, for example, 38 per cent of all "shooter" sorties flown from US Navy aircraft carriers were defensive counter-air or defensive combat air patrol sorties. During the same period, only 12 per cent of all shooter sorties flown by the US Air Force were defensive sorties.[16] These physical and psychological realities significantly constrain the perceptions and limit the options of sailors with regard to the use of aerospace power.

As the evidence indicates, if organised as part of a surface force and subject to the culture, customs, and mindset of the parent surface force, airmen will be much less likely to fully and appropriately exploit the unlimited employment options available to them. Air force leaders must understand and be able to articulate that the need to perform some mystical, "independent" mission is not the reason that a "full service" air force should be independent and co-equal with surface forces. Nor is the rationale for an independent air force based on notions of a stand-alone, war-winning capability. Rather, the most fundamental and most compelling argument for an independent air force is the imperative to fully exploit the essence of aerospace power. Exactly the same arguments lead to the inevitable conclusion that, within a theatre of operations, an airman should centrally control aerospace forces.

## The Space-Power Conundrum

The term aerospace occurs throughout this article, yet one finds much vacillation at the highest command levels concerning the medium in which the air force operates. Three successive chiefs of staff went from using the time-honoured appellation aerospace to air and space (which, it was said, would someday become space and air) and then back again to aerospace. Such inconstancy highlights the difficulty airmen face when considering mature air power capabilities, the promise of space power, and the nexus between air and space power.

Space and space power are subjects of obvious and growing importance, but our consideration of them is hobbled by a dearth of conceptual thinking about the role of space in military operational matters. For much of its history, scientific wizards rather than operational warriors dominated the military space community. As a result, military space power is still looking for its great theorist. A modern-day, space power version of Alfred Thayer Mahan or Billy Mitchell has yet to make his or her presence felt. The problem became so painfully obvious in the latter 1990s that Gen Howell M. Estes III, then the commander-in-chief of US Space Command, commissioned a civilian academic to develop a space-power theory "as the opening statement in what I hope will be a meaningful debate about space power theory."[17] Unfortunately, the project fell on hard times, and the results have yet to provide the spark that General Estes sought.

Despite the paucity of general theory, space operations unquestionably have become vitally important to US military operations. Command, control, communications, intelligence, weather, reconnaissance, surveillance, global positioning, and mapping are just the most obvious areas in which space plays a major role. But even with the growing importance of space operations, how should air force leaders think about space power? Without some overarching theoretical framework, space and space operations remain only a collection of capabilities, albeit very important capabilities. Three sets of fundamental issues must be vetted if we are to understand space power with the kind of clarity with which we now understand air power and if we are to understand their nexus.

First, we must determine whether the essence actually applies to space power, as we have assumed throughout this article. Can space power "apply great power quickly to any tangible target on the planet"? Many people would answer no to this question because of political restraints on weaponising space. Others would argue for an affirmative answer based on technical, if not political, feasibility. In either case, the question concerning the applicability of the essence remains assumed but undemonstrated. Or perhaps there exists a space power version of the essence that differs from all other military operations, including air power.

A second group of issues concerns the future of space power. What kinds of military operations are likely to migrate to space and why? Space may become another "battle space," or it may become only a home to military operations focussed on non-lethal activities in support of combat elsewhere. The horizon is wide open on the options and ramifications of these alternative futures.

The third set of issues has to do with the relationship between space power and air power. The defining characteristic of air power is an operational regime elevated above the earth's surface. Conceptually, space power would seem to be more of the same at a higher elevation, a concept tacitly endorsed by the air force in its current (as of this writing) basic doctrine.[18] The term aerospace, coined in the late 1950s, echoes this same theme, as do official pronouncements such as "although there are physical differences between the atmosphere and space, there is no absolute boundary between them. The same basic military activities can be performed in each, albeit with different platforms and methods."[19] But in our conceptual thinking, can we so easily ignore the vast differences between operations in the atmosphere and in space? It is difficult to analyse these and many more issues dealing with space without a general, overarching theory of space power. The task is made even more difficult by several other factors, such as the limited experience base in military space operations, the tight security classification concerning much of what goes on in space, and the thoroughly sub-divided responsibility for space operations.[20] Thus, we have a conundrum—a jigsaw puzzle that will someday picture how space power fits or doesn't fit with air power. Solving the puzzle represents a major leadership challenge.

## Explaining Aerospace Power and the Dilemma Airmen Face

Airmen generally try to explain aerospace power by using two broad themes that seem almost frozen in time at about the middle of the last century— updated technologically but not conceptually. The first and most common theme is some version of "higher, faster, farther" that emphasises the relative advantage of operating above the earth's surface. The new air force slogan "No One Comes Close" is the latest incarnation of the relative-advantage theme. The second theme emphasises the lists of things that aerospace power can do. Some of the listings are quite detailed, as in the Global Reach, Global Power White Paper issued in 1990. Others, such as the air force's core competencies, are much more abbreviated. Neither of these themes captures the uniqueness of aerospace power.

The essence of aerospace power, on the other hand, takes a much broader and more fundamental view, founded on the unique capability of aerospace power. It concentrate on concepts, possibilities, and virtually unlimited options rather than on comparisons and lists. It is instructed by the absolute requirements that make it work and is tempered by vulnerabilities and limitations. A thorough understanding of the essence reveals the intellectual imperatives for an independent air force and for theatre-level centralised command of aerospace forces. A thorough understanding of the essence makes clear that aerospace power is the key to the flexibility that we will certainly require in the new world disorder. In short, the essence provides the foundation for aerospace leadership in the 21st century.

Aerospace power would seem to have a very bright future. But dark clouds loom on the horizon. Just as an essence exists, so does a two-fold reality that produces a dilemma airmen must face. The reality is that because aerospace power has become so valuable to so many in so many different ways, the demand for it is virtually unlimited. As noted earlier, the reality is also that aerospace resources are very limited and becoming even more limited. In sum, we have a growing supply-and-demand mismatch. All of this produces a classic dilemma for tomorrow's leaders. How can airmen exploit unlimited options and satisfy unlimited demands with increasingly limited resources? How aerospace leaders deal with this dilemma across the entire spectrum of conflict will determine much about the future of aerospace power.

## Notes

1.  Air Force Doctrine Document (AFDD) 1, *Air Force Basic Doctrine*, September 1, 1997, p. 27.
2.  With all of these challenges, it is no wonder that the air force chief of staff initiated the "Developing Aerospace Leaders" programme, designed to ensure the production of future leaders capable of steering the air force through such troubled waters.
3.  There are several well-known examples of such unusual circumstances. Examples of ground forces directly attacking air forces are found in the Vietnam War, in which Vietcong sappers successfully attacked a number of US air bases in South Vietnam, destroying aircraft and material, killing American personnel, and disrupting operations. An example of naval surface forces directly attacking an air force is found in the struggle for Guadalcanal in the southwest Pacific theatre during World War II. Japanese surface warships made night time raids on Henderson Field on Guadalcanal, which was within the range of heavy guns on Japanese ships sitting just off shore.
4.  Col. Phillip S. Meilinger, *10 Propositions Regarding Air Power* (Washington, D.C.: Air Force History and Museums Programme, 1995), p. 20.
5.  One finds countless instances of gross errors in bomb damage assessment

(BDA). A classic example comes from the war in Vietnam and the effort to determine the number of North Vietnamese trucks destroyed on the Ho Chi Minh Trail as they infiltrated men, equipment, and supplies into South Vietnam. In April 1971, an Air Staff message to commanders in Southeast Asia noted that "Seventh Air Force is really concerned about the validity of the BDA reported by the AC-130 gunships in their truck killing operation. They stated all aircraft BDA for this hunting season indicates over 20,000 trucks destroyed or damaged to date, and if intelligence figures are correct, North Vietnam should be out of rolling stock. The trucks continue to roll however." Quoted in Donald J. Mrozek's *Air Power and the Ground War in Vietnam: Ideas and Actions* (Maxwell AFB, Alia: Air University Press, January 1988), p. 131.

6.   The relatively recent examples illustrate the point. During the Gulf War, the Joint Chiefs of Staff (JCS)/US Central Command (CENTCOM), the Defence Intelligence Agency (DIA), and the Central Intelligence Agency (CIA) each came up with widely different estimates of the percentage of Iraqi tanks, armoured personnel carriers, and artillery that had been destroyed by Coalition air strikes. For example, on February 23, 1991, JCS/CENTCOM claimed that 39 per cent of Iraqi tanks had been destroyed. DIA said only 16 per cent had been destroyed, while the CIA claimed only 12 per cent. Thomas A. Keaney and Eliot A. Cohen, *Gulf War Airpower Survey,* vol. 2, *Operations and Options: Effects and Effectiveness* (Washington, D.C.: Government Printing Office, 1993), pt. 2, p. 211, Table 13. For an even more recent example, refer to the controversy between *Newsweek* magazine and NATO concerning the number of Serbian tanks, armoured personnel carriers, and artillery pieces destroyed during Allied Force. For example, Newsweek claimed that only 14 Serbian tanks had been destroyed while NATO claimed 93. John Barry and Even Thomas, "The Kosovo Cover-up," *Newsweek,* May 14, 2000, pp. 23-26; and Stephen P. Aubin, "Newsweek and the 14 Tanks," *Air Force Magazine,* July 2000, pp. 59-61.

7.   This point is driven home by Michael R. Gordon and Gen. Bernard E. Trainor in their comments on the widely differing estimates of damage done to Iraqi tanks, armoured personnel carriers, and artillery (see n. 6). In essence, they argue that the bar had been set too high. The goal had been to destroy 50 per cent of the overall Iraqi armour and artillery, which, theoretically, was required to make the Iraqis combat-ineffective. No one's estimates came near the 50 per cent

level, yet "the air attacks made it impossible for the Iraqis to mount an effective defence. Air power crippled the Iraqi war machine." Initially setting the bar too high in the Iraqi case seriously hindered the ability to estimate Iraqi capabilities prior to the start of ground operations against Iraq. Gordon and Trainor, *The General's War: The Inside Story of the Conflict in the Gulf* (Boston: Little, Brown and Company, 1995), pp. 331 and 474.

8.   For an excellent discussion of "air occupation," see Maj. Marc K. Dippold, "Air Occupation: Asking the Right Questions," *Air Power Journal*, vol. 11, no. 4, Winter 1997, pp. 69-84. For a realistic look at British air control operations, see Dr. James S. Corum, "The Myth of Air Control: Reassessing the History," *Aerospace Power Journal*, vol. 14, no. 4, Winter 2000, pp. 61-77.

9.   Sappers and mortar teams destroyed 96 aircraft in attacks on US Air Force bases. Only 67 air force aircraft were lost in air-to-air combat, while surface-to-air missiles downed 110 air force aircraft. Walter Kross, *Military Reform: The High-Tech Debate in Tactical Air Forces* (Washington, D.C.: National Defence University Press, 1985), p. 98. Anti-aircraft artillery was the biggest threat to US aircraft, particularly radar-guided guns ranging from 57 mm to 10 mm. Lon O. Nordeen, *Air Warfare in the Missile Age* (Washington, D.C.: Smithsonian Institution Press, 1985), p. 13.

10.  The issue is not exactly how much aircraft cost or how much more they cost today than in the past. One can make such determinations in several different ways, using different sets of assumptions. Nor does the question concern the capabilities of the aircraft. Without question, modern aircraft are much more capable than their predecessors. But there is also no question that, by virtually any standard of measurement, modern aircraft cost considerably more than their predecessors. For a discussion of the different dimensions and difficulties of comparing the cost of aircraft and weapons, see Kross, n. 9, pp. 24-57.

11.  The decline in aircraft inventory over the past 40 years has been startling. "Snapshots" taken at 20-year intervals of bombers and fighters in the active inventory reveal the following:

|          | 1960  | 1980  | 2000  |
|----------|-------|-------|-------|
| Bombers  | 2,193 | 412   | 179   |
| Fighters | 3,922 | 2,804 | 1,594 |

See *Air Force Magazine* (almanac issue), May 1975, p. 137; May 1980, p. 162;

and May 2000, p. 66.

12. For further explanation, see the author's article "Joint Operations: The World Looks Different From 10,000 Feet," *Air Power Journal*, vol. 2, no. 3, Fall 1988, pp. 5-16.

13. Russell F. Weigley, *Eisenhower's Lieutenant. The Campaign of France and Germany, 1944-1945* (Bloomington: Indiana University Press, 1981), p. 35. Weigley notes that "by concentrating almost all their planning effort on the assault and the immediately following buildup, the planners neglected a maze of troubles awaiting behind the French shore. The greatest trials of OVERLORD... were to appear when the invaders plunged inland...in the region of Normandy called the Bocage."

14. US Army Field Manual (FM) pp. 100-5, *Operations*, July 1, 1976.

15. For example, because carrier aircraft must take off from, and land on, relatively small ship decks and must be able to "go below" for maintenance and so forth, their potential size is sharply limited; this puts limits on such capabilities as payload capacity, unrefuelled range, and the like.

16. Keaney and Cohen, n. 6, vol. 5, *A Statiscal Compendium and Chronology*, p. 232, Table 64.

17. Quoted in James E. Oberg, *Space Power Theory* (Washington, D.C.: Government Printing Office, March 1999), p. x.

18. AFDD 1, pp. 21-22.

19. Air Force Manual (AFM) 1-1, *Basic Aerospace Doctrine of the United States Air Force*, vol. 1, March 1992, p. 5.

20. In addition to the army, navy, and air force, other government agencies involved in space operations pertinent to this discussion include the National Imagery and Mapping Agency (NIMA), CIA, National Aeronautics and Space Administration (NASA), National Oceanic and Atmospheric Administration (NOAA), National Reconnaissance Office (NRO), and National Security Agency (NSA). Tamar A. Mehuron, "Space Almanac 2000," *Air Force Magazine*, August 2000, p. 40.

# 4

# RMA and Emerging Aerospace Technologies

*M. Matheswaran*

## Introduction

The term "RMA" or "Revolution in Military Affairs" has been in prominence and used very frequently since the last decade and a half. A revolution is, in the larger holistic sense, essentially the outcome of a confluence of seemingly disparate societal, technological and intellectual transitions, of which the RMA is merely one symptom. In a pure sense, a revolution brings change that is permanent, fundamental and rapid. A revolution, therefore, theoretically relates to a paradigm change brought about by organisational and functional discontinuity caused primarily by technological and conceptual breakthroughs. Practically there have been very few revolutions in human history, whereas most cases known as revolutions were in effect groupings of many smaller evolutionary changes over extended time periods.

Alvin Toffler identifies only three major waves/revolutions affecting the human civilisation. The Tofflers[1] say many technological evolutions have been confused for revolutions. This is quite relevant. In their opinion, revolutions are those that bring radical transformations in the way wars are fought, wealth is made, and in the way societies live and interact. If this is the criterion, then mankind has seen two waves of revolutions so far and the third is underway. Each wave of revolution spanned a large period, depending on the technologies involved, to complete the cycle of the transformation. This period would comprise many sub-revolutions that weave together to complete the transformation.

What emerges from the Tofflers' theory, however, is the fact that the larger wave of revolution has its moorings in technology. Thus, the first wave was related to the society dominated by agricultural technology; the second, driven essentially by the industrial revolution, was dominated by the culture of mass production and free market economy; while the third, which is underway, is knowledge driven and differs greatly from the previous waves. This concept makes clear that usually the RMAs become the sub-sets of a larger revolution. Thus, there can be many RMA sub-sets in each major revolution depending upon the change agents/drivers that initiate these RMAs.

## The Concept of RMA

Extensive discussions and considerable ink has been spent in recent years in trying to elucidate what many in the professional military, academic and research establishments claim is an impending "Revolution in Military Affairs." What constitutes this RMA? A good definition of RMA can be seen in the one given by former US Defence Secretary William Cohen: "A revolution in military affairs (RMA) occurs when a nation's military seizes an opportunity to transform its strategy, military doctrine, training, education, organisation, equipment, operations and tactics to achieve decisive military results in fundamentally new ways."[2]

The key words in the above quote are "seizes an opportunity." This opportunity could emerge from social, geopolitical or technological factors. Throughout history, technology has played a crucial role in bringing about the RMAs. The current concept of RMA owes its origins to the idea of "military technological revolution" propounded by the scholars and strategists of the erstwhile Soviet Union.

In the early 1970s, the Soviet theorists evolved the term "military technical revolution." They related this to two periods of fundamental military change in the 20th century: one, driven by the emergence of aircraft, motor vehicles and chemical warfare in World War I, and the second driven by the development of nuclear weapons, missiles and computers in World War II. The Soviet military theorists led by Marshal N.V. Ogarkovo began to write of the next "Military Technical Revolution" that would be driven by advances in microelectronics, sensors, precision-guidance, automated control systems, and directed energy. This concept of "military technical revolution" was seen by others, mainly in the USA, in the light of the revolutionary technological developments underway, and evolved as the

RMA. This RMA is all encompassing. As to what constitutes and drives this RMA would be discussed subsequently.

## RMA in the Modern Period

There are different interpretations on the number of RMAs that have taken place in the last 500 years. However, there are few that are incontestable in any view-point. The first and very significant RMA in modern times was ushered in by the invention of gunpowder and guns. This RMA did not occur instantly but spanned a few centuries, leading to a very comprehensive change in the nature of warfare that had remained unchanged for millennia.

The 100 Years War between the European Empires saw technological developments leading to an RMA that transformed traditional infantry and artillery. Here the infantry displaced the dominant role of cavalry on the battlefield. Similarly, advances in technology led to the development of effective cannons and siege warfare which could quickly degrade the formerly strong defence of cities.

The outcome of the Battle of Crecy—which marked the end of cavalry supremacy—is an example of the overwhelming dominance that becomes evident from the completion of an RMA. In that battle, the French lost 1,542 knights and lords, and suffered over 10,000 casualties among crossbow men and other support troops. The victorious English, relying on disciplined formations of infantry with unprecedented use of longbow men, lost two knights, one squire, 40 other men-at-arms and archers, and "a few dozen Welsh."[3]

In the 16th century, the advent of the sail powered warships and cannons triggered the RMA that changed the nature of naval warfare. Similarly, new technologies relating to fortifications led to a "fortress revolution" better able to withstand the siege artillery of the day. The development of muskets and tactics to overcome their weaknesses and exploit their power brought about revolutionary changes in land warfare. This RMA, started by what many today would see as a very elementary technology of muskets, ended the age of pike men and archers who had earlier overcome mounted cavalry, as they now became targets for artillery and musket fire.

The RMA ushered in by Napoleon stemmed from socio-political, technological, and military-strategic factors. The French Revolution established firmly the concepts of nationalism and nation-state. Napoleon exploited this with his brainchild of Levee-en-masse that brought in the concept of national armies. These factors combined with the new technologies were exploited by Napoleon to bring about radical changes in operational strategy and tactics. The RMA initiated by the Napoleonic wars was one of the most comprehensive ones that impacted on the nature of war and organisational structures.

The latter half of the 19th century saw two major RMAs. The first one evolved from the development of railroads and telegraphs, and the introduction of muskets and artillery. This RMA was all about the beginnings of modern communications and logistics and its revolutionary impact on military affairs. It brought about a significant "Land Warfare Revolution" which was demonstrated in the most telling manner by Bismark and the senior Moltke in the war against France, culminating in the comprehensive defeat of France at Sedan in 1870. Towards the end of the 19th century, technological developments such as the rifled cannon, steel ships, and steam power triggered a second "Naval Revolution" that changed the face of warfare at sea.

By the end of World War I, considerable level of technological and organisational changes had taken place which impacted on the militaries of nations. This had set the stage for the "Revolutions in Mechanisation, Aviation and Information" that took place in the inter-war period, which together formed an important RMA of this period. It led to a few great military innovations of World War II: *Blitzkrieg* by the German Army, carrier aviation by Japan and the United States, amphibious warfare by the United States, and strategic bombing by Great Britain and the United States. While the all basic elements of this revolution—the internal combustion engine, aeroplanes and radios—were present in the earlier war, it was the combination of their technical advancement in the 1920s and 1930s, along with new doctrines and organisations, that created revolutions. The invention of the nuclear weapon initiated the RMA of nuclear deterrence that evolved through combinations of nuclear weapons, their delivery systems such as strategic bombers, intercontinental missiles, various multiple warheads, accuracies and the nuclear strategy that evolved continually as weapons, delivery systems, early warning and command and control systems became increasingly more sophisticated.

History shows that technological developments were, although not in all cases, the primary drivers of most RMAs. The 20th century, the second half in particular, has been characterised by very rapid, accelerating, and unavoidable technical change. This means that technological development, which is a critical element for a revolution in military affairs, is always present. Thus, the current RMA is largely driven by technology.

## Dynamics of Technology

As brought out earlier, of all factors, technology is a critical one in driving a revolution in military affairs. This becomes clear when one examines the critical relevance of military power to national power. The noted economist Wallerstein's world economy model establishes the fact that economic, technological, and military factors are responsible in the build up of the national power of a state. The criticality of military power to a nation is well described by Paul Kennedy: "Wealth is usually needed to underpin military power, and military power is usually needed to acquire and protect wealth."[4]

A combined analysis of Wallerstein's model and the Russian economist Kondratieff's cyclical economy model establishes the fact that world economic growth is linked to the emergence of "critical technologies" in each period. Fig. 1 shows a simplified picture of the four K-waves beginning in 1780, and the dominant technologies. Every cycle tends to be associated with significant technological changes. The current fifth cycle is driven by aerospace and information technologies. Most importantly, analysis shows that the nation that develops and controls "critical technologies" dominates the cycle. Dominating a cycle inherently involves recognising, driving and mastering the associated revolution in military affairs.[5]

It is generally assumed that the technological dimension has been the driver to initiate changes in the nature of warfare. However, the changes affecting the nature of warfare during pre-modern times have been conspicuously few.[6] Historical analysis shows that technological innovation connects with continuity in the development of weapon systems only from the modern period with the onset of the industrial revolution. As Barry

**Fig 1**

Major New Technologies

| Steam Power Cotton Textiles Iron | Railways Iron & Steel | Electricity Chemicals Automobiles | Electronic Synthetic Materials Petrochemicals | Aerospace & Information Technology |
|---|---|---|---|---|

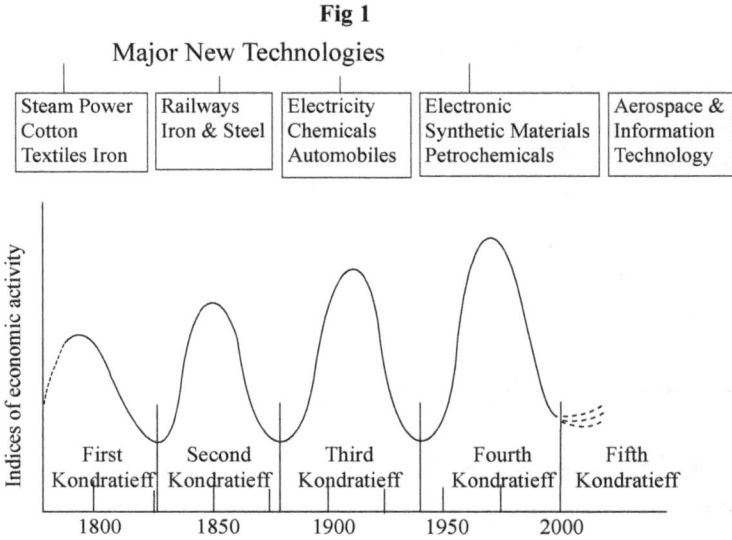

Buzan observes: "The military technology of Roman legions changed little in the six centuries between the conquest of Greece and the fall of Rome; similarly, the galleys used by the Ottomans and the Christians during their Mediterranean wars as late as the sixteenth century were quite similar to those used by the Greeks against Xerxes in 480 BC. Napoleon's astonishing victories at the end of the eighteenth century were based almost wholly on innovative use of existing types of weapons, and scarcely at all on innovations on weapons themselves. By the middle of the nineteenth century, however, a fundamental transformation in military technology was underway. The industrial revolution, with its ever expanding use of energy and machinery in the process of production by that time developed such momentum that major changes in technology began to occur frequently."[7]

Essentially, it can be seen that technological revolutions lead to revolutions in strategy and tactics, resulting in crucial transformations in military power and the conduct of war. This, in turn, has major ramifications for the security of the state. For example, the Pharoes of Egypt lost their long held dominance when they failed to recognise the technical superiority of the new harder iron swords as against their weapons made of bronze. Similarly, the ancient Greeks invariably overwhelmed their numerically superior Persian adversaries, primarily because their generalised body armour for troops allowed them to develop close-formation fighting tactics. The Romans further refined the Greek tactics and this enabled them to establish the largest empire in ancient times. The introduction of the longbow, the crossbow, and the pike put paid to the supremacy of the mounted and armoured knight in medieval Europe. The introduction of gunpowder and the cannon necessitated revolutionary changes in fighting methods and fortifications. Major empires in India and China, which were the richest and strongest in the world in the 15th-16th centuries, became vulnerable and collapsed as they failed to recognise the impact of these revolutionary technological changes. By the late 19th century, developments in shipbuilding, steam engines, and gun design were making it suicidal to go to war in the wooden sailing ships that had formed the backbone of naval power in the previous three centuries.

Significant technological changes have always allowed an alert state to bring about revolutionary changes in the methods of warfare and strategy. As brought out earlier, Germany's revolutionary use of the new rail transportation enabled her to mobilise her forces rapidly against France in 1870. This rapid mass mobilisation helped her to achieve critical advantage and crush the much-vaunted French forces at Sedan. The battle of Sedan initiated the RMA that gave birth to the concept of rapid mobilisation. It also gave a new dimension to the theory of manoeuvre warfare.

Colin S. Gray assets that the dynamics of technology is of permanent significance as a dimension of strategy.[8] Technology can become useful only when it is exploited through appropriate strategy and tactics. This is exactly what is achieved through the RMA. Thus, the invention of guns and muskets became effective only when use of these weapons brought about significant changes in the method of warfare. The states that recognised the need for these changes were the ones that evolved appropriate strategies, tactics, and doctrines to achieve enormous advantage over others, and dominate the international order. This was done when, after the initial recognition of an invention, it led to strategic changes; it was continuous evolution of strategy as a process of RMA that drove the technological growth and its application. This can be seen in the development stories of guns, cannons, ships, tank, aircraft, communications, weapons, nuclear technology, and space technology. Thus, artillery replaced traditional cavalry to transform land power, while steam and later diesel powered ships and submarines made sea power the most critical element of military power in the 19th and early 20th centuries. The advent of air power and nuclear weapons brought about major dimensional changes to the nature of warfare.

Traditionally, strategists drove technology to meet their demands of weapons with increasing destructive power. Air power and nuclear weapons were not spared of this strategy. Douhet's prediction that air power could terrorise cities and, thereby, populations, through the threat of mass destruction, became possible only after the invention and use of the nuclear weapon. Therefore, early strategists of nuclear weapons relied largely on Douhet's theory of massive destruction and, consequently, were happy with larger explosive power and yield. The natural progress of technology, however, led to improvements in performance such as accuracy, range, effectiveness, miniaturisation, yield to weight ratio, etc. Nuclear weapons, just like aviation, could not remain without the influence of the natural progress or dynamics of technology. As a result, nuclear strategy evolved from being governed by maximum explosive power alone to more realistic and effective deterrence through design of weapons with greater accuracy, range, lighter and multiple warheads, and improved kill probability. This development was not deliberate but inevitable due to the "trajectory of technology."[9]

## Aerospace Technologies

What exactly are aerospace technologies? A very common perception is to take a simplistic view to say that those technologies that deal with aviation and space are aerospace technologies. For a critical analysis, one needs to examine the issue in greater depth and detail. The current explosion of technology, when related to Toffler's "third wave," can be seen to have originated essentially in the 1950s with the beginning of space exploration. The post-modern period, however, can be said to have begun in the last decade of the 20th century when a critical level of maturity was attained in aviation, space, communication, and information technologies. The third wave is one dominated by knowledge-based technology. The roots of third wave technology can be traced to the four technologies of aviation, space, communications and computers. Aviation technologies matured and attained a critical mass for faster growth by the end of World War II. This led to explorations in space, communications, computers and other allied technologies.[10] The specific needs of the aviation and space sectors, small size (miniaturisation) and high performance (computation), led to rapid growth in the fields of computers and communications. Once critical thresholds, in terms of performance, miniaturisation and production, were achieved in all four sectors by the 1990s, we find that the integration and interaction of these technologies have fuelled an explosive growth in all segments, underwritten by the core factors of information and knowledge. All these four segments, when fused, emerge as aerospace technologies.

Aerospace technologies generate significant capabilities in the aviation, space, and information sectors. These capabilities combine and synergise to create very powerful capabilities and immense growth potential. This synergy of aviation, space and information capabilities is aerospace power. Aerospace technologies are, by virtue of their many dimensional impacts, beginning to have a major impact upon national power. The technological explosion emanating from aerospace technology has branched off into many segments such as information technology, computers, aerospace applications, sensors, biotechnology, etc. This makes it clear that the fundamental drivers of current technological revolutions are aerospace technologies. The aerospace revolution enabled by aerospace technologies is shown in Fig. 2.

**Fig 2**

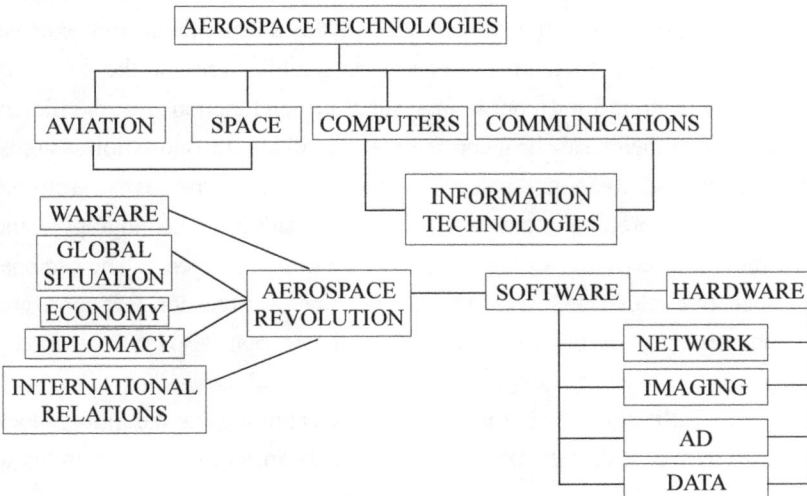

Aerospace technologies have ushered in a significant revolution in military affairs due to rapid strides being made in the areas of communication, information, intelligence, automation, navigation, artificial intelligence, precision weapons, aviation and space technology. It is obvious now that these technologies are becoming interdependent, commercially and militarily. The rapid developments in high speed computing, increase in capabilities of aviation and space platforms, enormous developments in sensor applications and data fusion, and realisation of real-time analysis have made use of aerospace technologies a vital necessity for all military arms.

Aerospace power realised through exploitation of aerospace technologies is bringing about radical changes in the characteristics of the military power of a nation. These manifest themselves in four crucial areas of warfare in such a manner that these are responsible for major changes in the very nature of warfare, which is what the current RMA is all about. The four areas are:

— Information.
— Command and Control.
— Precision.
— Penetration.

The much discussed aerospace dominance of military affairs flows from the above four characteristics. Aerospace dominance allows a state to achieve dominance in precise and decisive military force application, coercive ability as well as diplomatic advantage. The synergistic function of air and space technologies provides immense potential in the development and exercise of national power. For example, space-based satellites provide the necessary information for aircraft and other aerial systems in their function towards efficient achievement of their tasks, be it commercial or military transportation systems, communications, weapons, rescue, disaster management, early warning, survey, weather prediction and warning, remote sensing, oceanography, and many more. The coverage of the aerospace spectrum is immense. The personal computer, live television, worldwide 24-hour news, precision weapons, and cyclone/hurricane warnings are just a few of the estimated 307,000 secondary applications from aerospace systems development and use.[11]

Ashley Tellis emphasises that the focus on technology, as a building block of national power, is centred exclusively on understanding a country's ability to produce the most sophisticated "critical technologies" identified today. While these span areas of information and communications, materials, manufacturing, biotechnology and life sciences, aeronautics and surface transportation, energy, and environment, it is clearly evident that aerospace technologies form the most "critical technologies" of the 21st century.[12] These technologies tend to develop in clusters of related areas simultaneously. According to Kotler, modern technological development tends to function in clusters, and results in tremendous spillover, fusion, and interactive effects, leading to developments in many other areas.[13] Aerospace technology is particularly effective in leading to various spillover, fusion and satellite effects.

Currently, there are nearly 30 emerging technologies that are related to aerospace technologies and which would significantly affect the national power of major nations. Space related technology alone is advancing at such a rapid rate that space has already become a crucial centre of gravity in the international power struggle. Military, civil, and commercial space sectors are converging—if they have not already converged—and this is leading to an inevitable necessity for major nations to have space-faring ability. In 1996, more than 1,100 commercial companies across 53 countries were developing, manufacturing, and operating space systems. This is increasing at an exponential rate. By 2010, there are likely to be over 1,000 satellites in orbit, of which nearly 60 per cent would be launched by countries other than the USA and Russia. Aerospace technologies, therefore, impact on every aspect of tangible factors of national power.

## Current RMA

As brought out earlier, the current RMA is being enabled by aerospace technologies. The 20th century began with rapid developments involving largely physical principles. These principles focussed on technologies such as aviation, explosives, communications, guidance, lasers, etc. The RMAs associated with these developments operated by exploiting combinations of various systems and technologies or a single system. For example, the inter-war innovations such as armoured warfare by the German Army, the *Blitzkrieg* strategy of the German General Headquarters (GHQ), amphibious warfare by the US Marine Corps, carrier warfare by the Japanese and US

Navies, and strategic bombings by the Royal Air Force (RAF) and the US Army Air Forces have been characterised as "combined system RMA." Their revolutionary nature derived from a collection of military technologies put together in new ways to achieve a revolutionary effect. On the other hand, the nuclear revolution of the 1940s and 1950s was driven by a single technology—nuclear fission/fusion.[14]

Since aerospace technologies flow from the fusion or integration of the four core technologies of aviation, space, communications and computers, it becomes obvious that the RMA triggered by these is neither a combined-system nor a single system RMA but an integrated system RMA. The fusion of the four sectors leads to rapid evolution of many new technologies, eventually leading to the development of several advanced military systems. These systems, when joined with their accompanying operational and organisational concepts, will become integrated systems. It becomes a system-of-systems approach that aims to take advantage of the cumulative effect of employing each of the new capabilities at the same time.

### *Exploitation of Aerospace Technologies*

The current RMA is centred on exploitation of emerging aerospace technologies. The vital importance of these technologies to the new way of war is becoming clear as we see their impact in critical areas such as information. Aerospace technologies, therefore, are becoming critical tools of the new way of war emerging from the RMA. The tools of war have, as we know, largely influenced the transformation in the conduct of warfare. The emergence of the aerospace revolution has resulted in the development of many tools that are contributing immensely to the changes that are underway in the conduct of war. The technology that has driven the development of many of these tools, and that lies at the heart of this change, is the microchip. With each passing year, computer processors are becoming more agile, lighter, and less power hungry. According to David Shukman, "There'll be chips in everything."[15] It means that aerospace weapons will become more robotic, doing more for themselves, and far more accurate. These tools of aerospace power can be seen to be influencing the conduct of war through their impact in four broad areas: information, command and control, penetration, and precision.

*Information*

Probably the most important area where aerospace technologies have made the greatest impact is information. Information has always been, and will remain, central to the conduct of warfare. Modern aerospace power has enabled an enormous availability of information for military forces. Current technologies and developments for the future are enabling the availability of information on real-time basis. Aerospace information tools are spread from satellites to unmanned aerial vehicles (UAVs) and sensors of various sizes and capabilities. Apart from gathering technologies, modern aerospace technologies provide processed information to a variety of users; intelligence compilation, targeting, decision-making, and automation through artificial intelligence, surveillance, reconnaissance, and data bank updating. Today, aerospace technology enables collection of data on an enormous scale, processing it to create the right information, and translating this information into knowledge and wisdom. A variety of sensors, platforms and processors has evolved as a result of aerospace technologies to make information available on a scale as never before. This availability of information in terms of quantity and timeliness is a prime element of the current RMA.

Today, major aerospace powers operate satellites and other information gathering systems, with the USA leading by a huge margin. These sensors fall into two categories: stand-off systems that operate from space or sea; and intrusive systems that operate from air or ground. Currently the space-based sensors are low earth orbit (LEO) satellites and geo-synchronous orbit (GEO) satellites. LEO satellites, orbiting between 150-800 km altitudes, have the advantage of taking high-resolution pictures in the visible, infrared, and microwave bands, using the synthetic aperture radar (SAR).[16]

Space-based satellites are critical to vital information activities for modern warfare such as surveillance, reconnaissance, intelligence, navigation, communications, early warning, weather and electronic warfare. Space-based information platforms form a most important component of aerospace power and contribute to a range of vital functions such as integrated tactical warning and attack assessment (ITW & AA), weather/ environmental monitoring, satellite communications (SatCom), surveillance and reconnaissance, navigation and positioning, space control, ballistic missile defence (BMD), and force application.[17]

Information tools are crucial agents of the observation and orientation processes of aerospace power. Achievement of information dominance is a mandatory requirement for success in future wars. These tools consist of a plethora of platforms: satellites, UAVs, manned aircraft, COMINT (communications intelligence) SIGINT (signals intelligence) and ELINT (electronic intelligence) systems, and many other electronic sensors and information networking systems. Today's satellite technology permits real-time coverage via staring sensors down to one metre resolution. Micro-satellite technologies have already been established. These smaller satellite packages such as the MSTI or the Clementine satellite can provide similar coverage and much wider synoptic range apart from being stealthy, and, therefore, more easily survivable against future threats. A most important development in information technology is the commercially available information. For e.g. IKONOS satellite pictures with resolutions of one metre or even less are available internationally. Even smaller nations can access far greater information today, which can be of great use in their asymmetric strategies against much stronger foes. Surveillance and reconnaissance capabilities have increased by many orders of magnitude during the last decade. As a result, the aerospace dimension has truly acquired global reach in information gathering capabilities.

Increasing sophistication and operational capability of the UAVs have made their relevance in place of manned aircraft for many risky operations very attractive. The US operated the Gnat 750 over Bosnia. The experience gained from this operation led to the development of the Predator UAV.[18] The Predator with its UHF and Ku band SATCOM links broke out of the tactical usage restriction that was imposed on earlier UAVs by their line of sight communications. The Predator, in theory, could operate pre-programmed missions without ground receiver stations in theatre. In Bosnia, its data was fed into joint surveillance and tracking radar system (JSTARS) GSMs. In addition, line of sight C band command uplink enables in-flight override of a pre-planned mission if the ground link is close enough. The Predators over Bosnia operated from Hungary, thus, establishing the transition of UAV missions from tactical to operational and strategic levels. The UAVs were very effectively used in the Kosovo War in 1999. The USAF's Predator was used to provide real-time video-imagery of targets to commanders and planners, which could then be used for planning effective strikes and BDA (battle damage assessment).

The Predator, equipped with SAR and 24-hour endurance capability, enabled the North Atlantic Treaty Organisation (NATO) commanders to track targets through clouds and, thereby, augment the two E-8 JSTARS aircraft that were operating adjacent to Kosovo out of Germany. It also provided significant SIGINT capability through its ability to approach threat emitters more closely than manned aircraft and to monitor low-power transmissions, such as those from cell phones and portable radios operated by enemy ground troops.[19] The versatility of the Predator UAV was also demonstrated in a clever fusion of UAV sensor and specialised command and control procedures: "Two Predators orbiting at 5,000 ft would provide electro-optical and infra-red identification of mobile targets, and a third Predator would then use its laser designator and mapping software to provide geolocation, after which orbiting A-10s or F-16s could be called in on the detected target. Several confirmed hits on VJ tanks were made possible by this technique."[20]

Vast increases in processing capabilities and miniaturisation of microprocessors have been crucial elements in contributing to the rapid growth in employability of UAVs. A variety of payloads covering intelligence, hyper spectral sensors, communications, and information warfare aspects have made UAVs very effective and essential at all levels of warfare. Today, larger UAVs like the USAF's Global Hawk, which is almost the size of a Harrier aircraft, has strategic capabilities.[21] This UAV can link with a global network and operate anywhere in the world. When operated in conjunction with its successor, the stealthy Dark Star, and JSTARS, these systems become very potent facilitators of information dominance.

The criticality of space is becoming more obvious day by day. "In a series of US war games conducted in 1996, satellite destruction or neutralisation was assumed to have taken place at the outset of hostilities. The impact on military intelligence and communications systems was catastrophic."[22] Major military powers like the US are critically dependent on the indispensable satellite information related to imagery, navigation, communications and weather. The development of SAR technology and its integration in the satellite has provided enormous capability to the satellite and other aerospace platforms. For example, the US satellite Lacrosse is believed to produce a SAR resolution of less than 10 metres. The EU's Helios I satellite, launched in 1995, was used over Bosnia and could provide a resolution of one metre from an orbit of 680 km. The French series of SPOT satellites were used in the Gulf War. After the experience of inadequate intelligence in the lead-up to the Kargil conflict in 1999, the Indian Space Research Organisation (ISRO) launched the TES satellite which supposedly can give one metre resolution pictures. The Kargil experience has accelerated India's decision to launch satellites with dedicated military applications.

The invention of the global positioning system (GPS) is one of the greatest scientific achievements of the modern world. GPS information constitutes a vital requirement in most applications, civil and military. But the most important aspect of its usage is for navigational information for all kinds of users; aircraft, ships, vehicles, foot soldiers, and weapon guidance. GPS satellites, therefore, have become a vital requirement for the entire world. Navstar, the first US GPS satellite, was launched in 1978. Today, Navstar GPS comprises 24 satellites. Freely available GPS signals provide accuracy to less than 10 metres. Specialist signals for the US military can provide an accuracy of 1-2 metres.[23] The Russians have similar GPS satellites of their own called Glonass, consisting of a similar number of 24 satellites. The European Union (EU) has planned to launch their own version of GPS satellites called "Galileo." The European Space Agency satellites will provide data to interconnect, augment and refine signals from GPS and Glonass. Thereby, more signals would be available at any point in the globe with increased accuracy.

Jeffrey R. Barnett emphasises that the information campaign will be integral to any future conflict. Consequently, the importance of information tools is gaining critical relevance, as information supremacy is vital for victory in war.[24] Observation platforms are the most vital information tools as they provide the basic data, which then gets processed as information, knowledge and wisdom that are essential steps towards achievement of information superiority or dominance.[25] In short, information superiority is achieved through the development of core capabilities in the development and use of information tools.

## Command and Control

An important development of aerospace technologies involving information, communications, digitisation and satellite technologies, is the enhancement that has been made in command and control functions. The impact of aerospace power on command and control has been revolutionary to say the least. While, on the one hand, it has led to a trend of increasing centralisation of decisions due to better situational awareness and clarity of communications, real-time information flow, and rapid processing of information, on the other, it has made decentralisation effective as lower level commanders are more confident of their decisions due to greater awareness and reliability of information. Consequently, the impact of aerospace technologies has led to the concept of centralised command and decentralised execution.

Martin van Creveld says that the ideal system of command and control is to follow Clausewitz's famous dictum on strategy. That is, have a genius in charge, first in general and then at the decisive point.[26] In reality, geniuses are hard to come by and, therefore, the effectiveness of command and control functions is largely governed by how technology is exploited. Fundamentally, the process of command and control is done through four phases: situational analysis, planning, directing and controlling.[27] This is essentially Boyd's OODA (observation orientation decision, action) process.

The Gulf War first demonstrated the capability of aerospace driven command, control, communications, computers, intelligence, surveillance, reconnaissance (C4ISR) systems. Since then, a lot of improvements have been made, and these capabilities have been put to use in the Gulf, Kosovo, Afghanistan and Iraq. Alan D. Campen calls the Gulf War the "First Information War" primarily due to its extensive impact on command and control. As Joseph S. Toma says: "A major factor contributing to the coalition victory in Operation Desert Storm was that the Coalition commanders had a picture of the battlefield, and the enemy did not. It was made possible through communications, while the Iraqis were denied theirs. This is the first conflict of such size and complexity in which C4 systems technology made a big difference. The difference is not just in conducting operations more effectively. Communications and computing capabilities made it possible to do things very innovatively. For example, resources 7,000 miles away from the battlefield, were used to assist the commanders and staffs. Technology was adapted quickly to meet operational needs. Communications, sensors, and computer systems that allowed the impressive array of sophisticated weaponry to be employed with such precision and impact are yet to be fully understood by others."[28]

The Gulf War gave an overview of the importance of aerospace communications in modern war. The electronic dimension is an important element of aerospace power. In this war, 16 military and five commercial communications satellites made the command and control of Coalition forces possible. Fourteen US military communications satellites were in orbit when the crisis began, and two others, one British (SKYNET) and one NATO spacecraft, augmented them. Five leased commercial satellites and communications circuits were also added. Together, these systems provided a transmission rate of 200 million bits per second, or about 39,000 simultaneous telephone calls. These space systems carried 90 per cent of the inter-theatre communications and an undetermined, but substantial, portion of the intra-theatre.[29] The entire Desert Storm communications architecture was a collection of interconnected landline, radio, and satellite systems, thus, demonstrating the vast potential of the electromagnetic spectrum of aerospace power. Since then, the use of aerospace technologies to enhance command and control in all the wars that followed has been exponentially high.

If communications form the foundation of aerospace command and control, a variety of sensor platforms have revolutionised the concepts of force application. The platforms such as airborne warning and control system (AWACS), JSTARS, etc are mandatory requirements for any major power if it wishes to establish aerospace superiority or dominance at the initial stages of the war. These platforms provide near real-time situational analysis of the battlefield to the commander and, thus, aid his decision. The AWACS provides a total picture of the relevant air space.[30] In the Gulf War, the US deployed eleven of its E-3 AWACS aircraft. The AWACS has been an integral element in all types of operations since then: Kosovo, Afghanistan and Iraq.

While the AWACS component provides the command and control of air situation, the JSTARS is a development that completes the ground picture of the theatre. The technology of JSTARS was tested out in the Gulf War. Originally, it was not designed to perform command and control, but it did, in part, serve in that role. JSTARS had advanced radar to detect and track ground targets. The JSTARS contribution in the Gulf War was a revelation of its enormous potential. Of the two aircraft that were fielded, one flew every night of the war, performing reconnaissance of Iraqi ground formations and suspected Scud sites, passing targeting information to the ABCCC and AWACS aircraft, and even coordinating target information directly with the strike aircraft. JSTARS has evolved as an exceptional platform for targeting decisions.

*Precision*

Precision has emerged as the most significant development of aerospace technologies and is largely the reason for the current RMA. If the information revolution has transformed the nature of warfare due to its capability to enhance situational awareness of commanders and planners, it would not have been deemed successful had it not been for the quality of precision that followed in all operations—from navigation to weapon accuracy. The Gulf War was the testing ground to validate most precision weapon technologies and their employment doctrines. The success of PGMs in the Gulf War turned the traditional concepts of mass, concentration and economy of effort on their head. Traditionally, weapon developments were oriented towards increasing destructive power and, as a result, mass and concentration implied overwhelming application of firepower. For aerial weapons, the degree of assurance on destruction of a target was dependent on the accuracy of hit, which further led to a minimum number of weapons required to be dropped to achieve the minimum assurance level desired. All these concepts had to change when precision munitions were developed. With their exceptional accuracy and their fusion with sensors and satellite information, their assurance levels went up phenomenally, and, as a result, traditional calculations of over the target requirement (OTR) of aircraft and weapons became irrelevant.

PGMs consist of a variety of armaments ranging from laser-guided bombs (LGBs) to various terminally guided weapons such as air-to-air missiles to air-to-ground munitions like the HARM anti-radiation missile. At the higher end, cruise missiles and GPS aided munitions have added significant capability to modern air forces. But it is primarily the sensor-fused weapon such as the LGB and the cruise missile that have revolutionised strike philosophy. The Gulf War was a watershed because the effectiveness of the LGB surprised even the US.[31] Precision strike capability, coupled with long-range penetration using air-to-air refuelling, electronic warfare aids, and stealth technology enabled even tactical aircraft to undertake strategic missions. More importantly, this capability demonstrated the deep strike potential to become a decisive factor in future wars. Precision strike, then, has become "the ability to locate high-value, time-sensitive fixed and mobile targets; to destroy them with a high degree of confidence; and to accomplish this within operationally and strategically significant timelines while minimising collateral damage, friendly fire casualties, and enemy counter-strikes."[32]

The effectiveness of precision strike can be seen when comparing the empirical data of the past.

**Fig 3: Orders of Magnitude Improvement in Precision Munitioms**

| Conflict | CEP | Bombs Required? |
|---|---|---|
| WW II | 3,300 ft | 9070 |
| Korean/Vietnam | 400 ft | 176 |
| Desert Storm | <10 ft | 1 |
| Future | <10 ft (all weather) | 1 |

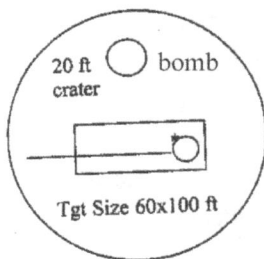

CEP (circular error of probability)=Radial distance from a point in which 50% of all bombs will land.

\* 90% probability of hit 2000—lb bomb.

The dramatic impact of PGMs can be gauged from the increase in capabilities to strike strategic targets. During the entire year of 1942-43, the US Eighth Air Force prosecuted only 50 strategic targets. In the first 24 hours of Desert Storm, the Coalition air forces prosecuted 150 strategic targets—a thousand-fold increase over 1943 capabilities. As Jeffrey Mckitrick et al observe, "By the year 2020, it is not out of the realm of possibility that as many as 500 strategically important targets could be struck in the first minute of the campaign—representing a five thousand-fold increase over Desert Storm capabilities."[33]

While the number of PGMs used in the Gulf War formed less than 10 per cent of the total weapons dropped, this increased to a large 29 per cent in the Kosovo operations (Operation Allied Force). PGMs altogether hit 64 per cent of the 9,815 aim points, for a total hit rate of 58 per cent.[34] The fusion of sensors and advanced weapon systems exemplifies the modern precision capability. The B-2 bomber demonstrated its long reach and precise attack in a single pass. Each B-2 flew non-stop to its targets directly from the US mainland base on 28-32 hour round-trip missions, delivering up to 16 GPS-guided GBU-31 joint direct-attack munitions (JDAMs) from 40,000 ft, usually through cloud cover, against Serbian targets including hardened command bunkers and air defence facilities. In all, 49 B-2 combat sorties were launched, of which 45 were successful sorties. Although that was less than half a per cent of the 9,500 strike sorties flown in Allied Force altogether, the B-2 dropped 11 per cent (some 700) of the bombs delivered against fixed targets in Serbia and Kosovo. It also dropped a full third of all PGMs expended during the air effort.[35] The use of PGMs was substantially higher in the wars in Afghanistan and Iraq.

Precision strike capability has emerged as an important aerospace force as it has transformed the traditional concepts of mass and firepower. A precise strike on a target is far more effective as it neutralises or incapacitates the target system. Consequently, precision strike creates a more important psychological effect apart from the first effect of neutralisation. As a result, precision strike is far more attractive as compared to attacks aimed at pure destruction. Precision strike produces effect-based results that are long lasting as compared to traditional destruction-based attacks. The vast differences between precision strike and non-precision strike have been well brought out in a RAND study. Fig. 4 shows the differences in the number of bombs required destroy a bridge with a reasonable assurance level.

Aerospace precision capability has not only become a great force multiplier, but more importantly, it has facilitated the breakdown of traditional compartmentalisation of warfare such as strategic, operational

**Fig 4: Improved Accuracy of PGMs and Effectiveness**

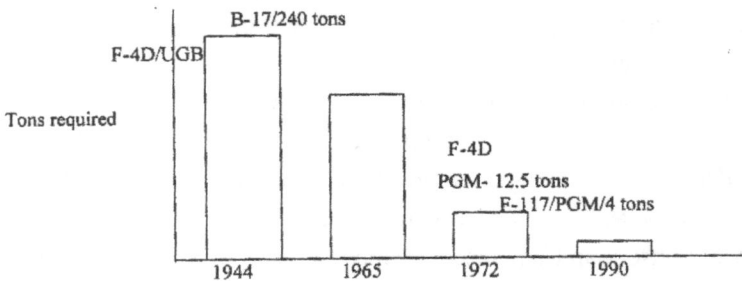

Note:    Data represent tons of bombs required to destroy a bridge span with 90 per cent
         assurance level.

Source:  Eduard Mark, *Aerial Interdiction in Three Wars* (Washington D.C.: Government
         Printing Office, 1994), pp. 236, 387; and Zalmay Khalilzad et al, ed., *Strategic
         Appraisal: US Air and Space Power in the 21st Century* (RAND study, 2002),
         pp. 35-39.

and tactical battle areas into a seamless scenario. It is precision capability that has enabled the development of Warden's Five-Ring Targeting model and Deptula's Parallel Warfare theory, or has made possible for air power strategists to contemplate simultaneous prosecution of strategic, operational and tactical levels of war. As David Goure and Stephen A. Cambone observe: "The ability to control the skies and to deliver precision ordnance with impunity virtually anywhere in the theatre marked a qualitative leap in the capability of air power. For the first time, aerospace power can deliver almost fully on the vision put forward by the early air power advocates."[36]

### *Penetration*

Penetration signifies the ability of aerospace power to reach out to strategic, operational and tactical levels simultaneously, accurately and deliver weapons with precision. By virtue of aerospace technologies such as information access, satellite aided global navigation using GPS, real-time target update, sensor integration, and smart weapons, allied with force multipliers such as stealth technology, aerial refuelling, and electronic counter-measures (both passive and active), modern aerospace power is now capable of attacking any target at any place and at all ranges and times. This penetrative ability of modern aerospace power makes future wars truly three-dimensional.

Stealth technology has enabled aerospace power an exceptional capability to penetrate enemy defences and carry out successful precision attacks on targets deep inside enemy territory. The technology is known as stealth or low observable technology. The F-117A aircraft was designed purely with the aim of evading radar detection. Using angled surfaces to deflect radar returns such that they do not reach the source, and radar absorbent materials in its construction, the F-117A produces exceptionally low radar signature for hostile radar to detect. Stealth platforms were the keystones of Coalition attacks against the Iraqi air defence system, leadership, and communications targets early on the first day of the war, even in heavily defended targets. Throughout the Gulf War, the stealth aircraft attacked with complete surprise and were nearly impervious to Iraqi air defences. The US forces used three aerospace platforms during the Gulf War that were in the stealth, low-observable category: the F-117 stealth fighter and two long-range cruise missiles, the Tomahawk land attack missile (TLAM) and the conventional air-launched cruise missile (CALCM).[37]

The impact of the stealth technology is reflected in the statistics: "The F-117 flew only two per cent of the total strike effort, but struck nearly forty per cent of the strategic targets and remained the centrepiece of the strategic air campaign for the entire war. Two hundred and eighty eight TLAMS were launched, with sixty four per cent within the first two days. Only thirty-five CALCMs were employed, all launched from B-52s on the first day of the war."[38]

The F-117 and cruise missiles had their limitations, but the advantages resulting from their stealth characteristics far overshadowed the limitations.[39] Most of these limitations were overcome eight years later in "Operation Allied Force" over Kosovo. The B-2 stealth bomber is an advanced product of the stealth technology and was made operational in 1997. The B-2, with its advanced navigation and attack systems, is provided with advanced electronic counter-measures (ECM) suite. These together enhance the stealth bomber's survivability manifold. It is equipped with advanced secure communication systems designed to preserve real-time communications with minimum electromagnetic exposure. The aircraft is designed to deliver all kinds of conventional precision munitions as well as nuclear weapons at an unrefuelled range of 6,900 miles.

The B-2 was exceptionally successful in Kosovo. Operating from the US mainland, the B-2 was not hampered by weather. A significant capability was its SAR that was used in the initial approach to eliminate inherent GPS error in locating the aim point. The B-2's average miss distance with JDAM was less than half the 13 metres stipulated for unassisted JDAMs.[40] The B-2s were never tracked by any radar let alone shot at by surface-to-air missiles (SAMs). The B-2, along with the B-52 and B-1, showed the penetrating ability of modern aerospace technologies and power.

Aerospace's penetration capability, relying on stealth and precision, has restored a measure of surprise to air warfare. The vast potential of the combination of precision and penetration was reflected in a RAND study of 1992. The study explored the implications of using B-2s to attack armoured columns with sensor fused sub-munitions (SFS). Each B-2 could locate inertial navigation system (INS) guided dispensers to within SFS range of the targets. It was claimed that three aircraft could expect to destroy 350 out of 750 armoured combat vehicles in an armoured division travelling in three columns, while the psychological shock of a sudden, mass attack without warning from unseen aircraft could increase the neutralisation further.[41]

### RMA and Transformation of War

The current RMA, driven primarily by aerospace technologies, has enabled the maturation of the third dimension of war that began at the turn of the 20th century. While technology per se is an enabler of this RMA, it must be appreciated that the exponential improvements afforded by these technologies in the areas of information, precision, penetration, and command and control have necessitated a complete revolution in the nature and conduct of war. Fundamentally, this RMA has identified the overwhelming impact of aerospace power on military affairs and, consequently, is radically transforming the concept of military operations that has been prevalent over thousands of years.

## Maturing of the Third Dimension

Aviation and the 20th century are synonymous. For the first time, man learnt to exploit the medium of air when, in 1903, the Wright Brothers demonstrated their first flight in a heavier-than-air machine. Since then, aviation has developed at a breathtaking pace, as the century progressed, making the 20th century the century of air power. However, for most part of the 20th century, air power theorists tended to be far ahead of the prevalent technological capability. While the arrival of the nuclear weapon may have vindicated their theories to a certain extent, it soon became clear that the nuclear weapon cannot be a weapon of war but only a weapon of deterrence. It was left for "space" to bring about a sense of completeness to the third dimension in its span of effectiveness and control.

Attempts to exploit space for military purposes could be said to have begun by the Germans with their use of V-2 ballistic missiles in World War II. Since the launch of the SPUTNIK in 1957, man has realised that space is an endless frontier affording limitless possibilities for its exploitation. Within the next four decades, man's ability to exploit space has grown exponentially. Today, space technology has matured to such an extent that it has become a critical source of vital inputs for operations on land, sea and in the air. While space is uniquely different in its character when compared to the atmosphere, it is important to note that the third dimension became truly viable only when both technology and strategies in the use of air and space achieved critical maturity for integrated operations.

This maturing of the third dimension becomes clear when we review the development of air power. Unlike navies and armies, which evolved to protect national interests, investments, trade and project power, air power emerged differently because it evolved to support land and sea operations. Over time, however, air power became a separate instrument of warfare, protecting national interests and ensuring freedom of action in the air. However, technological limitations during most of the 20th century with respect to air power, limited air power's scope. Only when space exploration and its technology expanded in scope, did it begin to drive many other technologies such as communications and computers. The result was an enormous expansion in the capabilities of air power in terms of intelligence, surveillance, reconnaissance, command and control, precision, and long reach. These capabilities have become a source of vital inputs for air operations as also for land and sea operations. In short, air and space synergise to become aerospace operations and their impact on military operations is growing exponentially. This is primarily due to the fusion of the core sectors of aviation, space, computers and communication. The restriction of size, weight and complexity of computational, communication and system requirements demanded by aviation and space operations naturally led to developments in advanced computers, miniaturisation, microelectronics and a host of breakthrough technologies, leading to the aerospace and information revolution. It has resulted in rapid advances in automation, very high-speed computation, and wide variety of capabilities in surveillance, intelligence processing and artificial intelligence. The technological fusion of these four sectors and the resultant maturation of aerospace power would impact enormously on the national power of states in the 21st century. Thus, the "Third or Aerospace Dimension" has become the sole reason for the current RMA.

### Impact on the Nature of War: Linear to Non-Linear Paradigm

While the essential nature of warfare is characterised by constant factors that affect war irrespective of its period in history, people, location, and technology, the dynamic nature of war is characterised by the ever-changing nature of the technique of war. Transformations in warfare were conditioned, fundamentally, by technology, and resulted from revolutions in military affairs. Nations that recognised and took the lead in these transformations were better able to manage their security as well as achieve their national objectives. Technology leads to the need for changes in strategy. The two together necessitate the third dimension of organisational change as an imperative. The factor of "time" becomes the fourth and a very important dimension that completes the dynamic nature of warfare. Technology enables these four factors to combine and give rise to the RMA.

In earlier times, wars between states or monarchs consisted primarily of one or two decisive battles. These battles, on account of their close combat nature, were confined to small areas, and, therefore, they had very little distinction in terms of operational, tactical or strategic sense. The technique of warfare revolved primarily around the technology in use. This technique was destruction-centric and sequential in nature. Accordingly, development of weapons followed a sequential pattern. From times immemorial, most combatants viewed that the objective of war was to defeat the enemy physically. This, as most believed, could only be achieved through the destruction of the enemy forces. Although scholars such as Sun Tzu[42] have highlighted the importance of winning without destruction or fighting, history shows otherwise on almost all occasions. On most occasions, state leaderships preferred destruction of the enemy to defeating him strategically.[43] Accordingly, weapons were also designed with the intent of maximising destructive power.

Fundamentally, modern wars have continued to be fought on sequential patterns. The brilliance of Napoleon's early campaign, which demonstrated a mastery of manoeuvre strategy, was overshadowed by the changed focus towards large size of the army and attrition war in Spain in the later years. In fact, the beginning of mass armies, combined with radical improvements in weapons technology, was the primary cause of massive destruction associated with modern war. The Clausewitzian concept of "absolute war" and Jomini's insistence on "total destruction" of enemy forces were instrumental in driving the technique of war towards the concept of "total war." Accordingly, "firepower" was sought to be maximised over the next two centuries through both increase in numbers as well as improvement in technology. Thus, the concept of decisive battles was replaced by a policy of devastation.

The policy of attrition and devastation was evident on a large scale in the American Civil War. The American Civil War was a sequential war of attrition, won by the slow mobilisation of the industrial and technical superiority of the northern states. Major increases in firepower capability began in the second half of the 19th century. The combination of railways, telegraph, internal combustion engine, and mechanised armour, artillery, and steam ships increased the speed of engagement and the area of the lethal zone. Robert Scales analyses the last 150 years of warfare to find that the lethal zone, responsible for maximum casualties due to massive proliferation of repeating arms, has increased tremendously. The deadly or lethal zone expanded from approximately 150 metres during the Napoleonic times to

1,000 metres or more by the end of the American Civil War, and further by at least a factor of 10 or more in the 20th century. The risks of crossing this lethal zone have been expensive in terms of lives. As Robert Scales observes: "Images of the terrible slaughter of World War I remain as testimony to the cost and blood exacted by an operational method that relied principally on killing effect to achieve decisive results."[44] Although technology has enabled warfare, as Robert Scales emphasises, to be dominated by the offence-defence cycles, the sequential nature of its conduct has continued to remain its basis. The fundamental reason why it has been so has probably been due to the belief that the destruction of the enemy's armed forces ought to be the first object of strategy. This was evident in sea power as well as air power strategies as evidenced by the influence of Mahan's and Douhet's theories. It was also because the technological limitations of the day prevented the prosecution of the war in anything other than sequential mode.

The Newtonian paradigm of linearity governed this sequential nature of war and, consequently, the development of technology. All developments and inputs were perceived to follow the principle of linear inputs and linear outputs. This approach was due, primarily, to the inability of the then prevalent technology to compute complex inputs and outputs. Thus, wars were planned and conducted along linear increases in force structures and battle outcomes were predicted and studied in the same vein. But today, modern scientific theories and computing capabilities have led to the development of complex analytical and simulation techniques. In a departure from the Newtonian Paradigm, the impacts of the smallest event can now be calculated. In short, modern developments such as quantum mechanics, chaos and complexity theories, and exponential increases in computing capabilities have enabled warfare to be analysed and planned in a complex manner, thus, leading to a transformation in the paradigm of warfare. Since aerospace power introduces the third dimension in all its complexity and makes war a complex phenomenon, it is only logical that analysis and conduct of warfare are done using the paradigm of complexity or non-linearity. This has been made possible largely by developments in modern aerospace power, particularly the developments in information technology. The aerospace capabilities in precision, penetration, real-time information flow and data analysis make it possible to prosecute the modern war simultaneously at all levels and depths, thus, enabling the non-linear paradigm. The first exposition of the non-linear paradigm using aerospace technologies, albeit in a very limited manner, was practised by the Israeli defence forces in the Bekaa Valley in 1982. A full scale validation was carried out in the Gulf War 1991.

### Enabling OODA Principle

Another important development of the aerospace RMA is its enabling the exploitation of the OODA principle. The benefits of this usage were evident in all the wars since 1991. It was particularly significant in the Afghan War of "Operation Enduring Freedom" where the Taliban and Al Qaida were psychologically outmanoeuvred, dislocated and defeated. The OODA principle is extremely relevant in the emerging non-linear paradigm for the conduct of war.

The OODA, identified by Boyd, becomes the ideal tool in the light of space technologies to initiate a revolutionary transformation in the nature of war. This is primarily because the efficiency of the OODA process revolves around information dominance, for which space becomes a critical resource. The surfeit of information that is available through aerospace systems and its rapid processing through the appropriate use of technologies enables one to observe and orient rapidly which then leads to rapid decisions and actions. By identifying the crucial activities of observation, orientation, decision and action, Boyd established the centrality of any conflict or activity in terms of the mind-time-space frame of reference.

Any conflict, be it a duel between two individuals, battle between two opposing formations, war between states, struggle for power by nation-states in the international system, or even business competition between rival corporate houses, could be viewed as a duel wherein each adversary observes (O) his opponent's actions, orients (O) himself to the unfolding situation, decides (D) on the most appropriate counter move, then acts (A). The competitor who moves through his OODA loop cycle the fastest gains an inestimable advantage by disrupting his enemy's ability to respond effectively. Since aerospace capabilities dominate the information focus in the 21st century, the process of achieving "information dominance" will dominate military operations. Achievement of "information dominance" is central to the OODA cycle.

Essentially, the OODA principle involves the process of analysis and synthesis. Analysis involves pulling things apart while synthesis is putting things together in new combinations. The side or force that does this faster will achieve a faster tempo of operations and, thus, gain significant advantage over the adversary. Aerospace technologies that allow information dominance, reach and precision, allow one to exploit aerospace power to cycle faster in one's own OODA loop and, thus, increase one's situational awareness and reduce the fog and friction, which, in turn, helps to increase the tempo of operations. The idea is to get "inside" the loop by transitioning from one mode of action to another before the other party can react. The winner will be the one who repeatedly observes, orients, decides and acts more rapidly (and accurately) than his enemy. As Boyd emphasises, "The ability to operate at a faster tempo or rhythm than an adversary enables one to fold the adversary back inside himself" so that he can neither appreciate nor keep up with what's going on, leading the adversary to become disoriented or confused. Boyd analysed that fog and friction, which is an essential nature of warfare, is a crucial factor affecting one's orientation in conflict. The strategy should be to disrupt the adversary's orientation while improving one's own. The key to attaining a favourable edge in the OODA loop, speed and accuracy (and, hence, to winning instead of losing), is efficient and effective orientation. Thus, orientation becomes the centre of gravity that needs to be targeted in a conflict.

Successful strategy is, therefore, a game in which one must be able to diminish the adversary's ability to communicate or interact with his environment while sustaining or imposing one's own. Aerospace capability enables one to achieve dominance of the OODA cycle, thus, leading one to simultaneously compress own time and stretch out the adversary's time to generate a favourable mismatch in time/ability to shape and adapt to change. This will collapse the adversary's system into confusion and disorder by causing him to over-and under-react to activity that appears simultaneously menacing as well as ambiguous, chaotic or misleading.

Boyd's OODA theory aims to paralyse the enemy through "control warfare." It concentrates on disorienting the mind of the enemy command by disrupting the process for exercising command and control. In short, one ensures victory in conflict by securing a temporal advantage over one's opponent in transiting the OODA loop, which, in turn, produces a psychological paralysis of his decision-making and action-taking processes.

In a nutshell, one needs to tighten one's own OODA cycle while, at the same time, expand or slow down the adversary's OODA cycle. That is, success in conflict stems from getting inside an adversary's OODA loop and staying there. This is achieved by reducing one's own friction while increasing the adversary's friction. This decrease in friendly friction acts to "tighten" own loop i.e. to speed up own decision-action cycle time. The increase in enemy friction acts to "loosen" the adversary's loop i.e. to slow down his decision-action cycle time. This combination ensures one's continual operation within the enemy's OODA loop, leading to the adversary's strategic paralysis in terms of inability to decide and act correctly. As Boyd observes through his analysis of military history over many centuries, OODA dominance leads to dismemberment of the "moral-mental-physical being" of the enemy by getting inside his mind-time-space paradigm. In Fig 5 below, Fadok uses Robert Pape's analytical model to explain Boyd's theory in terms of strategic paralysis.

**Fig 5: OODA and Conflict**

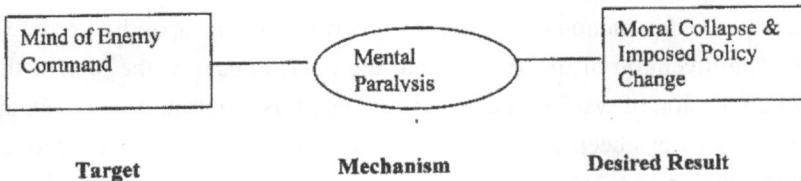

| Target | Mechanism | Desired Result |

Modern aerospace and information technologies are ideally suited to exploit Body's OODA loop theory. The flow of information from a surfeit of observational sensors, allied with real-time processing of information enables command and control systems to be very effective by aiding the decision-making process. Modern technology is leading to the build-up, process and archival of vast databases for analysis and synthesis at appropriate times. The synergistic application of aerospace and information technologies has increased information-gathering capabilities enormously. Because of the current technological developments, the importance of functioning along the OODA loop has even increased. Adhering to the OODA principle is an essential requirement to successfully practise the non-linear war paradigm, and aerospace technologies are vital for it.

## Revolutionising the Conduct of War

The major result of the ongoing aerospace revolution in military affairs would be seen in the conduct of wars in the 21st century. Because wars were fought on the surface of the earth for thousands of years, man has been conditioned to view war in a surface perspective. Earlier, conduct of wars could not but progress in a sequential fashion, as each layer of defence had to be broken or defeated, one by one. Accordingly, wars were fought by professional armed forces. It became incumbent on the national leadership to believe that to defeat another state, the enemy forces must be defeated or destroyed in battle. Wars then became affairs involving decisive battles. All this, as discussed earlier, led to the attrition warfare model.

The above factors did not change drastically when the world was affected by large-scale industrialisation. It only enhanced the concept of destructive warfare into the total war model. While complexities of industrialisation inevitably led to the involvement of all sectors of the nation in war production and waging, the total war concept still derived its idea from the basic model that required destruction of the adversary's war-waging capability to defeat him. The invention of the aircraft, and the development of the idea of the third dimension of warfare did little to change this mindset. As a result, air power has always been seen as an extension of firepower to support surface forces' objectives.

As Daniel Goure and Stephen A. Cambone observe, "Throughout the twentieth century, air power was captive of horizontal perspectives, differing from surface combat only in that air combat was conducted at altitude."[46] Essentially, air power was viewed as a method to restore to the battlefield manoeuvre via indirect and remote fires. Development of classical air power theories did not escape the influence of the sequential and attrition warfare model. The "strategic bombing concept" was a historic blunder that evolved from this influence. Air power application, whether in counter-air or ground support roles, all followed the attrition and sequential model.

Aerospace power is now capable of exploiting the third dimension in a way that is free of the surface perspective of thousands of years. The explosive growth of space technology, information and computer technologies have given aerospace power the ability to see, reach and impact at levels and distances that was never possible earlier. As seen earlier, aerospace tools involving information, precision, penetration and command and control effectiveness, have given new shape to the concepts of targeting and centres of gravity.

## New Ways of War in the Aerospace Age

The capabilities of precise and surgical strikes, information dominance, penetration, and real-time command and control aerospace technologies have allowed wars to be begun, dominated and concluded through the use of the third dimension, which is aerospace power. More importantly, these capabilities enable a nation to prosecute the war at all levels, strategic, operational and tactical, simultaneously. In short, the non-linear paradigm ushered in by the aerospace revolution has resulted in the seamless integration of the three levels of war.

## Targeting and Centre of Gravity

Aerospace tools have enabled targeting to be far more accurate, reachable, and cover the entire spectrum of the adversary's country. As a result, the objective of war can now be transformed from destruction of enemy forces to paralysis of the adversary. This paralysis applies primarily at the leadership, but also at various other levels. The feasibility of this concept has evolved primarily from capabilities of aerospace power derived from various aerospace tools. Because of this capability, an adversary's centres of gravity can be identified, not from the point of view of destruction, but more from the point of view of dislocation, disruption, and paralysis. This also becomes possible because aerospace power has also broken down the traditional tactical, operational, and strategic divisions of warfare, entirely on account of aerospace power's ability to prosecute the war at all levels simultaneously.

An important outcome of precision capability is the maturation of targeting philosophy. The essence of precision strike is the ability to sense the enemy at operational and strategic depth, recognise his operational concept and strategic plan, and select and prioritise attacks on enemy targets of value. All this is intended to achieve decisive impact on the outcome of the campaign. Even in limited conflicts or when the adversary employs asymmetric strategies or tactics, precision weapons can produce results entirely out of proportion to the force employed.

### *Strategic Paralysis and Effects-Based Operations*

There is nothing novel about the concept of strategic paralysis or effects-based operations (EBO). In earlier times, the Mongol leader Chengiz Khan used it very effectively. In recent times, Napoleon and the Germans employed the concepts within the technological capabilities available to them. But it is only after the emergence of aerospace technologies that these concepts appear far more feasible for effective application. Real-time targeting, precise force application and information dominance through the OODA process give an entirely different meaning and effectiveness to these concepts.

**Strategic Paralysis** of the enemy occurs from a combination of psychological paralysis and physical paralysis of the enemy. This is entirely in contrast to the conventional destruction-centric, attrition-based and linear approach to warfare. Psychological paralysis results from information dominance. Physical paralysis results from destruction/neutralisation of critical elements. Both these strategies depend on time relevance. Boyd's OODA theory aims to paralyse the enemy through "control warfare." It concentrates on disorienting the mind of the enemy command by disrupting the process for exercising command and control. In short, one ensures victory in conflict by securing a temporal advantage over one's opponent in transiting the OODA loop, which, in turn, produces a psychological paralysis of his decision-making and action-taking processes.

Just as aerospace capabilities exploit the strategy of information dominance to make Boyd's OODA theory a very viable tool for achieving psychological paralysis of the enemy's decision-making system, Warden's five-ring theory and Deptulla's parallel war theory focus on physical paralysis of the enemy's decision system. Warden emphasises that precision, speed, stealth and information management are the essential ingredients of parallel warfare. The role of space-based assets in providing or enhancing these capabilities is significant and is becoming increasingly vital.

Both Boyd's OODA process that aims at psychological paralysis and Waden's parallel war that aims at physical paralysis are two parts that complement each other and result from the enormous capabilities that aerospace power has ushered in. When the two complementary aspects are considered in totality, we arrive at the war strategy of "strategic paralysis." This is the singular transformation in the nature of war from the age-old pattern of "destruction-based warfare."

**Parallel War** is a concept that developed from Col John A. Warden's five-ring model of targeting theory, and Lt Col Deptula's parallel warfare method. The concept rests on the foundation of aerospace technology's strengths of precision, penetration, information and fast tempo of attacks. Warden conceptualised the adversary country as an entire target system. When this is done, the target becomes a living organism whose brain is the core, that is, the leadership. Obviously, if the leadership is neutralised, the war is won, but for obvious reasons it would be the most difficult task to achieve. The next in importance would be the command and control system, which, if disrupted, will break the ability of the enemy leadership to communicate with his forces for the conduct of the war. The third outer ring consists of infrastructure, which, if destroyed, would incapacitate the population and the military force to communicate or provide logistics. The last two rings are population and fielded forces. The concept is to attack all five rings simultaneously so as to paralyse the target nation.

The theory of near-simultaneous attack across multiple target sets is nothing new. A large number of attacks in a day have more effect than the same number of attacks spread over weeks or months. Earlier, air power lacked the military capabilities to implement near-simultaneous attacks. During all of 1942-1943, for example, the Eighth Air Force attacked a total of only 124 distinct targets. At this low rate (averaging six days between attacks), the Germans had ample time to repair and adapt between raids. In all these air campaigns, force was applied sequentially to "roll back" enemy defences before attacking targets of the highest value. In contrast, in the first 24 hours of

Operation Desert Storm, Coalition air forces attacked 148 discrete targets. Fifty of these targets were attacked within the first 90 minutes. Targets ranged from national command and control nodes (strategic) to key bridges (operational) to individual naval units (tactical). The goal was to cripple the entire system to the point where it could no longer efficiently operate, and to do so at rates high enough that the Iraqis could not repair or adapt. Such targeting, conducted against the spectrum of targets in a compressed time period, is called parallel war. The goal of parallel war is to simultaneously attack enemy centres of gravity across all levels of war (strategic, operational, and tactical), at rates faster than the enemy can repair and adapt.

Parallel war exploits three dimensions—time, space and levels of war. This would not have been possible without the maturity of the technologies of aerospace power. Simultaneous application of force (time) across each level of war uninhibited by geography (space) describes the conduct of parallel warfare. It differs significantly from the traditional use of force, in that use of force is to control rather than destroy an opponent's ability to act. This lends a different perspective to the most effective use of force. As Col David Deptula observes, "The crux of parallel war is not its physical elements, but the conceptual ones."[47]

**Swarming** is an operational concept that has historical origins. In the context of today's global connectivity due to aerospace technologies, swarming as an operational tactics and strategy can become very effective and feasible at all levels of war. It is a concept that leverages strengths of mobility, small force size, long-range weapons, rapidity of attacks from different directions, and use of psychological warfare. Swarming can be conceptually broken up into four stages: locate, converge, attack, and disperse. Swarming forces must be capable of sustainable pulsing: swarm networks must be able to come together rapidly and stealthily on a target, then redisperse and be able to recombine for a new pulse. It is important that swarm units converge and attack simultaneously. Each individual swarm unit is vulnerable on its own, but if it is united in a concerted effort with other friendly units, overall lethality can be multiplied, because the phenomenon of the swarm effect is greater than the sum of its parts. Synergistic application of force in three dimensions enabled by aerospace power provides unbroken connectivity, situational awareness and rapidity of operations, leading to immense effectiveness. Swarming as a concept provides for immense flexibility through the use of small, effective and rapidly moving forces in all three dimensions. The concept of swarming is particularly important in the aerospace environment, as traditional massed surface forces on land and at sea would be very vulnerable.

The concepts outlined above resulting from the strength of aerospace technologies have given a completely overarching perspective to the concept of **Effects-Based Operations (EBO)**. Throughout history, leaders have tried various strategies to realise the objective of EBO. This remained elusive because technology has always been the limiting factor and more so the sequential or linear nature of operations. Examples abound, such as the strategic bombing in World War II. Today, aerospace technologies have provided the wherewithal to operate at all levels and depths of war simultaneously with precision and surgical clarity. This has made EBO highly feasible and the most logical development in the RMA.

Targeting becomes a very important basis of EBO due to the reliability and timeliness of information that aerospace technologies make possible. Targeting and parallel operations are the main factors that make aerospace operations conform to the objective of EBO.[48] Using the strengths of aerospace technologies, EBO allows one to achieve rapid dominance. It relies on the employment of a series of unrelenting waves of powerful strikes across many targets combining sea, air, land and space forces to affect and influence the adversary's perception and includes the physical capture and occupation of territory if necessary. The execution of Operation Iraqi Freedom demonstrated this where cruise missile strikes and air bombardment were conducted on hundreds of targets in parallel with the employment of manoeuvre forces on the ground.

The culmination of the aerospace RMA appears to be in the development of the concept of **Network-Centric Warfare**. Without doubt, networking in the military domain is entirely a development that has been made possible by aerospace technologies. The concept of network-centric warfare proposes interlocking links between a sensor network, a weapons network as well as a command, control and planning network to increase the tempo and responsiveness of forces.

## Conclusion

The major transformation in the nature of war necessitated by the RMA due to aerospace technologies is a shift from the linear to the non-linear war that plays the mental game as against the physical destructive pattern of the 20th century war. This is due to the preponderance of information flow that would take place on a much larger scale. Accordingly, the results of war games, as we have been used to until now, will tend to be far less accurate as the influence of the number of variants will increase. This is because we have, until now, relied on linear modelling and simulation. Aerospace technology driven RMA is changing the conduct of war towards the paradigm focussing on strategic paralysis, using the concepts of effects-based operations and network-centric warfare.

The focus of 21st century wars will be to understand the factors that affect the adversary's decision process and apply the appropriate force/ power/influence to direct the will of the enemy leadership to a more desirable conclusion. As defined by Clausewitz, the focus of military action is on the will of the enemy leadership, irrespective of the levels of engagement— strategic, operational or tactical. What really matters is the effect of the action of the enemy leadership's decision cycle. In short, the change would be from attrition or destruction-oriented warfare to manoeuvre-oriented warfare at all levels and in the three dimensions to produce a rapid impact on the enemy's leadership and will. This transmission has become evident increasingly since the Gulf War through the Bosnian and Kosovo operations, Afghan War and Iraq War. Aerospace technology has made all this possible and, thus, future wars, irrespective of the type and level, would be dominated by aerospace power.

## Notes

1.   Alvin Toffler and Heidi Toffler are noted futurologists. Their book *War and Anti-War* is a very well researched analysis on the concept of revolution as applicable to the human civilisation.

2.  Annual Report to the President of the United States (Washington, DC: Government Printing Office, GPO, 1999), p. 122.

3.  The following section draws upon an article in *The National Interests*, Fall 1994, "Cavalry to Computer: The Pattern of Military Revolutions" by Andrew K. Krepinevich. See also CRS Report for Congress: Revolution in Military Affairs by Theoder W. Galdi, December 1995, Online, CRS 95-1170F, 2005.

4.  Paul Kennedy, in his sweeping analytical study of the Great Powers in modern times, establishes the interdependence of economic and military capabilities in the power of nations. According to him, the process of rise and fall of Great Powers—fundamentally related to differentials in growth rates and technological change, leading to shifts in global economic balances, which, in turn, gradually impinge upon the political and military balances—has not ceased but will continue to be the norm of the international system. Paul Kennedy, "Introduction" in *The Rise and Fall of Great Power* (New York: Vintage Books, 1987), p. xvi.

5.  Scholars like Alvin Toffler, Freeman, etc have said that the world is witnessing an unprecedented technological revolution. Some researchers have identified four generic technologies as being at the heart of this revolution: biotechnology, materials technology, energy technology, and aerospace and information technology. Thomas Clarke & Stewart Clegg, *Changing Paradigms: The Transformation of Management Knowledge for the 21st Century* (London: Harper Collins Business, 2000), pp. 150-155.

6.  Generally, military historians more often use the categorisation of pre-modern, modern, and post-modern when techniques of warfare have changed significantly, particularly due to technological revolutions. Viewed from a larger perspective, the modern period deals with the industrial revolution culture, spanning a period commencing from approximately 1500 AD to the late 20th century. Taking a cue from Alvin Toffler, the pre-modern period signifies the period before 1500 AD, characterised by agricultural technology, while the post-modern period has come into effect with the knowledge revolution of the 21st century.

7.  Barry Buzan, *An Introduction to Strategic Studies: Military Technology and International Relations* (New York: St. Martin's Press, 1987), pp. 17-19.

8.  Colin S. Gray, *Modern Strategy* (London: Oxford University Press, 1999), p. 37.

9.   Raja Menon has argued very convincingly that the trajectory of technology or the progress of technology is inevitable. Those who attempt to ignore or stifle it would be doing so only at their peril. He has analysed in detail various aspects of technological progress that have shaped nuclear strategy over the years in spite of efforts by many to stifle this progress. See Rear Admiral Raja Menon (Retd), *A Nuclear Strategy for India* (New Delhi: Sage Publications, 2000), pp. 69-131.

10.  Entry into space automatically projected the need for exploiting the vertical dimension for human civilisation's perennial requirement: 'information.' Obviously, a lot of effort in terms of research and development went into developing reconnaissance and surveillance systems, apart from high-speed communications.

11.  National Aeronautics and Space Administration, *NASA Facts*, August 1995, document FS-JSC-95(08)-004, and James E. Oberg, *Space Power Theory*, Online, www.peterson.af.mil/usspace/SPT/overview.htm, Internet, 2000, p. 124.

12.  Ashley Tellis, *Measuring National Power* (Santa Monica: RAND Publications, 1999), pp. 53-65.

13.  Philip Kotler *et. al., Competitive Advantage of Nations* (New York: The Free Press, 1997), p. 207.

14.  Jeffrey Mckitrick, et. al., "The Revolution in Military Affairs" in Barry R. Schneider and Lawrence E. Grinter, eds., *Battle of the Future: 21st Century Warfare Issues* (Alabama: Air University Press, 1995), p. 68.

15.  David Shukman, *Tomorrow's War: The Threat of High-Technology Weapons* (New York: Harcourt Brace & Company, 1996), p. 6.

16.  LEO satellites provide tremendous flexibility in their use. As a result, there has been, in the last decade, a sharp increase in demand for LEO satellites, particularly in communication roles. These are being deployed in three categories: "Big LEO" systems in the 1-2 GHz range, which provide voice and data communications, especially mobile data service (e.g., Globestar, Iridium); "Little LEO" systems which operate below 1 GHz and provide data communications such as e-mail, two-way paging, and messaging to remote locations; and "Broadband LEO" systems, which provide high-speed Internet access primarily using Ka Band. The USA plans to launch 512 commercial

payloads in the ten-year period from 1997-2006. In today's context, all commercial satellites are fully capable for military use, that is they are dual use platforms. See RAND, *Space: Emerging Options for National Power* (Santa Monica: RAND Publications, 1998), Online, Internet: www.rand.org/publications/MR/MR517, p. 25.

17. RAND, Ibid., p. 13.

18. The Predator is a reasonably large aircraft with a 48 ft wingspan, 28 ft length and 3.17 ft high. It has a ceiling of 25,000 ft, a maximum endurance of 24 hours over a mission radius of 3,000 miles, a loiter speed of 60 kt and can carry a payload of 450 lb. It carries SAR, a 900-metre spotter scope lens and IR sensors.

19. John D. Morocoo, David Fulghum, and Robert Wall, "Weather, Weapons Dearth Slow NATO Strikes," *Aviation Week and Space Technology*, April 5, 1999, p. 29. See also Benjamin S. Lambeth, *NATO's Air War for Kosovo: A Strategic and Operational Assessment* (Santa Monica: RAND, 2001), pp. 94-95.

20. Benjamin S. Lambeth, *NATO's Air War Over Kosovo* (Santa Monica: RAND Publications, 2001), p. 95.

21. The Global Hawk has a 14,000 mile range and 42-hour edurance. It cruises at 343 kt at 65,000 ft and has a primary task of wide area surveillance, with a resolution from 100 km of three ft and a spot resolution of one ft. Its 2,000 lb payload includes SAR, MTI, electro-optical visual and IR sensors. It can survey 40,000 square miles and focus on 1,900 spot target in 24 hours, day and night and in all weathers. It has multiple SATCOM and line of sight wideband data links which can transmit 50 megabytes per second, allowing real-time relay of video imagery.

22. Air Vice-Marshal Tony Mason, *The Aerospace Revolution: Role Revision & Technology—An Overview* (London: Brassey's 1998), p. 100.

23. The fully operational global positioning system of 24 satellites is placed in six orbital planes at 20,000 km. This constellation will ensure that a user anywhere on the earth will be able to view a minimum of 4 satellites simultaneously. Each satellite transmits at L-Band (1.2 GHz) precise (P) encrypted signals for military users and coarse acquisition (C/A) for other users. In 1997, a new series of NAVSTAR satellites, GPS Block 2R was launched. The 2R will increase positioning accuracy to less than 6 metres.

24. Jeffrey R. Barnett, *Future War: An Assessment of Aerospace Campaigns in 2010* (Alabama: Air University Press, 1996), Chapter 1, pp. 1-7, Online, Internet, www.au.af.mil/au/oas/aupress.

25. For elaboration on the relevance of data, information, knowledge, and wisdom, see R.N. Swarup and M. Matheswaran's "Wisdom Warfare: Transformations in Modern Warfare due to Aerospace Technologies" in Rajendra Prasad, ed., *India's Security in 21st Century: Challenges & Response* (New Delhi: Dominant Publishers and Distributors, 2002), pp. 144-176.

26. Martin van Creveld, *Command in War* (Cambridge, Massachusetts: Harvard University Press, 1985), p. 268.

27. "Out of the Sun," *Aerospace Doctrine for the Canadian Forces*, Chapter 6, p. 9, Online, Internet, www.airforce.forces.cal/libradocs/library8e.htm

28. Joseph S. Toma, "Desert Storm Communications" in Alan D. Campen, ed., *The First Information War* (New Delhi: Bookmart Publishers, Indian Edition, 2002), p. 5.

29. Thomas A. Keaney and Eliot A. Cohen, *Gulf War Air Power Survey Summary Report* (Washington D.C.: GAO, 1993), p. 193.

30. The AWACS has evolved over the last three decades into a very capable early warning and control system. The American E-3 Sentry AWACS aircraft has set a benchmark in capability for other aerospace nations. The Sentry is based on a Boeing 707-four engine platform with a AN/APY-1/2 S band, high pulse repetition frequency (PRF), pulse Doppler, multi-mode look-down radar. The aircraft operates at a cruising height of 30,000 to 35,000 ft, scans a detection range of 250 miles. It can register 600 aircraft tracks with surveillance volume divided into 32 azimuth sub-sectors. Each sub-sector can operate in a distinct mode providing surveillance to the radar horizon, target elevation, beyond the horizon operation for long-range surveillance for medium and high-altitude aircraft, passive scanning with the transmitter switched off to derive ECM information and, by a very short radar pulse, high resolution to detect slow moving or anchored ships.

31. Keaney and Cohen, n. 29, p. 226.

32. Jeffrey Mckitrick "The Revolution in Military Affairs" in Barry R. Schneider and Lawrence E. Grinter, eds., *Battlefield of the Future: 21st Century Warfare Issues* (Alabama: Air University Press, 1995), p. 77.

33. Ibid., p. 78.

34. Lambeth, n. 20, pp. 87-88.

35. Ibid., p. 91.

36. Daniel Goure and Stephen A. Cambone, "The Coming of Age of Air and Space Power" in Daniel Goure and Christopher M. Szara, eds., *Air and Space Power in the New Millennium* (Washington DC: The Centre for Strategic and International Studies, 1997), p. 9.

37. Keaney and Cohen, n. 29, p. 224.

38. Ibid., pp. 224-225.

39. Because of its low speeds, the F-117 had to operate primarily at night to maximise its stealthiness. In addition, nearly 19 per cent of its strikes were affected by adverse weather. Cruise missiles were restricted by smaller payload, required lengthy targeting process, and could not be retargeted after launch.

40. Lambeth, n. 20, pp. 89-94.

41. Mason, n. 22, p. 120.

42. Sun Tzu epitomised the ideal strategist as one who wins or forces the enemy to concede defeat without fighting: "Those who win one hundred triumphs in one hundred conflicts do not have supreme skill. Those who have supreme skill, use strategy to bend others without coming to conflict." See Sun Tzu, *The Art of Strategy*, edited by R.L. Wing (London: Thorsons, 1998), p. 45.

43. Certainly there were brilliant leaders like Hannibal, Alexander, Chengiz Khan and Napoleon who were exceptional in their practice of strategy, and often won victories with minimal destruction or losses. The secret of their victories lay in their comprehensive understanding of manoeuvre and deception. Liddell Hart, in his analysis of the "Indirect Approach," emphasises: "Throughout the ages, effective results in war have rarely been attained unless the approach has had such indirectness so to ensure the opponent's unreadiness to meet it. The indirectness has usually been physical, and always psychological." See H. Liddel Hart, *Strategy: The Indirect Approach* (New Delhi: Jupiter Publications, Indian Edition, 1967), p. 25.

44. Major General Robert H. Scales, Jr., *Future War: Anthology* (US Army War College, Pennsylvania: Strategic Studies Institute Publications, 1999), p. 4. Online http://carlisle-www.army.mil/usassi/ssipubs/pubs99/futrwar.

45. David S. Fadok, *John Boyd and John Warden* (Alabama: Air War College, 1996), p. 35.

46. Goure and Cambone, n. 36, p. 25.

47. Col David A. Deptula, *Firing for Effect: Change in the Nature of Warfare*, in "Defence and Airpower Series" by Aerospace Educational Foundation, Virginia, August, 1995, p. 5.

48. Parallel operations exploit the three dimensions of time, space and levels of war (tactical, operational, strategic) to achieve simultaneity. See David A. Deptula, *Effects-Based Operations: Change in the Nature of Warfare* (Virginia: Defence and Airpower Series, Aerospace Foundation, 2001), pp. 3-6.

# 5

# In Search of a Twenty-First Century Air Leadership Model

## Fodder for Your Professional Reading

*David R. Mets*

*Read and reread the campaigns of Alexander, Hannibal, Caesar, Gustavus, Turenne, Eugene, and Frederick. Make them your models. This is the only way to become a great general and to master the art of war. With your own genius enlightened by this study, you will reject all maxims opposed to these great commanders.*

— Napoleon Bonaparte

The quest for a key to successful air leadership is as old as air power itself. An Air Force Academy was first proposed in Congress in 1919, and by 1913, Randolph Air Force Base (AFB) was known as "The West Point of the Air." Yet, until fairly recently, professional air warriors have had slim pickings when they looked for case studies in air power leadership. For a long time, we have had many biographies of soldiers and seamen, but common perceptions hold that airmen are not a contemplative lot and have little inclination toward literary efforts. Few of them have set pen to paper to tell either their own life stories or those of other flyers.[1] Still fewer scholars and foundations have felt sufficiently competent to undertake such studies. But in the past two decades, that void has begun to be filled.

This article first explores the nature of models. What are they? What are they good for? What are they not good for? It then turns to sources of biographical material on airmen and the nature of biography as a vehicle for

Reprinted courtesy *Aerospace Journal*, Summer 2001.

exploring the subject of air leadership. It further examines the advantages of the biographical approach and its shortcomings. The article illustrates these matters with reviews of two forthcoming books about air leadership—one on Maj Gen Mason M. Patrick and the other on Adm Joseph M. Reeves. It then suggests some possible benefits as well as the limitations of biographies and, in keeping with my "fodder" series of articles, closes with a "10-Book Sampler for Professional Reading."

I am not sure to what degree either Napoleon or his marshals followed his advice. Certainly, his interpreter Carl von Clausewitz held that it takes more than maxims, and that genius—intuitive judgment—is the crucial element.[2]

## What is a Model?

A model is an artificial construct; it is not real. It is a simplification of reality. At the very best, it is an approximation of reality. It has no more authority that the credibility of its originator. Its utility is that it yields a conceptual framework and perhaps a commonly understood vocabulary that enables us to analyse and discuss a problem. It is an academic device to facilitate explanation and learning. But it cannot be used as a definitive guide to action. It can help in thinking about leadership, but it will certainly not make anyone a good leader. Consequently, all the abstract literature on leadership and all the air-leader biographies can do nothing more than suggest. Thus, one should certainly consider Napoleon's maxims but should do so in the light of his or her own genius—that is, professional judgment.

We have about as many leadership models as leaders. When I attended Squadron Officer School (SOS) in 1959, the institution's model was body, mind, soul. Yet, we received instruction from a parade of dignitaries from the flights over Schweinfurt, Germany, and other unpleasant places who gave us their own prescriptions for successful leadership. They were all different, but as I saw it, they merely described their own leadership styles. Some left out the need for professional knowledge, and some even omitted courage— perhaps taking it for granted. West Point's motto for the last century has been duty, honour, country, and a recent version of the air force's core values calls for "integrity, service before self, and excellence in all that we do." Still another maxim depicted by Prof. Dennis Drew suggests, "Know yourself, know your job, set the example, accept responsibility, foster teamwork, and care for people." The point is that no universal model for leadership exists. Drew suggests that leadership is highly situational, with the exception that one cannot compromise the constants of integrity, service before self, and the continual search for excellence.[3] I suppose that is largely the old SOS model of body, mind, soul—just in other words.

We encounter so many models of a positive kind that they become a bit bewildering. Either they are so complex that no one can begin to use them in all their dimensions in a crisis, or they are so simplified that they become useless platitudes in the real world. Perhaps a leadership model cast in a negative way would prove more useful—specifying a set of things to avoid rather than identifying desirable practices. One should avoid being unlucky, unhealthy, short, ugly, hesitant, cowardly, reckless, lazy, careless, dishonest, tactless, reticent, and pushy, just as one should not become a workaholic, martinet, dummy, or an intellectual "geek." Readers will quickly perceive that many of those attributes, like luck, are not within the leader's control. They will also see that only a very fine line separates some of them. Officers never want to say a dishonest word. Neither do they want to appear tactless when the general's wife asks what they think of her new hat.

So what's an aspiring leader to do if these models are so ambiguous, uncontrollable, and contradictory? He or she can resort to autobiographies and biographies—some positive, others negative, and all imperfect in one way or another. Some very fine people provide examples to avoid. Near the end of his days, Adm William Halsey lamented that it would have been better had Adm Raymond Spruance taken his place during the Battle of Leyte Gulf and had Halsey replaced Spruance during the Battle of the Philippine Sea.[4] Gen Ira Eaker was one of the finest officers in air force history, but what led to his relief as commander of Eighth Air Force, just as it approached its culminating point?[5] Gen Haywood Hansell, as fine a southern gentleman as ever graced the portals of Maxwell AFB, Alabama, was relieved hardly six weeks after his first B-29 attack of Japan.[6] Why? Why was Air Marshal

Hugh Dowding, whose leadership proved essential to victory in the Battle of Britain, shunted aside soon afterwards? All of these people have biographies that might be useful in suggesting things to avoid—like bad luck, if possible. But people who try too hard to avoid bad luck will surely never accomplish anything positive. Any air leader knows that one sure fire way to bring the accident rate down is to stop flying.

We can do something about the "body" part of the 1959 SOS model. Indeed, we in the air force have done so. There are far fewer smokers among us now, and our air force gymnasiums are far more heavily populated than before. But dwelling on physical problems is pointless since only the individual can solve them.

The man who inspired this series of "fodder" articles in *Aerospace Power Journal*, Col Roger Nye, once remarked on the unlikelihood of leadership training doing much to change the basic value systems ("soul"?) of successful young people. He said that if a "crook" entered such training, he would likely remain a crook when he graduated.[7] The training does some good for the group as a whole through the process of elimination. Even if a few members of the group are more honest by graduation, the class as a whole may indeed have more integrity. Over the course of the training, some dishonest people will be expelled, and some will self-select out. But if crooks wiggle through, they will likely lack integrity forever after. The point is that our hopes of making substantial moral improvements in individuals through preaching or training may be pretty dim, despite all our efforts. Setting an example may help, but coercing or coaxing people to be honest, humane, and all the rest is a formidable task.

For individuals, perhaps the most promising area for improvement lies in the SOS' region of the "mind." They can strive for excellence during formal training and education, and they can enhance those results through a serious programme of professional reading when not so engaged. Unhappily, that will never eliminate the need for seasoned professional judgments (read guesses) because we can never know all the facts that bear on our strategic, operational, and tactical problems. But such striving might well reduce the number of "unknowns" and increase the number of "knowns," thus, improving the odds that the final professional judgment will be right—or more so than the enemy's, at any rate.[8] In other words, inherent in attributing success to luck is the danger of failing to prepare one's self to take advantage of good fortune when it does appear.

## Possible Sources for Leadership Models

Many possible sources can help in the building of personal leadership models. They might include after-action reports, end-of-tour reports, diaries, interviews, personal papers, leaders' published articles, visits to battlefields or the homes and schools of leaders, alumni magazines, memoirs, autobiographies, and biographies. All but the last two sources would prove difficult for the aspiring air warrior-scholar to use in the field. Most of the others feed into autobiographies and biographies, but we know that the very act of selecting such material filters things and skews interpretations. Thus, although we know that completely unbiased biographies don't exist, they are nonetheless the most usable resources we have for the greater parts of our careers.

## Advantages of Biography as a Vehicle for Studying Leadership

Many students of leadership have difficulty relating theoretical studies to the real world. Many such studies recognise this and employ case studies, either to prove their point or explain it. But these treatments still tend toward the abstract. Too, the cases employed will often seem superficial and open to question. Many aspiring leaders find biographies less abstract—more grounded in real-world experience. Moreover, because we all must look at the world through human eyes, the biography almost automatically has more appeal because it deals with an individual. That tends to make it more entertaining than other kinds of books. The publishing industry knows that, so we find many more biographies of leaders than we do books on the subject of leadership. For the officer in the field, that means that biographies may be much more easily available and easier to use than other sources of information on leadership. My earlier comment about bias does not mean that biographies are necessarily untrue—only that the positive side of the truth seems to get a much more thorough treatment than the negative.

## Shortcomings of Biography as a Vehicle for Studying Leadership

One of the most serious difficulties with biographies is the tendency to overemphasise the importance of an individual. Every biographer must ask the question "What if my subject had never lived?" Too often, the answer would be that it would not have made much difference. When Franklin Roosevelt died, Adolph Hitler in his bunker, as well as most people around me, predicted that the Allies would now lose the war and that a depression would ensue. Neither happened. Air force leaders for both the *Mayaguez* affair and the Son Tay raid were fine men indeed.[9] However, the success of the former and the failure of the latter had very little to do with leadership and a great deal to do with luck.

Yet another difficulty with studying leadership through biography is that pressures on the author tend to result in an embellishment of the truth—that is to say, one cannot write negative things without solid documentation. Most sponsoring organisations would not fund a biography for any purpose other than glorifying the subject's role and, by extension, that of the organisation itself. One observes a rather powerful tendency among survivors for their memories to mellow with the passage of years. The old school tie can play a role here. Veteran military-academy tactical officers looked upon drinking and gambling cadets as mortal sinners; 50 years later, they tend to see such things in terms of "boys will be boys." In any event, there is something admirable about "beating the system." Moreover, witnesses to a leader's role, more often than not, will be unwilling to speak ill of the dead—even less so as long as the subject is alive. In fact, the latter case can prove dangerous. Hitler's generals were much freer with their criticism after the fuhrer died. Commercial publishers have a tendency to get the product on the street as early as possible and to overdramatise the role of the leader—because it sells books.

Another problem is that leadership models drawn from the study of biographies tend to obsolesce quickly. As recently as Vietnam, probably no more than one in 10 colonels could manipulate a keyboard; now they all seem to be able to do it. A grasp of technology did not seem to matter much to Napoleon's marshals; it is crucial to air leadership today.

All that aside, military biographies have always been, and will continue to be, attractive tools for the study of leadership. Aspiring air leaders have found themselves handicapped in this until recent times because of the scarcity of good biographies of air leaders. In the last two decades, that deficiency has been partially repaired (see the "sampler" at the end of this article). Plenty of biographies will keep readers busy for some time to come.

## Samples of Biographies

Recent worthy biographies that one might use for the positive side of an air-leadership model include books about Air Force Generals Henry Arnold, Carl Spaatz, Hoyt Vandenberg, Billy Mitchell, Curtis LeMay, Claire Chennault, and Mason Patrick.[10] All of our potential subjects do not have air force ties, and, obviously, piloting is not the same as air leadership. Our list might include Navy Admirals William Moffett, Joseph M. Reeves, Raymond Spruance, and Ernest King.[11] Neither Moffett nor Reeves were pilots although both earned observer wings. Both King and Patrick won pilot wings, but neither ever really served on an air crew. Spruance had no wings at all but undoubtedly must rank among the most impressive air leaders in American history. Certainly, readers should not limit themselves to Americans, for good works exist on Air Marshals Arthur Tedder, Keith Parks, Arthur Coningham, and Hugh Dowding.[12] More recently, Lt Col Eric Ash, the editor of *Aerospace Power Journal*, has done a corrective to the picture we have of the early days of the Royal Air Force in his book on Sir Frederick Sykes.[13] Further, David Irving has written controversial works on Hermann Goring and Erhard Milch.[14] There are many biographies on Goring, but most explore the sensational side of his character and don't have much to say about air leadership that is worthwhile. Indeed, biographical literature on the senior leaders of the Luftwaffe is rather thin.

## Current Air Leadership Biographies

Here, we turn to a closer look at two brand-new biographies—one on Maj Gen Mason Patrick, who commanded the US Army Air Service and Air

Corps during their most formative years [Robert P. White's *Mason Patrick and the Fight for Air Service Independence* (Washington, DC: Smithsonian Institution Press, forthcoming in September 2001)]. The other, from the same period, is about Adm Joseph Mason Reeves, who was the commander of the first American aircraft carrier, the USS *Langley*, and, ultimately, of the entire US fleet [Thomas Wildenberg's *All the Factors of Victory: Admiral Joseph Mason Reeves and the Origins of Carrier Air Power* (Washington, DC: Brassey's, Spring 2001)].

Both Gen Patrick and Adm Reeves lived in the shadow of the more noted air leaders Brig Gen William Mitchell and Adm William Moffett. Patrick was Mitchell's boss, first with the American Expeditionary Force (AEF) Air Service in France in World War I and later as the chief of the Army Air Service from 1921 until Mitchell's resignation in 1926. Moffett was at the political vortex in Washington from his appointment as chief of the Bureau of Aeronautics in 1921 until his death in the 1933 crash of the airship *Akron*.[15] Moffett was not Reeves' boss, but he had visibility in Washington while Reeves was at sea doing the day-to-day labour to integrate aviation into the navy. Too, Moffett was an adept politician—at least as able as Mitchell at that art—and good at public relations as well. As with Patrick and Mitchell, Reeves lived somewhat in the shadow of the more visible Moffett. Many books and articles have been written about Mitchell, and a feature motion picture with Gary Cooper (a Mel Gibson equivalent of an earlier day) in the role of Mitchell enjoyed wide circulation.[16] Moffett's reputation benefitted from the work of a splendid biographer seven years ago, with the publication of William F. Trimble's Admiral William A. Moffett: Architect of Naval Aviation. Now, both Patrick and Reeves emerge from the shadows because of the labours of two fine scholars, Robert P. White and Thomas Wildenberg.

Robert White is well suited to do a work on Patrick. He is a retired air force officer with long experience in writing and teaching in the Air Force History and Museums Programme. He is now the civilian historian for the Air Force Office of Scientific Research. At one time, he was chief of the Air Staff History Office. A Pennsylvanian, White has a master's degree in history and government as well as a PhD from Ohio State. The biography of Patrick is an adaptation of his dissertation, but it does not suffer from the usual defects found in that sort of work. White also seems at home with technology, perhaps as a result of his military service with the National Security Agency.

Thomas Wildenberg has a varied but fine background for the work at hand. Like White, he is at home with technology, in part the result of having earned a bachelor's degree in mechanical engineering from New York University. He also holds an MBA from the same school as well as another master's in library and information services from the University of Maryland. His scholarship has focussed almost entirely on naval history. His second book, *Destined for Glory: Dive Bombing, Midway and the Evolution of Carrier Air Power,* is a fine piece of work and has received excellent reviews.[17]

Neither book is a complete biography. As always, authors are prisoners of their sources, limited to what they can find in archives and elsewhere. One finds a little more of the subject's personal history in *Mason Patrick and the Fight for Air Service Independence*, but the book focusses on Patrick's service in the 1920s rather than his World War I work—and still less on his personal life. He was a West Pointer, second is his class there, and a friend of Army Chief of Staff John Joseph Pershing. From the beginning, Pershing had very high regard for Patrick's intelligence, common sense, and mission orientation and sought him out to bring order out of the chaos that was the Air Service of the AEF. For practically identical reasons, Pershing drafted Patrick back into the Air Service to restore order among post-war airmen. One of the major instigators of disorder in both cases was Billy Mitchell.

In the years that followed, Patrick did manage to exert a measure of control over the behaviour of his assistant—no mean trick since Mitchell probably was politically untouchable and certainly rich. Patrick was far from the reactionary lackey of the General Staff that the Mitchell worshippers have sometimes made him out to be (although Mitchell himself made no such accusation). Rather, Gen Patrick was a low-profile man who operated within the system yet was adept at making many of the very gains for the Air Service that Mitchell sought but failed to effect. They differed not in ideas but methods. Both favoured an independent air force: Mitchell demanded it immediately, but his boss had a better grasp of what was possible. As White shows, the chief had enough sense to see that independence in the 1920s was beyond reach. Yet it was possible to take several very substantial steps toward that goal through less flamboyant methods.

Through his major influence on the army's Lassiter Board and his labour with friends on the General Staff, as well as his work with Congress and the Press, Patrick yielded several favourable outcomes. One was the General Staff's official blessing of the idea that air forces might have an independent role to play before mobilising armies came into contact. Another was gaining general army acceptance of the notion of two kinds of air power: air service and air force. Patrick won approval to reduce the number of resources applied to the first and increase those devoted to the second. Too, he managed to persuade the General Staff to accept the notion that the air force portion should not be farmed out to the control of divisions and other subordinate units. Rather, centralised control would permit the massing of air forces against targets in any threatened area and permit their use in independent operations, the ground situation permitting. Those ideas are not too far removed from the ones of the present-day air forces, although ground forces still seem discontented with centralised control (but they now have their own "air service" forces in the form of helicopters).

Benjamin Foulois, later the chief of the Air Corps, found himself constantly at odds with Mitchell, who remained a burr under Patrick's saddle.[18] Yet, all three men—and the Air Service in general—shared much the same view of the world and the role of air power in it. At times, Foulois was more radical than Mitchell and quite prone to "shoot from the hip." But for most of Patrick's tenure, Foulois was stationed in Germany, where he could not stir up chaos in the Washington arena. According to White, his man managed all these problems and kept a lid on things from the *Ostfriesland* bombing trials in 1921 to the relief of Mitchell as his assistant in early 1925.

Mitchell fans have denigrated Patrick over the court-martial trial, but the chief had, in fact, requested Mitchell's reappointment for another term as his assistant. However, the secretary of war did not honour the request. Mitchell was not demoted. Rather, the rank went with the assistant's position, and when Mitchell had to transfer out of it, he merely reverted to his permanent rank—as many, many Air Service men had done at the end of World War I (though not the senator's son).

Mitchell's court-martial in late 1925 is an oft-repeated tale. Unfortunately, Bob White cannot compete with Gary Cooper in dramatising that dimension of the story. But Mason Patrick went on to win a substantial "half loaf" with the Air Corps Act of 1926. He got the name changed to corps, which implied both a real combat mission and served as a step on the road to an independent air force. The Act also authorised a substantial air build-up that both he and Mitchell had fervently desired. Patrick retired the next year, and Congress never did appropriate the monies it had promised in 1926—but by then, Patrick was retired and no longer responsible.

With *Mason Patrick and the Fight for Air Service Independence*, Robert White does a substantial service for air power historiography. He balances the picture by providing an important corrective to the Billy Mitchell legend and, at the same time, gives due credit to Mitchell's boss, who lived out of the limelight but, nonetheless, did more than has been recognised heretofore. I recommend this book most strongly. The neophyte air leader could do worse than adopt Mason Patrick as a role model.

That young leader might do equally well to choose Adm Joseph Mason Reeves as yet another pillar of his or her study of air leadership. Unhappy, Tom Wildenberg could do no more with the youth and private life of Reeves than could White with Patrick. Young air warrior-scholars are at least as interested in how the people they study got to be great air leaders as they are in the way they behaved once they reached the pinnacle. Again, biographers can go only as far as their reliable sources let them, so we are inevitably left with a partial picture with some "knowns" and many "unknowns." Air leaders must simply make the assumptions that compensate for missing information.

Like practically all of the admirals of his day and well beyond, Reeves attended the US Naval Academy in Annapolis, Maryland. Born in 1872, he graduated in 1894, 37th in a class of 47, more distinguished for his football than his academics.[19] He spent much of the ensuing time at sea, but his only combat time came briefly in the Spanish-American War. Over the years, he gained substantial recognition as a master of technology and especially as a gunnery expert. As with army artillery, this was conducive to an association with aviation from the earliest times. As Wildenberg makes clear, the battleship admirals were not so disdainful of aviation as they were pursuaded of its precious contribution to gunnery warfare at sea.

Assuming one had established air superiority over a battle area, one's guns were quite able to take the enemy under accurate fire long before he could return the favour. In all probability, the admiral who could sink an enemy's carrier first would then use air superiority for gun spotting to destroy his adversary's battlewagons well before they could hurt him with observing fire from their upper decks. Thus, battleship sailors had powerful motivation to get behind the development of good carriers and aircraft even without the incentives Mitchell provided. But the clear and present threat remained that if the navy did not develop aviation on its own, then Mitchell would take it away—as had happened in Great Britain.

One of the reactions of the navy was to create the Bureau of Aeronautics and promote Moffett to rear admiral in charge—an admirable choice. It showed Congress that the navy did not need an external prod and, at the same time, brought in someone politically savvy and an expert in organisational development and public relations. Further, Moffett had powerful political backing from his friends in Illinois, which helped in the competition with Mitchell. He well understood that he had to have ships, money, and a protected career track for his aviators.[20] He himself was not a pilot. Immediately after taking office, though, he created an aircraft observer's course down at Pensacola, Florida, which included all parts of the pilot's flying syllabus except the solo. Thus, he was able to pin on wings of a sort, and that seemed to help with his own aviators—and even with Congress. Because Reeves was too old to undertake the whole syllabus, he too went through the observer's course.

Earlier, Reeves had served as skipper of the new collier *Jupiter*, and when the navy converted it to the first US aircraft carrier USS Langley in 1924, he became her first commander. For the next decade and more, Reeves laboured on developing the procedures, tactics, and carrier doctrine aboard the *Langley* and the third carrier, the USS *Saratoga*. Meanwhile, back in Washington, Moffett was providing top cover, funding, policy, and personnel, which allowed Reeves the time and resources to pursue other matters.

As Wildenberg and Trimble so adeptly show, the personalities of these two great leaders, both gunnery men and neither a pilot, enabled them to lead feisty aviators. Thus, they successfully integrated aviation into the US Navy, making it the leading naval force in the world—even after the disaster at Pearl Harbuor. This was no mean feat. The qualities in Reeves that the prospective air leader might seek to emulate include a solid commitment to excellence and a continual desire for improvement (this long, long before the Total Quality Management folks came along in the 1990s). His firm but understanding personality enabled him to impose his will on such spirited pilots as Marc Mitscher, greatly increasing the numbers in carrier deck loads and choreographing deck operations to significantly increase the sortie rate. He did so with far, far fewer accidents and injuries than the pilots thought would be inevitable. Like Patrick, Reeves operated in such a reformist (as opposed to a radical or conservative) manner, relating well with the Service heavyweights, that he had made a substantial advance toward making the carrier a capital ship long before Pearl Harbour. Clearly, he had the requisite imagination and initiative. But he, Patrick, and Moffett combined those virtues with endurance. Progress takes time, and all three officers stayed in the saddle far longer than usual. Had Wildenberg found more documentation on Reeves' family life, we might have a better estimate of his selflessness. Certainly, he was more dedicated to his profession than most officers. But it also appears that his family life may have been such that it required far less of his attention than one might expect. Evidently, he and Admiral King had this in common. Both men seem to have concentrated their time and attention on their profession to a degree rarely seen.

Undoubtedly, Moffett especially, but also Reeves, demanded much of their people. But they cared for their charges deeply and went to great lengths to take care of them. As with Patrick, the aspiring air leader could do worse than use Wildenberg's fine book as a building block for a personal leadership model.

## Possible Outcomes of Studying Leadership Through Biography

Perhaps the most significant gain young officers can realise through this approach to leadership would come in the form of additions to a personal database. Most models assert that professional knowledge is one of the primary foundations of leadership. When the moment of truth comes, people never have all the data they need. But armed with a lifetime of study, they can at least increase their inventory of "knowns" and reduce their shortfall of "unknowns." That does not guarantee that their choices will be correct. But it will improve the odds that their guesses will be better than their adversary's.

More than that, though, the biographical approach seems more enjoyable than other methods. It also does something to cultivate a critical—hopefully, not cynical—approach to decision-making. The biographical approach makes it much easier to identify poor choices and to say to one's self, "There, but for the grace of God, go I." Even if such study does not yield guidelines useful in dealing with immediate real-world problems, it may nonetheless preserve composure under stress. People have a strong tendency to feel alone under such conditions. But it helps to know that other leaders, in other places, in other times have always faced fatigue, danger, and uncertainty and survived—"This, too, will pass."

## Improbable Outcomes

The benefits of biographical study—and study in general—have limits. It will not guarantee wisdom, charisma, certain victory, wealth, fame, love, self-fulfillment, or good looks; neither will it eliminate the need for the final guess. It might improve the odds for some of those things, but let us hope that the future does not hold the same thing that confronted Patrick and Reeves, both of whom lived to see the horrors of World War II. It's difficult to imagine anything worse—except losing that war. Perhaps if we prepare well enough, were a third world war to occur, we could prevent an even more terrible outcome.

**A 10-Book Sampler for Professional Reading on Air Leadership***
**Two for an Overview**
*The Challenge of Command: Reading for Military Excellence* by Roger H. Nye. Wayne, N.J.: Avery, 1986.
One of America's greatest military educators, Nye was a West Pointer, an authority on George Patton, a tank commander in combat in Korea, and a long-time faculty member at the US Military Academy. He earned a PhD from Columbia University.
*Makers of the United States Air Force edited* by John L. Frisbee. Washington, D.C.: Office of Air Force History, 1987.
This book contains biographical chapters on many air force leaders. Frisbee, a retired air force officer, was an editor of Air Force Magazine and head of the History Department at the Air Force Academy.
**Eight for Greater Depth**
*Master of Airpower: General Carl A. Spaatz* by David R. Mets. Novato, Calif.: Presidio Press, 1988. Although I wrote this book in two-day-a-half years after I retired from the air force, it is based on my research and experience as an active duty air force officer.
*Hoyt S. Vandenberg: The Life of a General* by Phillip S. Meilinger. Washington, D.C.: Air Force History and Museums Program, 2000.
The author is a graduate of the Air Force Academy, an air force pilot, a teacher of military history, former dean of the School of Advanced Airpower Studies, and former faculty member at the Naval War College. Now a researcher in Washington,
D.C., he has a PhD from the University of Michigan.
*The Quiet Warrior: A Biography of Admiral Raymond A. Spruance by Thomas B. Buell. 1974. Reprint, Annapolis: Naval Institute Press, 1987. Master of Sea Power: A Biography of Fleet Admiral Ernest J. King* by Thomas B. Buell. Boston: Little, Brown, 1980.
The author is among the top three or four practising military biographers in America. A retired navy officer who once commanded a destroyer, Buell was a teacher at the Naval War College and at West Point.
*Admiral William A. Moffett: Architect of Naval Aviation* by William F. Trimble. Washington, D.C.: Smithsonian Institution Press, 1994.
Trimble, a professor at Auburn University, has also written an authoritative book on aircraft development in the US Navy.
*Billy Mitchell: Crusader for Air Power* by Alfred F. Hurley. New York: F. Watts, 1964.
Of the many books on Mitchell, this is the best. Hurley, a retired air force navigator and former head of the History Department at the Air Force Academy, is now chancellor of a large university in Texas. His doctorate is from Princeton.
*Mission with LeMay: My Story by Curtis* E. LeMay with MacKinlay Kantor. Garden City, N.Y.: Doubleday, 1965.

We have a biography of General LeMay, but it was written quickly for the popular market, leaving room for an authoritative, academic work on his life. Thus, the serving air warrior might as well use this book of memoirs, which is widely available.
*Sir Frederick Sykes and the Air Revolution, 1912-1918* by Eric Ash. London: Frank Cass, 1999.
As was the case with Mason Patrick and Joseph Reeves, Sykes was overshadowed by someone more notable—in this case, Hugh Trenchard. This book gives us a more complete picture. The author, who holds a PhD from the University of Calgary, is an air force officer and a graduate of and former teacher at the US Air Force Academy. At this writing, he is the editor of Aerospace Power Journal.
**One for Good Measure**
*American Airpower Biography: A Survey of the Field* by Phillip S. Meilinger. Maxwell AFB, Ala.: Air University Press, 1995.
This pamphlet summarises the status of biographical writing about air leaders. Easily available to serving air warriors, it amplifies many of the ideas in this article.
* I do not mean to imply that this is a definitive bibliography of military biographies— only a starter list of readable, widely available books, most of them should be readily available in the field.

## Notes

1.  Those few included Gen *George C. Kenney, General Kenney Reports: A Personal History of the Pacific War* (1949; reprint, Washington, D.C.: Office of Air Force History, 1987); Lt Gen Lewis H. Brereton, *The Brereton Diaries: The War in the Air in the Pacific, Middle East and Europe, October 3, 1941-8, May 1945* (New York: Morrow, 1946); and Lt Gen William H. Tunner, *Over the Hump* (1964; new imprint, Washington, D.C.: Office of Air Force History, 1985).

2.  Carl von Clausewitz, *On War,* ed. and trans. Michael Howard and Peter Paret (Princeton, N.J.: Princeton University Press, 1976), pp. 100-112.

3.  Col Dennis Drew (Retd.) USAF, "Leading Airmen into the Twenty-First Century: Meeting the Leadership Challenges of the United States Air Force," draft, Maxwell AFB, Ala., n.d.

4.  Halsey had been criticised at Leyte for leaving the amphibious force unprotected while he went off chasing a decoy Japanese carrier force; earlier, Spruance had been criticised during the landings in the Mariana Islands for failing to pursue the Japanese carrier force. The current biography of Halsey is Elmer B. Potter's *Bull Halsey* (Annapolis: Naval Institute Press, 1985); Thomas Hughes is

preparing a new one. See also Thomas B. Buell's fine work *The Quiet Warrior: A Biography of Admiral Raymond A. Spruance* (1974; reprint, Annapolis: Naval Institute Press, 1987).

5.  The answer is not really in the biography written by James Parton, *"Air Force Spoken Here": General Ira Eaker and the Commando of the Air* (Bethesda, Md.: Adler & Adler, 1986). Parton was General Eaker's aide during World War II.

6.  Haywood S. Hansell's *The Air Plan That Defeated Hitler* (Atlanta: Higgins-McArthur, Longino & Porter, 1972), and Strategic Air War against Japan (Maxwell AFB, Ala.: Airpower Research Institute, 1980), give his interpretation of the campaigns but do not answer our question. I believe he was too much the gentleman to explore such subjects in print.

7.  Col Roger H. Nye, *The Challenge of Command: Reading for Military Excellence* (Wayne, N.J.: Avery, 1986). Nye was one of the great but unsung heroes of military education. The "crook" comment came in a conversation with the author—not from his book.

8.  The inspiration for this paragraph is Michael Howard's "Military Science in an Age of Peace," Chesney Memorial Gold Medal Lecture, October 3, 1973, reprinted in *Journal of the Royal United Services Institute* 119 (March 1974), pp. 3-11.

9.  John F. Guilmartin's *A Very Short War: The Mayaguez and the Battle of Koh Tang* (College Station, Tex.: Texas A&M University Press, 1995), is the best work on the subject. See also Benjamin F. Schemmer's *The Raid* (New York: Harper & Row, 1976).

10. There is no complete, scholarly biography of Henry Arnold, but his own *Global Mission* (New York: Harper, 1949), is useful. The current, authoritative work on Arnold is Dik A. Daso's *Architects of American Air Supremacy: Gen Hap Arnold and Dr Theodore von Karman* (Maxwell AFB, Ala.: Air University Press, 1997). When Daso retires from the air force in the summer of 2001, he is slated to become a curator at the Smithsonian Air and Space Museum; hopefully, a complete biography will be forthcoming after that. My own *Master of Airpower: General Carl A. Spaatz* (Novato, Calif.: Presidio Press, 1988), covers the life of Spaatz, and Richard G. Davis's impressive *Carl A. Spaatz and the Air War in Europe* (Washington, D.C.: Office of Air Force History, 1993),

goes into great detail for that part of Spaatz's life. Philip S. Meilinger's *Hoyt S. Vandenberg: The Life of a General* (Washington, D.C.: Air Force History and Museums Program, 2000), covers the latter part of Vandenberg's life, while Brig Gen Jon A. Reynolds's dissertation "Education and Training for High Command: General Hoyt S. Vandenberg's Early Career" (Duke University, 1980), deals with the earlier years. The latter may be difficult to obtain for the officer in the field, but a copy does reside in the Air University Library. Alfred F. Hurley's *Billy Mitchell: Crusader for Air Power* (New York: F. Watts, 1964), is the best work on Mitchell. Evidently, a good academic biography on LeMay does not exist, but his and MacKinlay Kantor's *Mission with LeMay: My Story* (Garden City, N.Y.: Doubleday, 1965), is widely available. Martha Byrd's *Chennault: Giving Wings to the Tiger* (University, Ala.: University of Alamabad Press, 1987), is the best thing on Claire Chennault.

11.  William F. Trimble's Admiral William A. Moffett, Architect of Naval Aviation (Washington, D.C.: Smithsonian Institution Press, 1994), is an authoritative interpretation of Moffett. Thomas B. Buell's Master of Sea Power: A Biography of Fleet Admiral Ernest J. King (Boston: Little, Brown, 1980), is doubtless one of the three or four best American military biographies ever written—truly a model for all young biographers. It is in the same league with Forrest Pogue's biography of George Marshall and Stephen Ambrose's work on Dwight Eisenhower.

12.  See Vincent Orange's three books *A Life of Marshal of the RAF Lord Tedder of Glenguin* (London: Frank Cass, 2000); *Coningham: A Biography of Air Marshal Sir Arthur Coningham, KCB, KBE, DSO, MC, DFC, AFC* (Washington, D.C.: Centre for Air Force History, 1992); and *A Biography of Air Chief Marshal Sir Keith Park, GCG, KBE, MC, DFC, DCL* (London: Methuen, 1984). See also Robert Wright's *The Man Who Won the Battle of Britain* (New York: Scribner, 1969).

13.  Eric Ash, *Sir Frederick Sykes and the Air Revolution, 1912-1918* (London: Frank Cass, 1999).

14.  See David Irving's books *Goering: A Biography* (New York: Morrow, 1989); and *The Rise and Fall of the Luftwaffe: The Life of Field Marshal Erhard Milch* (Boston: Little, Brown, 1973). Undoubtedly, Lee Asher's *Goering: Air Leader* (New York: Hippocrene, 1972), gives another, but less controversial, view.

15. Trimble, n. 11, p. 266.

16. *The Court-Martial of Billy Mitchell*, Republic Pictures, 1955.

17. Thomas Wildenberg, *Destined for Glory: Dive Bombing, Midway, and the Evolution of Carrier Air Power* (Annapolis: Naval Institute Press, 1998).

18. On Foulois, see the late John F. Shiner's *Foulois and the US Army Air Corps, 1931-1935* (Washington DC: Office of Air Force History, 1984), although it is not the complete biography.

19. United States Naval Academy Alumni *Association, Register of Alumni, Graduates, and Former Naval Cadets and Midshipmen, 1845-1992* (Annapolis: US Naval Academy, 1992), p. 163.

20. Stephen Peter Rosen, *Winning the Next War: Innovation and the Modern Military* (Ithaca, N.Y.: Cornell University Press, 1991), 64-71; and Thomas C. Hone, "Navy Leadership: Rear Admiral William Moffett as Chief of the Bureau of Aeronautics," in Wayne Thompson, ed., *Air Leadership: Proceedings of a Conference at Bolling Air Force Base*, April 13-14, 1984, ed. Wayne Thompson (Washington, D.C.: Office of Air Force History, 1986), pp. 83-117.

# 6
# Leadership Training in the IAF

*A.S. Bahal*

## Introduction

In the recently held bilateral exercises with the air forces of the USA, UK, France, South Africa, Singapore and Russia, our men and machines put up outstanding performances, making the world take notice of our professionalism. Besides exercises, the contribution of Indian Air Force (IAF) detachments in peace-keeping operations too has been exemplary.[1] Similarly, the courage and strong leadership qualities displayed by our personnel in Andaman and Nicobar Islands, despite personal losses, highlights the high traditions of the IAF. At no time in its history has the IAF been so technically competent and well trained. In fact, we have cultivated our own brand image, that is, "Brand Air Force."

Air Commodore Jasjit Singh says that the IAF today is undergoing unprecedented historical changes. From being a subcontinental force, it is transforming itself into a force with continental reach and effect. We are acquiring state-of-the-art equipment and technology and are linking ourselves with space. The modernisation process includes acquisition of airborne warning and control system (AWACS), more air-to-air refuellers, aerostats and high technology aircraft and precision weapon systems.

At the same time, the Service has been embarrassed by the acts of a few leaders of the middle and, sometimes, higher echelons.[2] In fact, in the last five years, there have been a number of inquiries and court martials in the armed forces. These include sensitive information leaks and financial irregularities. This has made the media question whether the last surviving bastion of discipline and probity is crumbling.[3] Someone has aptly said, "Men of genius are admired, men of wealth envied, men of power feared but only men of character trusted." Without trust, one cannot lead. Therefore, whilst we bask in our achievements, there is a need to overcome our weak areas by strengthening our leadership development process.

## Aim

The aim of this paper is to identify the leadership needs for the future, identify the weak areas in the leadership development process and recommend measures to equip the aerospace leaders of tomorrow to cope with the complex challenges of the future.

## Scope

The subject would be covered under the following heads:
- Leadership requirements for the 21st century IAF leaders.
- Requirements specific to the IAF.
- Traits desired in future leaders.
- Leadership development process in the IAF:
  ○ Structured.
  ○ Informal development process.
- Existing limitations in the leadership development process.
- Recommendations.

## Leadership Requirements for 21st Century Leaders in the IAF

### *Manpower*

Unlike earlier times, the typical young officer who joins the air force today predominantly comes from the middle or low middle income group families. Nevertheless, he or she is more qualified, aware and better equipped to handle technology. He is also more ambitious, competitive and calculative than his seniors who joined decades ago.[4] Even the aspiring airmen are usually better educated and more aware of their rights than their earlier counterparts. However, there is a dichotomy here in that whilst the younger generation personnel are more aware and tech-savvy, they may actually not be more intelligent or possess better IQ in problem solving. Informal discussions with qualified flying instructors (QFIs) at the Air Force Academy

(AFA) have indicated that the standard of the lower half of the trainees has deteriorated considerably over a period of time. This could primarily be due to the best available not joining the IAF because there are better opportunities outside. This dichotomy is likely to lead to a different sort of challenge for tomorrow's leaders where the personnel may be more aware and tech-savvy but may actually possess lower IQ.

### Globalisation and Rapid Economic Growth

The Indian economy has been growing at a rapid pace in the last few years. The pay scales in the civil sector have seen a quantum jump. It has been estimated that they are likely to increase at an average of 18 per cent in 2006. This has resulted in a number of skilled air force officers, pilots and personnel leaving the Service to join perceived greener pastures. Though the IAF provides a very high quality of life, we cannot match the pay scales being offered in the commercial sector. Therefore, retaining, skilled manpower is one of the major challenges that the IAF leadership faces today and is expected to face in the future.

In consonance with the emergence of an economically strong and technologically advanced India, its role in global affairs is likely to increase further. IAF personnel too would need to remain prepared for a larger global role. They could be utilised in possible out of area contingencies (OOAC), coalition tasks or increased participation in UN peace-keeping operations. The younger officers are likely to get more exposure in working along with air forces of other countries. They may also be required to project India's views on complex issues in international fora. This would require them to possess more cognitive skills and better cultural awareness of international politics in general and of South Asia in particular. In fact, this process has already started and the number of IAF officers who have gone abroad for courses, exercises or seminars has increased significantly in the last two to three years. The young leaders of tomorrow would need to be conscious of the political implications of their actions as these can have a profound impact on our national interests. In international exercises or global interactions, they may be required to act as our diplomats. The requirement, therefore, is to prepare our officers to "Think Global."

### Technological Advancement

Today, the IAF is transforming itself to become an aerospace power. Towards this end, a number of projects are under fructification that include installation of aerostats, procurement of airborne warning and control system (AWACS), instituting an integrated air command and control system (IACCS) and establishing a networked environment that exploits the information revolution. The main problem would lie not in integrating technology *per se* but in adapting various levels of leadership towards exploiting technology to its maximum effect.

This problem is likely to be more evident at the middle and higher echelons as the younger officers are increasingly exposed to handle technology at an early age. Since the processing speed doubles every 18 months, the technology management differential would increase further. It would become a significant challenge for the emerging leadership who would need to lead young leaders who are more tech-savvy and better informed.

Modern communication systems provide us with so much information that it permits us to take almost instantaneous decisions. Sometimes, an instant decision may not be the correct decision. Future leaders would have at their fingertips all types of information, from the status of an operational unit to the details of the type, number and location of each aircraft, weapon system and equipment available in the air force. Every level of command can then oversee the functioning of each unit on the lines of George Orwell's 1984. Though human-computer interactive devices are likely to aid the war-fighter's information management, they would not be able to control overwhelming information overload. The modern work environment has already increased the stress levels; this would get further compounded by information overload and continuous monitoring of all activities by the higher echelons.

Therefore, two things would need to be done. First, empowering the present-day machine-age leaders to meet the demands of technology and information age by providing them with education. Second, enhancing their ability to sift between what is critical and what is important. One of the techniques that could be used is "technology focus" that allows us to search further, define better and identify critical issues clearly.

The easy availability of information is likely to tie down the IAF commander to his office instead of making him visit the field areas to obtain first-hand information. This may cut him off from direct human contact, which is so essential to build bonds. The subordinates too want to meet their leader, see that he cares, and share his vision to achieve the organisational objectives.

In future, the IAF personnel would be working with some of the most expensive and technologically advanced equipment. There would be a greater need for accountability and responsibility on the shoulders of junior and middle level leaders whilst handling this equipment. The IAF leadership too would need to show greater sensitivity towards cost effective utilisation of assets and towards factoring the cost factor in our decision-making matrix.

### Media Handling

The media explosion of the 1990s has resulted in more intimate involvement of the media with the Indian armed forces. The Kargil War and the Tehelka expose have highlighted two diverse facets of our relationship with the media. Increasingly, junior leaders may find themselves interacting with the national or international media. Many may also take the route of venting their real or perceived grievances through the print or visual media. Some of the dirty linen of the IAF would be washed in public. There is a requirement to run the organisation more efficiently, honestly and in a transparent fashion, and train our personnel in media and legal affairs, including air force, civil and international law.

### Tomorrow's Battlefield and Nature of Warfare

The future battlefield is likely to be digitised, networked and seamlessly integrated. Fusion of advanced ground, air and space-based systems would result in greater transparency, increased mobility, enhanced reach and accuracy and enlarged areas of influence. The impact of technology demands innovative operational concepts to fight a high-tech knowledge-based war.[5] The future leaders would need to effect a synergistic union between myriad technological capabilities and effective employment of IAF personnel. Yet, wars fought for territory would slowly lose their meaning in an economically linked global world order and also while operating under nuclear thresholds. Consequently, destruction of the enemy's military power may not remain as relevant in the future. The scenario that is most likely too prevail is the increasing threat posed by non-state actors and terror organisations propagating their own form of *jihad*. The future leaders may have to contend with a faceless enemy, high tensions, greater fatigue levels, increased media glare and no clearly defined agenda. They would need to develop unconventional responses to diverse threats ranging from high intensity conflicts fought under nuclear thresholds to challenges posed by terror organisations.

Another important issue that needs to be kept in mind is that in the future, political considerations would increasingly influence military decisions and operational art. Military plans based on domestic and foreign policies, real world considerations, sensitive human rights issues and economic constraints would find greater acceptability with the civilian leadership. IAF leaders, while remaining apolitical, would need to give political fundamentals their due weightage. A greater flexibility in mind would need to be exercised to enable matching the diverse nature of threats and politico-eco-military and technological considerations.

## What is Critically Required?

To cater to the challenges of the future, what is critically needed in the leadership development process is the ability to impart the right type of education that leads to knowledge, and inculcating in the officers the ability to transform knowledge into wisdom—knowledge not only related to military issues but also related to handling technology, analysing the global security environment and understanding civil and political imperatives. The future leader, therefore, should be both a generalist and a specialist.

## Leadership Requirements Specific to the IAF

In the Indian Army or Navy, the officers are trained towards fighting alongwith their men from the first day of their careers. Hence, the officers are better exposed towards exercising leadership qualities involving a group of men. However, in the IAF, it is generally the officer cadre that does the bulk of war-fighting. Therefore, two different types of leadership development training are required; one that trains officers to lead in the air or in activities related with flying, and the other that trains them to lead air force personnel on the ground to achieve overall organisational objectives. Leadership in the air requires a very high level of professional competence in aspects related to flying itself, and the initial career of an air crew in particular is focussed towards this aspect. On the other hand, leadership on the ground requires a high degree of administrative acumen. Since an officer's career in general, and a pilot's in particular, is devoted more towards developing professional competence in his formative years, his exposure towards leading men on the ground suffers.

## Desired Traits in Tomorrow's Leaders

After taking note of the variables that are likely to affect tomorrow's leadership, let us examine the traits that need to be present in future leaders to overcome these uncertainties. As we discuss these traits, we may feel that they were required earlier too in some form or the other. However, due to rapid technological advances, changing societal values and faster pace of development, the requirement to possess these traits has now become critical.

### Ability to Create a Vision

The Roman writer, Seneca once observed, "If a man does not know what port he is steering to, no wind is favourable."[6] The primary trait that the leader of tomorrow must possess is the ability to create a vision, a dream, a set of intentions and a frame of reference at all echelons of leadership. Thereafter, he must motivate and inspire his personnel towards achieving this vision. Most of us at Command and Air Headquarters (HQ) are caught up in our routine day-to-day activities. There is a need to evolve and promulgate a strategic vision statement or a document that includes all key issues related to the aims and objectives of the IAF and critical issues related to operations, maintenance, administration of human resource development (HRD). From this document, the commanders at all levels would identify their own key result areas (KRAs)n to be achieved to realise this vision.

The vision document should be modified periodically to take into account current realities.

### Effective Communication Skills

Merely developing a vision is not adequate in itself; the leaders at all levels should clearly be able to communicate an extraordinary focus of commitment and zeal which in itself attracts people towards them. They would need to be like orchestra conductors to get potentially diverse and talented people to work towards a common goal.

### Technological and Professional Competence

The IAF places considerable emphasis on training leaders to be professionally competent. However, the junior leaders would need to develop the reading habit from a young age, in order to stay abreast of technological advancements and remain professionally competent.

### Dynamic Optimism

The personnel in the future would be working under considerable stress and in challenging situations. It is here that a leader's belief in himself and in his ability to make a difference in people's lives could act as a catalyst in enhancing the motivation levels of those placed under him. The output of an individual is equated to multiplying "ability" with "motivation." Here, motivation is a major force multiplier. Dynamic optimism is a key trait to develop if one wants to create transformational leadership. The outward manifestations of this trait are a positive attitude, unwavering enthusiasm and endless energy.

### Ability to Empower

Since the education and awareness levels of the junior leaders would be high, there is a need for the leader to be able to empower them with intellectual space and goals to be achieved. He would need to curb his natural instincts of micro-management and provide space to the subordinates to develop.

## Self-Discipline
To achieve goals, it is important that one possesses self-discipline. All great leaders do the basic things right such as they wake up on time, are punctual and usually exemplify a disciplined approach in their way of work. This habit would need to be inculcated at an early age.

## Time Consciousness
Time consciousness includes not only time management but also a major quality that all able leaders possess: they do not waste people's time.

## Character
Men trust leaders with character. This essential trait encompasses integrity, honour, moral uprightness and impartially. This is one critical trait of a leader that can be developed when the officer is young.

## Courage
Besides, bravery and valour, the leader of tomorrow must possess moral courage to pull up an erring subordinate, stand by his men when they are right, and have the ability to share credit for the work that comes to the unit.

## Ability to Show They "Care"
In this materialistic world, people want others to care, and will do wonders for those who care for them. Technology tends to drive leaders away from people. The basic adage that must never be forgotten is, "Effective leaders spend at least 25 per cent of their time with their men."

## Linguistic/Ability to Work with Multiracial Organisations
Increasingly, junior leaders would need to participate in multinational endeavours. They must develop the curiosity to learn about other cultures and have the ability to speak at least one additional international language like Spanish/French/German/Chinese/Russian.

## Physical Fitness and Spiritualism
The computer age has made today's leader more desk-bound. With increased

stress levels and more complex tasks, there is a need to be physically fit and mentally strong. Meditation provides a leader with spiritual insights and the ability to concentrate while it also acts as an effective de-stressor.

## Developing Leadership Training in the IAF

Field Marshal Viscount Montgomery had once said, "It is almost true to say that leaders are made, rather than born." It is a proven fact that the officers who excel during the training period, do not necessarily maintain their superlative performances during their service careers.[7] On the other hand, even officers with average scholastic ability can develop into highly effective leaders, provided they are trained properly. Let us evaluate our leadership development process.

The armed forces selection system consciously looks for candidates who may be academically average but have a balanced and upright disposition as well as possess basic essential leadership traits. In academies, initially the focus is on followership training to instil discipline and unquestioned obedience of orders. This is necessary to transform them from the civilian life to the military order and discipline. There is equal stress on academics, basics of warfare, physical and mental toughness and development of leadership qualities. In the IAF, the leadership development process is executed in a two-fold fashion: structured and informal.

### *Structured Leadership Development Programme*

The structured leadership development programme includes IAF academies, unit training and courses. The air force courses of instruction are so structured and spaced that an officer can constantly upgrade his knowledge commensurate with his years in service. Table 1 provides a summary of the existing structured leadership development process.

The Air Force Academy (AFA) shoulders the prime responsibility of initiating the leadership development programme in the IAF. The essential focus at the AFA is on teaching basic flying skills, enhancing knowledge on flying related subjects and developing physical and mental toughness.

When young officers reach the operational units, the responsibility for continuing with their leadership development process lies with the commanding officer/station commander. For the pilots, initially the officer focusses on learning how to fly an advanced aircraft and how to use it as a weapon system. Subsequently, he is taught how to lead in the air. Flying itself relates to an unknown environment and to an extent develops physical courage. Whilst they are learning advanced flying skills, the officers are also exposed to secondary duties that deal with administrative aspects like adjutant, UFSIO or Oi/c (officer-in-charge) messes, though in an ad hoc fashion. During the formative years, there is very little structured exposure for the pilots towards administering and leading men on the ground. This deficiency stands out when they become commanding officers.

After six years of service, the young officer is eligible to undergo the Junior Commander's Course (JCC). The Air Force Administrative College (AFAC) teaches him aspects related to administration, air force law, psychology of leadership and air power. Further, the officer is prepared to effectively function as a junior commander. At the Tactical and Combat Development Establishment (TACDE), the fighter and helicopter air crew learn about qualities of leadership in the air, while undertaking the FCL/FSL/HCL/MFC/SAGW courses. However, the training of young leaders till now deals only with the tactical level.

The next step in the officer's leadership development programme is to undertake the Air Staff Course at the Defence Services Staff College (DSSC), Wellington. The course enables officers to perform effectively in command and staff appointments tenable by squadron leaders to group captain ranks.

After the officer has finished command of a unit, he could be detailed for the Higher Air Command Course (HACC) at the College of Air Warfare or the Higher Defence Management Course (HDMC) at the CDM. The aim of HACC is to train selected officers of the three Services to occupy senior command and staff appointments, as they will be involved in planning of air operations and for command of stations.

The NDC is the last structured course in the leadership development process. This is pitched at the strategic level to provide insight into issues related to national security and higher leadership requirements.

*Informal Training*

In better run units, the commanding officer (CO) takes it upon himself to train newly commissioned officers. He exposes them slowly to various secondary duties that improve their administrative capability and professional acumen. The basic values and core ethics of the armed forces are learnt by the young officer in the first few units that he is posted to. He learns how to conduct himself as an officer, how to lead men and to develop the habit of reading and communicating. It is here that the role of a CO is crucial and it is here that the greatest challenge lies today in developing the leadership qualities of future leaders. During his career in the IAF, the officer carries out multifarious duties in a number of diverse appointments, thereby, learning his profession and the art of leadership simultaneously.

## Role of CLABS at CAW

The Centre for Leadership Training and Behavioural Sciences (CLABS) was established at the College of Air Warfare (CAW) on October 19, 2001. CLABS conducts capsules for officers between 5-13 years of service with an aim to expose them to concepts and theories of leadership and behavioural sciences and for officers with more than 13 years service, to enhance their understanding of organisation behaviour and the peculiarities that exist at the higher leadership levels. They have so far conducted around 70 courses in field units of different commands and have interacted with over 1,500 officers. The feedback of the capsules has been very positive. On an experimental basis, a capsule was conducted at Pathankot for the entire air force station to enhance vertical integration.

## Existing Limitations in Leadership Development

The major limitations in the present system of leadership development are:

- Most of an officer's time is spent in an operational unit learning the basic professional skills. However, there is no structured leadership development plan for leading men on the ground at the unit level. Therefore, the leadership development process depends largely on the individual CO's interest and his vision in developing his officers.

Table 1: **Existing Structured Leadership Development Process**

| Grade | FLT Cadet | 1-5 Yrs | 6-10 Yrs | 10-20 Yrs | 20-30 Yrs | 30-40 Yrs |
|---|---|---|---|---|---|---|
| Level of Education | BSC/Graduate | — | — | MSC (Def | M Phil | — |
| Training Institutes | AFA/Hakimpet/ Bidar | Op units | — Op Units — AFAC-JCC — TACDE — FCL/FSL/HCL | — Air Staff Course at DSSC — FCL/FSL/ HCL courses at TACDE | CAW — HACC — CDM — HDMC | NDC |
| Levels of Warfare Emphasised | Basic level | Tactical level | Tactical level | Tactical/ Operational level | Operational/ Strategic level | Strategic level |
| Focus of Training | Introduction to service training and developing basic flying skills | How to employ the aircraft as a weapon system | Leadership in air at unit level — FCL/FSL/ HCL at TACDE — Adm and junior staff appts at AFAC | — To hold staff and command appointments from Sqn Ldr to Gp Capt ranks — Courses on Combat Tactics at TACDE | Op Art and Senior command and staff appts | To hold senior appts and develop strategic thinking. |
| Leadership Traits Developed | Basic professional competence and physical and mental toughness | Professional competence courage and self-discipline | Professional competence, knowledge, communication skills, courage and self-discipline | Professional competence, leadership in air and on ground, Comn, Comd and staff work and exposure to other air forces | Op strategy, comm skills, leadership on ground and exposure towards conceptual skills | External interactions and conceptual skills |

- The formal training for a large percentage of air force officers is focussed mostly at the tactical level. For a majority of officers, there are limited avenues for developing operational or conceptual skills.
- Not all air force officers undergo all the desired training courses. Further, adequate importance is not being given in detailing suitable officers for these courses. Performance during courses is also not given due weightage and recognition.
- Structurally, there is a direct link between professional higher level courses and transition to higher ranks. However, the higher training institutions such as CAW, Army War College, College of Naval Warfare and CDM do not get the best and brightest officers of the IAF to attend HACC or HDMC courses as they cannot be spared from their present appointments. A number of air force officers detailed for HACC/HC/NHC/HDMC either miss their next rank or get superannuated within a few years of completing the course. Thus, we are imparting operational and conceptual skills to a sizeable number who may never actually employ them, thereby, missing out on the golden opportunity provided by a vibrant formal training structure in training potential higher level commanders. Further, the number of officers who undergo such courses is very limited, as only limited vacancies are available in these institutions.
- There is no in-Service institution that provides an intellectual framework for the development of doctrine and strategy, or to conduct research on aerospace issues or evolve doctrinal and philosophical thought for the IAF.
- No specialised training is given on space issues. With increased dependence on space for war-fighting, this indeed is a serious deficiency.
- A considerable amount of micro-management takes place in the IAF due to the zero-error syndrome and also because we tend to remain rooted to the Flt Cdr level, as that is our comfort zone. This reduces the intellectual and working space available to the young, leaders for developing their leadership skills.
- In consonance with the outside environment, there is a general

degradation in the qualities of integrity, honesty, ethics, values and moral courage in our officers today.

- Adequate emphasis is not being given to building physical fitness and mental strength, especially in the flying units.

## Recent Training Developments in the IAF

To overcome some of the existing limitations, a review of training courses was carried out by Air HQ and HQ TC in 2005. The aim was to reduce the duration of the absence of officers from the operational units, streamline the course syllabi and provide "just in time" training. It was felt that the basic learning should be carried out more by "distance education" with a short contact programme. Distance education leverages existing technology to provide more learning to a wider audience at different locations, and that too at low cost. There is also a proposal to grade all the courses and link the grade point average with promotions. In the new system, instead of JCC, there would be a Basic Air Staff Course at AFAC for all officers between 3-4 years of service, Basic Professional Knowledge Course for all air crew between 5-6 years, Intermediate Staff Course at AFAC for all officers between 6-8 years, QFI/FCL/TP courses between 8-11 years, Advance Professional Knowledge Course between 10 to 101/2 years, Advanced Air Staff Course between 10-12 years and HACC between 19-21 years of service. The main benefit of the new training policy is that in a methodical manner, a greater number of officers would benefit from these courses as it would be mandatory for all the officers to attend them, current issues would get speedier dissemination to an wider audience and the knowledge bank would be continuously updated as the information would eventually be available at the Air Force WAN to any one who wants to access it.

## Recommendations for the Future

One of the greatest assets of the IAF is that it provides officers with progressive and comprehensive professional training. The training system synchronises an officer's intellectual growth in line with increasing rank and responsibilities. Further, the IAF is moving towards "just in time" training and e-learning. To reduce the remaining limitations, there is really no need to make major changes with the established structures—what is required is to empower those structures that bring about a "Revolution in Leadership Affairs." The IAF would need to focus on four pillars of leadership development; viz unit training, institutional courses, operational assignments and self-development. Let us look at some of the recommendations.

### Develop a Vision

There is a need to promulgate a clear and achievable vision document at all echelons of the leadership that clearly highlights the KRA that need to be achieved at that level and the core values of the organisation that cannot be compromised.

### Structured Leadership Development Plan at Unit/Station Level

Unit-based learning and leadership development achieved should be considered part of a unit's overall operational readiness. A CO/ Station Commander (Stn Cdr) of a unit is intimately involved with the professional and personal development of newly commissioned officers. At this impressionable age, the officer can be moulded in any fashion. Therefore, the major responsibility for developing leadership traits in the budding leaders would lie with the COs/Stn Cdrs; the vision they communicate, the values they propagate and the professional skills they develop in these young officers. Whilst each of us as CO has worked within our capabilities towards developing leadership traits in the young officers, each one of us has done it in our own way and each one's way has been different. Presently, there is no systematic method that lays down guidelines for leadership development in the units. Some of these guidelines could include the following:

- Develop a structured leadership development programme at the unit/ station level for the newly commissioned officers.
- Identify buddies among senior colleagues who can assist junior officers in all spheres of personal or professional growth.
- Encourage development of ethics and moral values in the junior leaders by acting as role models, communicating core values of the organisation and taking firm action on acts relating to moral turpitude.
- Create a balance between focus towards development of professional

skills and developing physical fitness and administrative acumen.

- Provide opportunities to young officers in holding diverse secondary duties. It must be ensured that within the first five years of his service, each young officer has been exposed to all the secondary duties such as UFSIO, O i/c Airmen Mess/SNCO's mess, Oi/c Work Services, adjutant, etc in a systematic manner. This could be recorded in his PRB/Personal Occurrence Book (for non-air crew) and would assist the CO of the next unit to identify future development areas.

- Develop the young leaders' habit to read by asking them to give periodic lectures, briefs and analysis on global issues. This also means that at least one day in two weeks should be mandatorily devoted towards maintenance and leadership development activities. Further, encourage them to write articles and papers. The aim is motivate an officer to become more of a warrior-philosopher than merely a warrior-scholar.

- Empower the young leaders by providing them intellectual space. This could be carried out by giving them challenging tasks and providing them with appropriate guidance.

### Training Courses

The focus would now need to shift towards e-learning and distance education with a short contact programme. The fundamentals should be learnt at the unit level through the distance education programme; the training course could focus more on enlarging the horizons of the officers and solving problems many levels above their rank. In this, the COs and station commanders have a major role to play. The Staff and War Colleges would need to focus less on basics and more on developing operational and conceptual skills. The air force too would need to give greater importance to developing the operational and strategic thinking at the middle and higher echelons of leadership. The professional higher level courses such as HACC/HDMC/NDC that encourage intellectual and conceptual development must find a link with transition to higher ranks. The IAF would need to spare its upcoming leaders to attend these courses. Having selected the best for these courses, they should get promoted to higher ranks so that the expertise gained can be utilised gainfully by the organisation.

### *Resident and Non-Resident Programmes*

Towards ensuring that a wider audience benefits from courses i.e. Air Staff Course at DSSC, HACC at CAW/AWC/CNW and HDMC at CDM, there should be two types of programmes: resident and non-resident. The resident programme could be for those who have been selected for undergoing the course. For all other officers who meet basic QRs and are interested in undertaking these courses, a distance education non-resident programme could be designed with a short contact period for holding exams and submitting dissertations.

### *Mandatory Courses and Appointments*

Courses such as the Air Staff Course and higher level professional courses as well as command of units and stations should be made mandatory for career progression in the IAF.

### *Empowerment*

There is a need to develop the culture of empowerment at all echelons of leadership. The IAF leadership should be willing to share power with its subordinates in terms of developing an organisational vision. The first step towards empowerment is providing knowledge. Thereafter, providing an environment where we are not looking for scapegoats but adequate rope is given to those who want to exercise their intellect. The progress starts with giving small challenging tasks at all levels of leadership and demanding innovativeness and creativity. The senior leader must be seen as a coach and a guide and not as a micro-manager. Here, one would be reminded of what Lao Tzu had emphasised about empowerment, "But of a good leader, who talks little, when his work his done, his aim fulfilled, they will all say, we did it ourselves." In empowerment, the credit must go to the doers. These highly skilled leaders would need to be retained in service by providing them a stimulating environment for growth.

### *Moral Values*

Decisive action would need to be taken against officers found indulging in indisciplined activities or acts not commensurate with the high traditions of the armed forces.

### Aerospace Issues

Selected officers should be trained at the Indian Space Research Organisation (ISRO) or at an appropriate agency on space issues such as launch and recovery of satellites, satellite tracking and anti-satellite warfare.

### Media Training

Media training is being carried out at Staff and War Colleges. It should be part of all training courses, including the Basic and Intermediate Staff Course.

### Rewards

The officers standing first in training courses should be rewarded either with choice postings, posting abroad or promotions. This should be visible to all the officers of the organisation so as to motivate them to take the training courses more seriously.

### Flt Cdr/CO/Stn Cdr Capsules

For the short term, Flt Lt Cdr/CO/Stn Cdr capsules should be organised at a suitable location where case studies on practical aspects relating to leadership, discipline, law, administration, work services and media could be covered in a short, two-week capsule for potential COs/Flt Cdrs/Stn Cdrs just before they take on these appointments. There are plans to hold such capsules at a central location.

## Conclusion

The requirements of the IAF leadership in the future would be diverse. This would include adapting to technological advances, matching a diverse range of threats, remaining within budget constraints and preparing leaders to operate under the media's glare while employing air power even against non-state actors. To develop matching leadership traits, the IAF would need to follow a four-fold strategy: structured unit training, institutionalised training courses, diverse operational assignments and self-development programmes.

The key to success in future would be to bring in a more institutionalised role of the CO/Stn Cdr in the leadership development process, provide an empowered environment, reward deserving officers and link training courses with career progression in the armed forces. Whilst we all have talked the talk for a long time, let us have the courage now to walk the walk with greater resolve.

## Notes

1. Para 5 of speech given by the Chief of Air Staff (CAS), Air Chief Marshal S.P. Tyagi PVSM, AVSM, VM, ADC at the Air Force Day parade on October 8, 2005.

2. "Leadership in the IAF," unpublished Service paper written by Air Cmde A. Raha, Dy Comdt AFA.

3. Rajat Pandit, "6000 Cases of Court Martial in Armed Forces Since 2000," TNN.

4. Lt Yogesh V. Athawale, IN, "Changing Nature of Leadership in the 21st Century."

5. V.K. Shrivastava, "Indian Air Force in the Years Ahead: An Army View."

6. Talk by Robert D. Blackwill, "The Quality and Durability of the US-India Relationship."

7. Lt Gen H.B. Kala, PVSM, AVSM, SC, "Demystifying Military Leadership."

# 7
# Managing Future Space Capabilities

*K.K. Nair*

It is reasonably well known that space enabled information and information enabled warfare comprise the crux of modern military war-fighting, the much touted revolution in military affairs (RMA) of the 1980s, network-centric warfare (NCW) of the 1990s and, finally, defence force transformation architecture concepts of the new millennium. Briefly, the very base of most of these concepts is contingent on the exploitation of space. Talk on the above concepts has been rampant in the armed forces across the world (and ours) for quite some time. As a matter of fact, a veritable cottage industry has grown around these concepts. However, the pace of the translation of the concepts into military operations has been significant only in the case of a few countries like the United States (US) and the former Soviet Union (FSU).[1] Most countries, including ours, are yet to venture beyond healthy discussion and debate into actual development of capabilities. In most cases, this is primarily because of the usual inihibiting riders of high cost and technology as well as immature doctrines and inadequate comprehension of the operational utilities afforded by integration of space into military capabilities.

Nevertheless, the impact of these riders in our unique context is not as significant considering that space capabilities do exist and a growing economy would be able to sustain reasonable military demands. Matching US levels of space utilisation to revolutionise military operations apparently is too ambitious, but making a beginning certainly is not.

## Matching the Revolution in Civil Affairs
The above assumes greater significance considering that a more intense,

more powerful and yet less famous revolution in civilian affairs is already underway. The revolution is driven by our civilian space capabilities and is silently revolutionising national well-being, commerce and development as never before. However, the development of national space capabilities and their integration into civil development is apparently not concurrently matched in a military context. Far from concurrent matching, the reality is that there exists a serious mismatch.

One of the primary factors contributing to the mismatch is the absence of leadership, both organisational and institutional, for integrating space into military operations. This has, consequently, led to absence of an institutional space vision and absence of resources (both human and otherwise) for fulfilling aspirations. Fulfilling these lacunae would be essential for systematically integrating space into conventional military capabilities and then refining the broad strategy and operational doctrines for translating the concepts of RMA, NCW, etc into operational solutions.

## Challenge to Leadership

While fulfilment of the leadership vacuum appears a fairly simplistic solution in theory, in actual practice, it would be fraught with enormous difficulties and challenges. Inclusion of the space paradigm into military affairs and the near-chaotic pace of change and confusion that it generates would present enormous leadership challenges at a variety of levels, ranging from the national, organisational to institutional levels of squadrons, units, personnel, etc. The inherent pace of technological innovation in the realm of air and space is so intense that even aerospace superpowers like the US and the FSU are yet to fully come to terms with the immense potential afforded by the vertical dimension, the challenges in integrating the media of air and space, the doctrinal challenges, the challenges to operational integration, and a host of other issues.[2]

The complexities of integration and utilising space for military purposes assume greater significance in our context considering the fact that, unlike in the case of most countries where space programmes evolved to serve military needs, our space programmes were tailor-made purely to support civilian rather than military endeavours. Hence, civil to military spillovers are by exception rather than design. Redesigning for military purposes would be neither possible nor desirable or even acceptable. Our requirements in the present and near foreseeable future would demand optimal exploitation of extant capabilities, in keeping with the technological, cost and other limitations.

Hence, integrating and operationalising space as well as developing military specific space technology in the future would demand a reexamination of the operational attributes afforded as well as the roles, missions and employability of space in support of national security objectives. Enormous changes would be forthcoming; the changes would need to be comprehended and engaged in their entirety. The change driven by the advent of space would need to be viewed not in isolation but in relation to the dynamics of the prevailing geo-economic and geo-strategic issues, its impact on national empowerment in a broader context and on military instruments of power in a narrower context. Managing the change would call for effective leadership. The challenge to leadership would be in anticipating changes, accepting changes, keeping pace with changes and, finally, in managing changes to support objectives. In order to undertake the above, it would be essential to briefly dwell on optimally utilising existing capabilities, envisaging future capabilities and then exploring the options for developing leaders to manage future space capabilities.

## Optimally Exploiting Extant Capabilities

At the outset, it needs to be borne in mind that space-based assets as in the case of aircraft are complex, costly and scarce instruments which have multiple applications and also apply at multiple levels of strategy, operations and tactics, as also during peace, crises, wars, etc. Hence, a broad-based comprehension of the operational possibilities as also the technological limitations would be an essential prerequisite for managing future space capabilities. This would dictate a deeply cooperative and even integrated approach between the military and the Department of Space (DoS) to understand the impact of space on military operations, as well as for building and managing capabilities. Space shares a large degree of commonolity with air power in terms of characteristics, attributes, doctrinal utility, etc and, hence, air power expertise would be an essential prerequisite to develop leaders responsible for managing future space capabilities.[3] A reservoir of air power expertise is already available with the Indian Air Force (IAF), and the same would need to draw upon the space expertise available in the DoS, and an initial effort could be undertaken which would be primarily aimed at:

- Comprehensively exploring the realm of possibilities afforded by space.
- Based on the possibilities, enunciating a dynamic vision and a road-map.
- Developing leaders to translate possibilities, vision and roadmaps into operational solutions.
- Application and integration of space into conventional capabilities for providing solutions to national security challenges.

The above is a vast field and initially would primarily aim at fulfilling two aspects. The first would be generic space familiarisation and dissemination of operational utility and knowledge across the military, and the second would deal with detailed studies aimed at building capabilities. The latter would rely heavily on consultations and discussions with a large variety of experts in the DoS as well as in different components of our security establishments.

## Future Uses Envisaged

We have a fairly advanced space programme for economic and development purposes which already provides inputs and resources for defence, especially in communications and imagery. Further programmes with dual use potential are on the anvil. Space capabilities for defence, hence, would largely be built around these endeavours. The challenge to leaders would be to optimally manage extant capabilities and judiciously build future capabilities. Our utility in the near term and foreseeable future would largely be limited to missions of "force enhancement." Broadly, the near foreseeable future would demand the following space capabilities.

### Observation/ISR

- The constantly expanding reach of the air force would demand accurate targeting, intelligence and information for efficient delivery of military power. Our long-range precision strike capability would be only as good as the accuracy and timeliness of targeting inputs available. The expanding reach of the IAF also implies a vastly expanded number of targets from which to select priorities in keeping with operational goals. A larger geographical coverage would expand the number and type of targets, thereby, demanding precise intelligence, surveillance, reconnaissance (ISR) capabilities which could only be augmented and made more efficient by space-based assets. Political air space restrictions would restrict acquisition of targeting intelligence and, hence, to match strategic reach with adequate intelligence and targeting information, the availability of space-based assets would be imperative. Permanent postional space-based imagery intelligence (IMINT) and electronic intelligence (ELINT) would complement and compensate for the prevailing airborne capabilities, which are transitory and temporary in nature. For example, while the entire spectrum of aerial platforms ranging from aircraft, unmanned aerial vehicles (UAVs), aerostats as well as balloons in near space are of a transitory nature, satellites would enable safe, permanent presence and persistent over-watch over the area of operations during peace, crises and war-time. In brief, the prevailing strategic breadth, reach and vertical depth of the IAF would be more efficiently exploited for national security and defence goals.

## *Navigation*
- In view of the enormously expanding reach of the IAF, these capabilities would be necessary for enabling precise navigation, targeting and delivery of scarce and costly platforms, munitions, personnel, humanitarian assistance, etc well beyond national borders, thereby, increasing the contingency support as well as contingency management of the government in keeping with our rise as a global power.
- Increasing crowding of the aerospace continuum would demand augmentation, assistance, etc by navsats for aerospace management (in both civil and military terms) and eventual phasing out of radar-based manual systems.

- It would enhance the efficiency of special operations by enabling insertion of personnel and materials well beyond our borders as well as search and rescue, and recovery of stranded combatants from deep within enemy territory.

### Communication

- India's stated nuclear doctrine would demand availability of survivable communication links for a retaliatory strike by elements of the nuclear triad that could be provided only by space-based systems.
- The enormous strategic reach and mobility of the IAF enables rapid response and insertion of military forces at long distances and the same would demand extensive coordination, command and control, etc that could be addressed only by space-based communications.
- Enormous information would be available from aerospace elements inclusive of aerial platforms like aircraft, UAVs, satellites, etc. This would require real-time, transfer and distribution, vertically and laterally. Efficient, secure real-time data transfer would dictate the need for communication satellites.
- Apart from enhancing efficiency of command, control communication computers, intelligence (C4I), the information-decision-action cycle, etc, the requirement of aerospace management would also demand real-time, immediate transfer of data that could be enabled by communication satellites.

### Other Applications

The above are some of the operational gains forthcoming on harnessing of capabilities of air and space power. Apart from these, numerous other applications are available though they are still untapped. Space applications, as previously mentioned, have multiple applications and would be of use across a wide spectrum of occupations, branches and trades. In addition to the above well known applications which would impact the entire armed forces and the IAF in particular, various other applications are presently available and would need to be harnessed. For example, prevailing telemedicine applications would need to be exploited by the medical branches (as well as the general populace); education officers could tap the immense potential of tele-education; signals officers could utilise the immense potential of satellite communications for an independent mobile communications system;[4] administrative officers could use the geographical information system (GIS) for estate planning, formulating key location plans (KLP), etc; flight safety officers could use GIS applications for plotting power grid lines, helipad location and a host of other utilities. Junior level leaders like unit warrant officers (UWOs) would have immense use of the global positioning system (GPS) locator chips to keep track of their work force; senior non-commissioned officers (SNCOs) in charge of mechanical transport, catering, etc would have immense uses of space-based location and positioning devices to keep track, manage and distribute resources more efficiently. The overall impact on efficiency would be enormous. The best manner to promote integration would be by demystifying space, making space capabilities familiar and by broadening the space user base, no matter how rudimentary the uses and applications. Increasing use in multifold aspects would increase the employability and utility awareness across the IAF and the armed forces, thereby, enabling systematic integration at a later stage. Once space capabilities become demonstratively apparent and make their presence felt, the demands for greater and better integration would automatically follow. The above would initially perhaps result in chaotic growth and demands for services. The challenge to leaders would be in anticipating the changes, managing the chaos, and judiciously balancing the conflicting requirements of demand and supply.

## Translating Space Capabilities into Strengths

Comprehensive exploitation of space and concurrent building of capabilities and their conversion into strengths would demand intense broad-based efforts in terms of developing human resources, training and education, familiarisation of missions, concepts, uses and a host of other factors. The challenge to leadership would be in terms of building, sustaining and managing space capabilities and enabling percolation of these capabilities to the lowest level possible. Penetration of space-based facilities into cockpits, soldier back-packs, operation rooms, etc would demand enormous efforts and training to disseminate operational knowhow and widen user participation and involvement. Increased user involvement would ensure greater demonstration of capabilities, leading to greater demands, greater integration and greater operationalisation of capabilities. Nevertheless, ad hoc and haphazard growth would be self-defeating; containing the conflicting demands of widening user participation and streamlining the supply and demand chain would be essential to avoid chaos and confusion. The test of effective leadership would be in managing conflicting demands, balancing requirements and ensuring judicious procurement and distribution.

Considering that the above venture would continually be impacted by new and unfamiliar technologies, enormous efforts would have to initially go into basic familiarisation, adaptation and broad dissemination of missions possible by integrating new technologies, evolving concepts, etc. The above effort would have to ensure that the dynamics of technological change and evolving operational requirements are factored in at the planning stages, for less wastage on consumption of capabilities. Foresight, vision and ingenuity tempered by adequate knowledge and analysis would distinguish leaders tasked with managing future space capabilities.

## Developing Leaders for Managing Future Capabilities

To translate capabilities into operational strengths, purposeful and deliberate efforts would have to be put in to develop leaders who are adept at converting concepts into operational solutions, are knowledgeable and possess cross-competencies in a variety of disciplines. These leaders would gradually comprehend the desired mix of space power competencies and provide space solutions to operational problems. Demands presently and in the future would exceed supply in the case of air and space assets as well as personnel and, hence, development of cross-competencies and multi-tasking would be the norm rather than the exception.

Correct identification, education, training and formation of a human resources pool would be the key to developing space competencies. In essence, the foundations for human resources development would rest with the IAF, on the one hand, and the DoS, on the other. The requirements could be centrally collated by the IAF and after due deliberation, could be developed upon in consultation with the DoS. Such an endeavour would fulfil the requirement of an educated and trained leadership pool which would be charged with translation of possibilities into capabilities.

### Building the Leadership Pool

Akin to air and space assets, military human resources are a scarce commodity. The leadership pool tasked with converting space possibilities into capabilities would, hence, need to be sourced or multi-tasked (at least initially) from prevailing resources and, thus, the model is proposed (Fig. 1).

**Fig 1**

| Higher Levels: Shallow depth of knowledge, greater breadth of cross-competencies. | | |
|---|---|---|
| | Intermediate & Middle Level: Enormous depth of knowledge, less breadth (number) of personnel occupied. | |
| Foundational Level: Shallow depth of knowledge, greater breadth by dissemination of space knowledge amongst personnel. | | |

### Foundational Level

The emphasis here would be on familiarising space to a wide cross-section of personnel and building a reservoir of people aware of the impact and utility of space to military operations. The idea would be to demystify and democratise space capabilities. This could be fulfilled by a two-pronged approach. On the one side, basic space familiarisation courses could be conducted at training and educational institutes and, on the other, the same could be incorporated at the induction stage itself. For example, while elementary space capsules could be introduced along with general service knowledge (GSK) and basic air power syllabus at the induction stage itself to familiarise the coming generations, the prevailing generations could be educated by conducting the same at the Centre for Air Power Studies (CAPS), College of Air Warfare (CAW), or any other suitable institute. The course content could be suitably modified to apply to both officers and enlisted personnel. The depth of knowledge would be shallow but breadth of space familiarisation would be enormous; consequently, the pool of resources to draw upon for building space capabilities would be enormous over a period of time. Rotation and integration of space qualified leaders would lead to a domino effect, thereby, increasing the resource base. Later, space specialists of the middle and intermediate levels would be extracted from this general pool for managing space capabilities. Over a period of time, the IAF could become the lead service in providing quality space education (in terms of application to security needs) not only within the IAF or the military but also to other security agencies like the paramilitary forces, police, intelligence agencies, etc. After all, space applications transcend a variety of applications ranging from military specific strategic imagery to even crop analysis to detect illegal cocaine/opium plantations hidden in farms, tracking prisoners, jail parolees, emergency services, disaster management, etc. The above endeavour, thus, would provide the foundation upon which national space competencies for security applications are built over a period of time.

### *Middle and Intermediate Levels*

This, as the name suggests, would target leadership at the aforesaid levels. The emphasis at this level would be on developing leaders with expertise in particular niche areas related to space like particular mission areas of navigation, communication, ISR, etc. as well as areas related to concepts and doctrines, technology, space law, operational integration and application, planning, training and education, policy, etc. The endeavour would be to develop a narrow core of specialists with enormous depth of knowledge and expertise in their respective fields. This, in the near term, would be the most challenging arena, considering that there exists no specialisation, and competencies would have to be built upon as collaborative efforts with the DoS and other foreign training institutes. Notwithstanding the same, within a period of around five years or so, it would be possible to identify, select, train and develop leaders with expertise in niche areas. These leaders would form the core of space specialists who would be tasked with integrating space and developing space competencies. These leaders would be responsible for vetting the possibilities, mitigating the technological challenges, adapting technology and doctrine, streamlining demands and acquisition, formulating policies and tackling a host of other issues which would demand expertise, innovation and ingenuity. This level would, over a period of time, provide a ready leadership cadre for enabling vertical and horizontal integration of space into mainstream military operations. The challenges related to career progression, personnel matters and growth would have to be suitably met considering that this core would need to be characterised by continuity and specialisation.

### Higher Levels

The emphasis here would be on developing leaders with a reasonably less depth of expertise but enormous breadth of awareness regarding space related affairs. This could be obtained by providing the requisite space education as well as brief space assignments to develop leaders with cross-competencies in as many space disciplines as possible. Brief assignments would not compensate for expertise, but a balanced mix of education and exposure would develop leaders with the requisite competencies to grasp the contextual elements of issues, problems, etc. While initial efforts would be focussed largely on education, as capabilities develop, a judicious mix of education and exposure could be undertaken. Secondly, over a period of time, these levels would also be fed by competent experts from the intermediate and middle level of space specialists.

## Familiarising Space

It would be imperative to familiarise leaders with space capabilities and increase military space presence as much as possible to ensure optimal comprehension, application and exploitation of capabilities. It could primarily be undertaken by:

- Including space in education and training by designing suitable courses and curriculum.
- Exposure to space capabilities, possibilities and applicability. This would entail cross-training and study tours at the Indian Space Research Organisation (ISRO) and other institutes of the DoS, etc.
- Incorporating space capabilities in exercises, war games, simulations, etc.

## Education, Training and Integration

There are numerous definitions and interpretations of education and training. However, for our present purpose, the premise that education serves to provide knowledge and a broad intellectual understanding of issues whereas training provides the requisite skills to apply knowledge would suffice. Both education and training would be essential prerequisites to meet the challenge of developing leaders to manage and integrate space capabilities. Optimal exploitation of prevailing capabilities and systematic building up of capabilities would be dependent on the quality of these two factors. Education and training would not only refine the tactics, techniques and procedures for optimal exploitation, they would encourage use and employment of space capabilities to meet operational challenges. Education would enable comprehensive understanding of the impact of space on military operations and proper training would ensure gradual integration and incorporation of space capabilities into both operational combat as well as support units.

Overall, it would enable the development of leaders who use their specific branch/trade skills to collectively produce and disseminate space-based information and other facilities for integration into routine day-to-day tasks and specific operations. For example, personnel devoted to imagery processing, navigation, etc. would provide information for combat military operations whereas personnel in other areas could use tele-medicine, tele-education, etc. for general utility of personnel and their families. The impact on military efficiency would be manifold.

Space education would demand a judicious mix of operational utility and technical education. Personnel would need to be educated by means of preliminary, intermediate as well as advanced education. The emphasis of education would need to be on operationalising and integrating space rather than space sciences. As a consequence, the accent of education would be more on how space enhances military efficiency, on its utility and less on orbital mechanics, systems engineering, etc. A rudimentary knowledge of space science to enable comprehension of the technological limitations and operational possibilities would suffice. In our unique case, the entire space programme is managed by the DoS and, hence, our focus (initially at least) would be on utilising extant capabilities and judicious planning for future capabilities unlike in the case of countries like the US or Russia wherein the space programmes are actually run by military bodies and, hence, demand enormous efforts in space technology education. The point is, operator-level education rather than launch or systems designer level would suffice. The above is validated considering the fact that even hugely successful and highly complicated military space systems like NAVSTAR GPS are operated by personnel without engineering or even science degrees. Most satellite vehicle operators do not hold (and are not required to hold) technical degrees. In fact, satellite systems operators who generate and transmit commands to satellites are young airmen, often only a few months out of basic training and possessing only high school diplomas.[5] By contrast, the IAF already has a vast pool of technologically qualified engineers and personnel who could adapt their competencies to include space operations. In view of the foregoing, the following education model is proposed for incorporation at various levels (Fig. 2).

**Fig 2**

| Levels | Yrs of Service | Officers | Airmen | Hours | Content |
|---|---|---|---|---|---|
| Induction | 00 | Pre-commission | Pre-enlistment | 10 | Basic |
| Entry | 1–2 | Branch Specialisation | OJT/equivalent | 20 | Intermediate |
| Junior Leaders | 2–6 | Junior Commanders | Equivalent | 20 | Intermediate |
| Middle level | 6–13 | Customised Space Course | Customised Space Course | 30/30+ | Advanced |
| Senior Leaders | 13+ | Customised Space Course | Customised Space Course | 20 | Intermediate |
| Air Ranks | — | Space Familiarisation | — | 10 | Broad-based |

The above model is conceptual rather than instructive and based on the concept, further refinements could be undertaken. The space curriculum would broadly revolve around the following:

- Military and civilian uses of space.
- Role of space in conflicts.
- Missions and role of space.
- India's space capabilities, limitations and vulnerabilities.
- Basic space science.

- Space law and legalities.
- Space simulation and war gaming with computer generated visualisation tools, etc.

Apart from education, personnel would need to be trained in a variety of areas to provide skills required to plan and conduct space operations. The primary emphasis would again be on integrating space-based information capabilities, hence, skills would need to be honed accordingly. Practising skills aimed at providing space-based information, analysing capabilities and limitations, recommending space applications to support operational requirements and decision-making, etc. would provide the decisive edge in conflicts.

### *Simulated Training and War Gaming*
However, education and training by themselves would be artificial experiences, and affordable virtual (or real-time) experiences with effective space models and simulation would need to be integrated into field level exercises, war gaming, etc. The models and simulation would need to be as realistic as possible and should attempt to realistically duplicate extant space capabilities. This would enable near-accurate comprehension of impact and incorporation of space capabilities into operations. Based on this, leaders could plan for, demand, distribute and use capabilities accordingly. To begin with, space visualisation and analysis kits like the satellite tool kit (STK), etc. could be procured off the shelf.[6] Later on, software, based on our own capabilities and environment, could be designed for our unique purposes. This would enable reasonably accurate modelling of our space systems, their capabilities, vulnerabilities and impact on military efficacy and national security. During major exercises, actually available capabilities could also be tasked for assessing the efficacy of systems, their integration into military capabilities and their overall impact.

Integrating space education and training across the IAF would also ensure that personnel apply their space knowledge to operational tasks and subsequently come up with ingenuous and innovative applications. Numerous instances of innovative applications of knowledge to security needs exist. For example, the impact of Indian ingenuity was demonstratively manifest in May 1998 when India surprised the world with its nuclear tests in spite of persistent coverage by US spy satellites. American space power had clearly failed to deter India from conducting nuclear tests "when sand storms normally swept across the Thar Desert and intense heat could disrupt surveillance sensors. Activity was also timed around the flights of spy satellites."[7]

Similarly, while the impact of space systems like GPS and precision guided munitions (PGMs) like HARM air-to-ground missile is well known, what is less famously known is that innovative use of domestic microwave ovens, low power GPS jammers, etc. was sufficient to blunt the impact of high technology space systems. During the Allied Forces' Yugoslav campaign, based on Russian advice, the Serbs lured away North Atlantic Treaty Organisation (NATO) aircraft and PGMs from their intended targets by switching on microwave ovens and aiming them upwards. American HARM missiles would home in on any strong source of radio emission in the 400-10,000 MHz range, exactly the range of conventional household microwave ovens. Hence, the Serbs used household microwave ovens to simulate the emissions of armoured transport systems and lured away NATO planes from their intended targets onto domestic microwaves.[8] The point is, Russian knowledge of space systems enabled blunting of the American space offensive.

### Gains Envisaged
Correct identification, education, training and formation of a human resources pool would be the key to developing space competencies over a period of time. Such an endeavour would broadly fulfill the following requirements:

- Streamline the selection, education and training for developing leaders who would form the core group committed to developing space concepts and applying them to resolve national security issues.
- Increase the understanding of the impact of space on military operations by education, training, battlefield simulation, participation in exercises, etc. This would serve to familiarise space operations across the rank and file. With adequate encouragement, it would enable a reciprocal flow

of ideas from across the air forces and other agencies which could be
developed into operational concepts.

- Develop leaders who understand the changing dynamics of national
  security issues, adapt space competencies to support national objectives
  and plan development of space capabilities accordingly.
- Develop leaders who envision, develop, manage, acquire, sustain,
  support and employ capabilities which exploit the space domain to
  create military effects.
- Develop leaders to implement space power doctrine and strategy.
- Develop leaders to strengthen space capabilities for credible nuclear
  deterrence.
- Enable systematic and professional development aimed not only at
  producing space leaders, but also providing the foundation upon which
  aerospace competencies are built over a period of time.

## Conclusion

The above recommendations are by no means exhaustive and would primarily
serve to broadly guide the development of space competencies at the
prevailing nascent level. Further refinements and incremental development
of capabilities would follow once the leadership issue is deliberated upon and
resolved. Resolving the leadership issue would be the first step to building
aerospace competencies and heralding any form of a revolution in military
affairs or networking, etc.

## Notes

1.  The Former Soviet Union (FSU) is not known to have evolved beyond the RMA
    stage and as of 2004, its space capabilities and overall military capabilities have
    seriously dwindled.
2.  The complexity of the issues can be gauged considering the fact that the world's
    leading military space driver, the US Air Force, within a span of 10 years
    (1990–2000), attempted thrice to integrate space into an air and space force
    and yet did not meet unqualified success in its endeavours. See Lt Col Mark P.
    Jelonek, USAF, "Toward an Air and Space Force," *CADRE Paper* AU Press,
    Maxwell Air Force Base, Alabama.

3. For a detailed brief on the commonality between air and space, see Sqn Ldr K.K. Nair, "Merging Frontiers of Air and Space," *Air Power Journal*, vol. 2, no. 3, Monsoon 2005.

4. Instead of relying on commercial vendors like Airtel, Hutch, etc. for mobile connectivity, it would be worthwhile to explore the possibility of an independent IAF cell phone network. Considering that most stations have VSAT terminals and the frequency spectrum is available, a network could be developed with confidential connectivity for personnel and open channels for families. This would serve the purposes of both security and welfare.

5. See 1st Lt Brent D. Ziainik, USAF, "Mahan on Space Education," *Air & Space Power Journal*, Winter 2005.

6. For details on computer-generated space software and models, see site of Air University, Centre for Space Studies at http://space.au.af.mil/teaching.htm

7. See Krishnan Guruswamy, "India Tricks US Satellites," *Associated Press*, May 19, 1998. Available at http://abcnews.go.com/sections/world/Daily news/india980519_nukes.html

8. Vladimir Bogdanov, "Anti-Weapon: Russian Scientists Threaten to Halt Space War," *Rossiyaskaya Gazeta* (Moscow), October 18, 2002, quoted by *Global Research.Ca*, November 2002, at www.globalresearch.ca/articles/BOG211A.html

# 8

# Demands on Future Aerospace Leaders

*Jasjit Singh*

*The air force must prepare officers today for the managerial and executive tasks to which they will fall heir tomorrow. The need exists for officers who can manage not only people but also ideas and concepts on a broad basis; these will be the future leaders, and it is important that the air force begin to prepare them now. Yet this preparation cannot be accomplished by confining ongoing educational opportunities primarily to scientific and technical fields; rather, it can be accomplished by a continuing emphasis on a broad-base education upon which can be built the professional competence necessary for development as career officers.[1]*

— William L. Anderson

Aerospace power has increasingly become the crucial factor in national defence and sovereignty. For nuclear weapon states concerned about the high potential for escalation in the employment of land forces, aerospace power offers unique opportunities and a range of options to use coercive military force in pursuit of national interests with or without war. Technology obviously plays a crucial role in enhancing the capabilities of aerospace power. But **aerospace power and its effectiveness is critically dependent upon the people who operate, command, control and sustain the systems ranging from platforms to warheads—the aerospace leaders.**

If one was to identify the single most important attribute of military leadership, the focus in all probability would go onto integrity. But if we were to search for the single most important asset of a leader in the profession of arms, able to conceive and plan a future force relevant to the future period and future enemy, and be able to employ that force with success within the parameters of political interests, then that asset would have to be **education leading to knowledge** and the ability to transform it into wisdom and use it. This is no doubt what William Anderson had in mind when he wrote the above lines. But in our country we accord little or no importance to this aspect related to leadership of our armed forces. In fact, we place a great deal of emphasis and invest a tremendous amount of effort and energy in "training" and very little on "education." Any education that does take place is as a consequence of personal interest and development in an environment where this is actually discouraged. This is not to suggest that training in, and for, skills needed in the profession of arms is not important. In fact, this is perhaps the most important aspect of the military profession, especially at tactical and the lower ends of operational levels.

We know that there are three levels of warfare—the strategic, operational and tactical—not in rigid compartments but quite distinct though characterised by seamless overlapping of the three. Each of these demands leadership that can guide and direct military power to achieve designated political goals and the military objectives flowing from the political aims and priorities. What we need is to strengthen the leadership at each of these three levels without compartmentalising them. **Such strengthening of leadership development for the future would depend on the degree of institutionalised professional military education that we invest in beyond what an individual pursues as his personal interest.** No wonder, we come across what we term as a "thinking general" once in a decade or two, implying that others were men of action, but no one was certain whether they were also thinkers!

Or we find endorsement of professional military education to be pursued through non-existent institutions (like an Air University, yet to be conceived!). And the National Defence University appears years away from reality in spite of the idea having been around for four decades. We recognise that one of the ways of encouraging professional military education is to permit study leave; but caught in the web of daily work schedules, we conclude that we cannot "spare" officers from that gruelling, almost debilitating, routine for such military education opportunities.[2] Where manpower in reality has proliferated.

History tells us that intellectual assets and inputs played a crucial role in statecraft and the profession of arms, when both were comparatively simple. Aristotle and Alexander, Chanakya and Maurya, Sun Tzu and the Chinese emperors, etc are all examples of repositories of knowledge and the ability to analyse events and actions in proximity to the decision-makers and sharing their assessments with them.[3] Although we used to put on the ground a flight supervisor who was expected to visualise the actual situation in the air of a fast-jet fighter, we cannot have a Chanakya or an Aristotle guiding the commander (of an aircraft or of the air force) through changing circumstances if for no other reason than that the pace of events and actions has accelerated well beyond the ancient practices. What we need is a symbiotic synergy of the intellectual and the warrior at all levels of leadership in a modern fighting force.

Times, of course, have changed. But **the principle that leadership requires intellectual rigour based on empirical understanding of facts, analysis of these facts and data, and the need for knowledge remains valid.** Unfortunately, there seems to be limited scope for professional education opportunities and expertise since they have not been created and the culture of reading beyond the list of aircraft emergencies is all but absent. Our training schedules at Staff Colleges, etc. leave less and less time for professional reading and critical thinking on issues and subjects beyond the listed syllabus. There are few opportunities and avenues for discussions on military history and lessons to be learned—or not to be learned. Unlike those in the United States (and even China) our military teaching institutions do not have research think-tanks to provide professional studies and output for study by serving officers. There is a gross deficit of professional journals in the country. What is needed in the words of General John C. Meyer is that the future air force leader must "...be part manager, part sociologist, part student of history."[4] This requires broad-spectrum military professional education of our future aerospace leaders.

## Employment of Military Power: The Context

Study, understanding, internalisation and dissemination of the qualities and attributes of leadership are important and integral elements in leadership training in our military forces. But there is much more to leadership than mere attributes. The problem is aggravated if our teaching and practice of military professional leadership starts and ends with defining and refining the attributes and does not go beyond them to understand the geo-political, operational, technological and human environment of the future that the leaders of today must prepare for.[5]

Even at the risk of restating the obvious, we must remember that the military power of a nation is not only its last and final instrument in pursuit of its interests—it represents a key instrument of policy to defend, support and enhance national interests. Thus, there is an obvious contextual salience of employment of military power being undertaken within the framework of political goals and objectives. These goals would actually define the military aims, the types of military capabilities required, and limits of military power. Here we must note that, unlike many militaries (including those of Pakistan and Bangladesh that grew out of the Indian military institution), our armed forces have prided themselves for six decades and more, in being apolitical. While this principle continues to be sound and relevant for the future, our military leaders would need to study the political context to help understand the limits and aims of employment of military power in pursuit of national interests. Such pursuit cannot be assumed to be a static phenomenon since the global and regional security environment, the enemy and its capabilities, etc. keep changing. But it is clear that many trends can be identified to provide a reasonably accurate understanding of the type of factors that will shape political-military goals in the future. Let us take a couple of examples.

One of the most influential factors that have altered the way we can use military power in future is the possession of nuclear weapons by our two major neighbours and ourselves. Our own political interests clearly require that nuclear weapons should not impinge on our security, and, hence, the need for universal disarmament. Meanwhile, nuclear weapons are part of the security and strategic environment and our interests demand that they should not be used against us at any time. This factor—one can define it as an "overriding factor" in military appreciation terms—influences conventional war and its aims. A broad conclusion would be that existence of nuclear weapons and the catastrophic destruction they would cause if used, impose a major political condition of restraint on the use of military power. The type of action undertaken in 1971, doable with our capabilities, can be replicated only at the risk of a nuclear holocaust. It is obvious that our military leadership should be thoroughly conversant with the theory and practices related to nuclear weapons and deterrence. The effect of nuclear weapons, thus, is to limit the political and military goals of a conventional war that we might be involved in our region.

How would we define our national interests and the political objectives of the use of military power under these circumstances? And if a local-border war is all that we can pragmatically plan for, how would we apply military power successfully, and for what feasible political and military goals? What would be the role of aerospace power under these circumstances? For example, if the political aims are to influence Pakistan's policy of prosecuting cross-border terrorism, then can the costs of its policy be raised by discriminate air strikes at economic and terrorist infrastructure like bridges and power stations across the Line of Control in Jammu and Kashmir (J&K)?

At another level, wars for territory have already reached their end state, the American war in Iraq four years ago being the classical climax to the centuries-old phenomenon. Occupation of territory was a central politico-military goal for centuries since it allowed the resources of the territory to be exploited by the victor. For a variety of reasons which we need not go into here, occupation of territory no longer plays the earlier role. Destruction of the enemy's military power was a prerequisite to occupation of territory; and, in turn, the successful execution of the two would naturally lead to change of regime in the target country and enable greater convergence with the attacker's interests. This, of course, does not imply that military power has become redundant. All it means is that changes in political goals, military objectives and the way military power has to be applied have been changing in many respects and in fundamental ways. Our future leaders would have to be fully conversant by with the political aims and strategy of the country in pursuit of our interests.

If territory is no longer the prime motivation of a viable strategy option for military action, then what is the role and mission of military power that we can rationally institute? For example, traditionally, there was a disjunction between diplomacy and war. Simply stated, the soldiers took over when the diplomats failed, and the diplomats came back into action when the soldiers either succeeded or failed. A state which allows disjunction to take place between its foreign policy and defence strategy today does so only at serious risk to its own interests. Secondly, even in peace-time, capable military power makes a substantive contribution to a country's ability to handle foreign policy issues through diplomacy. And in an age of information revolution, the political implications of every military action can have a profound impact on our national interests.

Thirdly, there would be many occasions and opportunities where military force may need to be applied without necessarily leading to war or even firing a shot in a process that has come to be known as "coercive diplomacy." At the same time, "military coercion" is an obvious tool available to countries to employ in pursuit of their interests. Both these require deep understanding of the history, culture, political interests, type of leadership, strengths and vulnerabilities, and military capabilities of the target country in relation to our own. No doubt, the United States and the former Soviet Union indulged in coercive diplomacy and military coercion over the decades. But India itself has employed this tool as and when necessary, though it could have done so more often. The Indian military operation which came to be known as the "rice bombing" of Jaffna in June 1987 was a classical example. The most recent example is that of Operation Parakram where the widely different assessments of its success or otherwise themselves indicate the weak understanding of the politico-military issues.

At the same time, we need to note that uncertainty would continue to be a major factor that has to be factored into military planning and operations (where military leadership tends toward dealing with issues where there is clarity and certainty). Successful strategy must be able to assess the implications of uncertainty and evolve a course of action that is well understood by the leader as well as those he leads. Uncertainty can be reduced to some extent through a study of the strategic personality of the adversary. We also have been taught over the decades that we need to study the capabilities of a potential adversary; but that his intentions can change any time and, hence, remain a major variable. But a detailed, continuing study of the adversary's history, its grand strategy, politics, economy, relationships with other countries, etc. can provide indicators of its intentions which could be partially validated by hard intelligence where available. These are but a few examples of the complexities of understanding the political-military factors that have to be factored into diplomacy, on one side, and the creation and employment of military power, on the other.

The foregoing provides a glimpse of factors that would have to be taken into account by aerospace leaders of today and tomorrow. It may be recalled that we failed to use combat air power in the 1962 War purely because of inadequate understanding of the role that the Indian Air Force (IAF) could play (in and beyond close support) while the White House Intelligence Summary was clear that such use would make a "material difference" to the war on the ground. The pace of change in the modern world since then has been remarkable, and its impact on demands on leadership is equally enormous. Management of change holds the key to maintaining the competitive advantage over the enemy. Our leaders of tomorrow would require quality education as a lifelong learning process which builds aerospace leaders for the future and develops leaders into critical thinkers who can think and learn faster than the enemy and through that process, dominate it in future operations. In a way, this is what the OODA (orientation, observation decision, action) loop is all about: not a loop by itself, but its relationship to the OODA loop of the enemy. We also need to remember that **we are likely to experience prolonged periods of peace with spurts of armed violence of great variety, including wars.** Hence, our leadership development has to take this factor into account. Some of the areas that such education process would need to include are briefly outlined below:

- National security and defence, including strategy issues, especially deterrence and escalation dynamics.
- International affairs and India's place in the international order. Without a thorough grounding in international relations theory and practice, our leaders would be handicapped in understanding political aims and objectives governing decisions about employment of military power and taking initiatives to preserve and promote our national interests. Foreign policy issues need close study to enable the military leaders to

provide the necessary synergy of military power with diplomacy and its political management.

- History, especially military history. A major handicap here is that our records of history are sketchy at best and misleading at worst. Take the case of the official history of the IAF in the 1965 War.[6] Eliot Cohen, who believes that historical education of civilian and military strategists is more, not less important in an age of rapid change, has made a strong case for not only the study of history, but also for the acquisition of the "historical mind—that is, a way of thinking that uses history as a mode of inquiry" by military strategists. He concludes, "If strategists don't even know what happened, they cannot be sure what succeeded and what went wrong; they cannot reinforce success or remedy failure. There is then, a desperate need for reliable histories as raw material for decision-making as well as for the use of military institutions."[7] Understanding of history is essential for learning the relevance of lessons from the past. This is one of the greatest deficiencies we have, at both the national and professional levels.
- Broad understanding of macro-economics and its place in the national comprehensive power and comparative power of nations.
- Deep understanding of the political enemy(s) and their history, culture, strategic personality, grand strategy and military capabilities and intentions.

## The IAF in 2030

It is in this context that we need to look at the needs of aerospace leadership in the IAF over the next quarter century. What is clear is that the top commanders of 2030 are already in service. What is less clear is the nature of challenges that our future leadership would have to cope with.

**What is patently clear is that our air force is undergoing an unprecedented historical transformation which would occupy most of the coming quarter century.**

During the coming two decades or so, the IAF would have:
- Remained the prime repository of India's credible conventional deterrence capabilities while providing critical components of credible nuclear deterrence.

- Changed from a subcontinental, geographically limited force to one with continental reach and effect.
- Acquired capabilities for the strategic effect and role while performing tactical tasks more effectively altering its role.
- Acquired ability to exploit space capabilities for enhancing military operations.
- Shifted from a pure line-of-sight capability to substantively beyond-visual-range capabilities, especially for air-to-surface operations.
- Integrated new technology systems like the airborne warning and control system (AWACS), etc. fully into service.
- Would have recovered force level to the authorised level, and so on.

This transformation is far more momentous than the expansion of 1962-67 forced on us by the Chinese invasion. The earlier expansion was essentially a matter of accretion and adjustment of the organisation to a larger force level; while the current one involves a series of paradigm shifts in aerospace capabilities and the way they can be employed in the future. The nature and direction of the current transformation would be deeply affected by the choices we have made in recent years and would make during this period in the future. Looking back at history, we observe that:

- The IAF came into being as one of the few air forces established as an independent force, not so much because the government of the day felt the need for air power in national defence but essentially under pressure for "Indianisation" of the military forces. In keeping with imperial policies, this was given the shape of a subsidiary role for the IAF like army cooperation and battlefield reconnaissance (with the Royal Air Force retaining the primary roles like bombing and air warfare) from which some leaders tried hard to break out over the decades. But support of the army has remained in practice the primary mission of the air force.[8] This is a legacy that the air force may be on the threshold of changing only now seven decades after it was established, at least in terms of strategy.
- In the early years (1930s-1950s), the air force was preoccupied essentially with survival, facing as it did the demobilisation after World

War II, the partition of India, and the lack of understanding of the role of air power among the decision-making elites of the country.

- The decade of the 1960s set the IAF on the path of increasing reliance on Soviet weapons systems which in politico-economic terms became attractive, especially with licensed manufacturing arrangements in the country. But at a different level, these led to reinforcing the concept of defensive employment (and deployment) of the air force, largely because Soviet combat aircraft had short radius of action, low payloads and limited avionics.

- The period 1970s-1980s was a period of consolidation where serious thought was given to optimising its size and building a balanced force. But even then, support for extending the envelope of operations (like aerial refuelling, AWACS, etc.) was limited.

- The 1990s was once again a period where the air force faced the struggle for survival, this time due to major budget cuts, the main source of weapons supplies, the Soviet Union, having collapsed and disintegrated in social-economic chaos, and the dominant assumption in the country of the primary challenge to the military power being "low intensity conflict."

It is not surprising, therefore, that the air force remained heavily committed to two missions: that of air defence and air support to the army which together consumed upwards of 85 per cent of the air effort in the 1965 and 1971 Wars, leaving the Indian Army still dissatisfied! It remained tactical in its outlook. But the more important point is that a RAND study concluded. "The IAF has not figured prominently in Indian thinking about defence... The (Indian) air force did not take the initiative in pushing concepts of air power or an air plan for the defence of India."[9]

It is against this historical backdrop that the IAF is entering a wide process of change. This would by itself pose a major challenge for the future leadership. But this also happens to coincide with a period when it is experiencing force depletion due to lack of modernisation and reequipment in the past. If the air force of the next quarter century is going to be qualitatively different from that of the past quarter century, then it is obvious that the nature of this transformation and its direction/success would depend greatly on the leadership that manages and directs it.

These and myriad other changes are what the leadership has to wrestle with in the coming years. This, no doubt, would require leaders of very high calibre and capabilities. But to enable them to energise the organisation to ever higher levels of performance, it would be necessary for everyone in the air force and outside it to understand the fundamental purpose of the IAF: why does it exist? What is its role in national defence and war? And so on.

To begin with, the leaders would need to understand the art and science of war. The art of war may be defined as the creation and exploitation of advantage in war that enable military power to achieve political objectives: "Military art concerns what military forces should or should not do and why" and how.[10] The science of war covers a discipline concerned with the nature of war and the methods of conducting war, knowledge of military hardware, force structures, technology, etc. plus knowledge of group behaviour, social sciences and history.

This leads us to the question of the "purpose" of the IAF? In other words, what would be the IAF's institutional mission over the coming quarter century? And how would this purpose be achieved under a variety of circumstances? What equipment, technology, organisation would be required to achieve it? What would be the basis of making the requisite judgment toward that end? In other words, what would be the theory of aerospace power that India needs for the next quarter century?[11] And how would the leaders achieve synergy between these two elements and the lessons learnt from history, as applicable to the geo-political, operational and technological environment of the future? In turn, how could we prepare them for the inevitable uncertainties and ambiguities inherent in the situation? And how would aerospace capabilities be applied?

An objective search for answers to these and many more questions would help us to design operational education and training to produce effective responses to them. Two examples can elaborate the issues involved.

The official doctrine of the IAF states "The ultimate purpose of the IAF is war." If that was indeed to be the purpose of the IAF, then it appears to be divorced from the political aims of that war, and the military objectives—

for example, to win that war?—remain unclear. In turn, how can a credible theory for employment of aerospace power be constructed if the institutional mission of the IAF is not clear? In the absence of clarity of purpose and theory, persons serving in the IAF are far more likely to pay greater attention to personal careerism and advancement rather than the organisational goals. This is much more likely to affect the leadership at the operational and strategic levels since they require clear conceptual abilities and goals affecting the whole force as compared to the tactical levels.

We could perhaps draw a few pointers from the United States Air Force (USAF). Soviet acquisition of nuclear weapons began to influence the operational doctrine from victory in war to include deterrence. During the 1950s, the USAF leadership had reached two important conclusions: "(i) The defence of the United States must be based on air power; and (ii) in this thermonuclear age, defence is best assured by a strong air force in being."[12] In the words of Gen Curtis LeMay, one could reduce the air force's purpose in the late 1950s and early 1960s to a single statement: "Our mission is to deter war by providing our nation with the primary forces to gain and maintain general aerospace supremacy—and if deterrence fails, to repel and defeat the aggressor's forces." This deterrence mission—both conventional and nuclear—should guide the development of air force leadership for the future.

Today, the IAF, like the USAF, finds itself struggling with issues that parallel those faced by the latter Service after it won its independence from the army in 1947 or the former faced during the first two decades after Indian independence. The integration of new platforms, systems, and doctrine; the definition of emerging missions; the identification of opponents; fiscal austerity; and competition with the other Services for money and technology were among the challenges airmen confronted in the 1940s and early 1950s. The same holds true today. The difference is that the USAF has a Service-specific leadership manual that serves as an important doctrinal declaration which defines the mission, capabilities, and limitations of air and space power, coupled with a sense of dedication to the air force. On the other hand, we have no easily available publications or literature to guide our future leadership.[13] As Morris Janowitz has aptly pointed out, "The military establishment requires a balance between the three roles of heroic leader, military manager, and military technologist..."[14] To this, we should add, leader with a historical mind.

I would like to end by citing Samuel P. Huntington's 1957 assessment of this requirement which holds important lessons for our leadership needs for the future:

The military skill requires a broad background of general culture for its mastery. The methods of organising and applying violence at any one stage in history are intimately related to the entire cultural pattern of society...To understand his trade properly, the officer must have some idea of its relation to these other fields and the ways in which these other areas of knowledge may contribute to his own purposes. In addition, he cannot really develop his analytical skill, insight, imagination, and judgment if he is trained simply in vocational duties...The fact that, like the lawyer and the physician, he is continuously dealing with human beings, requires him to have the deeper understanding of human attitudes, motivations, and behaviour which a liberal education stimulates. Just as a general education has become the prerequisite for entry into the professions of law and medicine, it is now almost universally recognised as a desirable qualification for the professional officer.[15]

Ask a sailor about sea power, and he'll give you a speech on the maritime strategy. Ask a soldier about ground power, and he'll tell you about AirLand Battle. But ask an airman about air power, and he'll tell you what time happy hour starts at the club.

— Gen Michael Dugan, former US Air Force Chief of Staff

National safety would be endangered by an air force whose doctrines and techniques are tied solely on the equipment and process of the moment. Present equipment is but a step in progress, and any air force which does not keep its doctrine ahead of its equipment, and its vision far into the future, can only delude the nation into a false sense of security.

— Gen Henry H. "Hap" Arnold

But if we limit our efforts only to applying space technologies to existing modes of war-fighting, we have undershot...It is no different than all the ways our armed forces once found for air power to support ground operations—and do no more.

— Hon. Peter B. Teets, Undersecretary of the Air Force

## Notes

1. William L. Anderson, "The Whole Man? A Look at the Neglected Half of Air Force Education," *Air University Review*, September-October 1972.

2. Even study leave, having been sought by Air HQ since 1968, has not moved forward seriously in all three Services partly because of the mindset that (i) such education process does not contribute to professional acumen, leave alone ability to conduct warfare; (ii) the distorted focus that study leave must lead to the award of a "degree." In spite of a cadre specifically catering for study leave, and colonels spending as many as nine years in the same rank before being considered for promotion, the quota remains unfilled; (iii) the terms and conditions of study leave are such that officers seeking to enhance their professional military education lose a lot of their basic entitlements, making it a disincentive; and (iv) the belief that time spent on study leave does not enhance the individual's career prospects.

3. For one of the finest studies on how Alexander was trained to be a conqueror of the world at a young age, see Partha Bose, *Alexander The General's Art of Strategy: The Timeless Lessons of History's Greatest Empire Builder* (New Delhi: Penguin Viking, 2003).

4. Gen John C. Meyer, "Managing the USAF: The Now and Future Challenges," *Air Force and Space Digest*, vol. 53, January 1970, p. 51.

5. Brigadier Rameshwar Roy, "Leadership for the 21st Century Environment of Empowerment," *War College Journal,* Army War College, Mhow, pp. 39-48 provides a vivid example of enunciation of qualities of leadership with nothing stated of the environment of the 21st century under which the leader would have to lead and how he should equip himself for the task. He also seems to believe in the positional authority of the leader rather than his ability to think critically.

6. The Official History of the 1965 War, compiled in the late 1980s by the Historical Division of the Ministry of Defence, remains unpublished though

the text was placed on the Internet by *The Times of India* in the late 1990s.

7. Eliot Cohen, "The Historical Mind and Military Strategy," *Orbis*, Fall 2005, pp. 575-588.

8. As late as 1995, a RAND study concluded, "Support of the army is a top mission of the Indian Air Force...The current air force leadership consider air support to the army as one of the highest priorities." (RAND MR-424-AF) p. 91.

9. George K. Tanham and Marcy Agmon, *The Indian Air Force: Trends and Prospects*, MR-424-AF (Santa Monica: RAND 1995) p. xii.

10. Lt Col Dennis M. Drew, "Military Art and the American Tradition: The Vietnam Paradox Revisited," *Air University Review*, January-February 1983, pp. 31-34.

11. It is worth noting here that a major RAND study had concluded that the major reason why the USAF had lost its original elan, and careerism had replaced professionalism was due to the Service having failed to evolve an appropriate theory of air power after the nuclear missiles came into service. See Carl H. Builder *The Icarus Syndrome: The Role of Air Power Theory in the Evolution and Fate of the US Air Force* (New Brunswick: Transaction Publishers, 1994).

12. *Principles of Leadership and Management* (Montgomery, Alabama: Air University, 1954) p. 11.

13. Our apathy toward institutional education can be gauged from the fact that as part of the reorganisation of Air HQ in January 1970, a Directorate of Air Staff Publications was established. But it soon dissipated without producing a single document!

14. Morris Janowitz, *The Professional Soldier* (Illinois: Free Press, 1960), p. 21.

15. Samuel P. Huntington, *The Soldier and the State* (Cambridge: Harvard University Press, 1957), p. 14.

# 9

# The Leadership Imperative in a Transforming Air Force

*R. Joe Baldwin*

The last decade of the 21st century promises to be one of the most eventful in modern history. These truly revolutionary times mark a defining moment for the United States Air Force. Sweeping change in the international arena, coupled with irresistible domestic pressures to cut the defence budget, has produced a dramatic shift in America's national security strategy. Fortuitously, in 1990, the senior leadership of the air force got out in front of events and promulgated a strategic planning framework for the post-Cold War era.[1] Subsequently, efforts to realise the promise of global reach—global power— and to implement organisational realignments have put the air force in a good position to meet the demands of a regionally focussed military strategy while building down to lower force levels.[2] However, merely restructuring the air force in accordance with an overarching strategic framework is insufficient to ensure the vitality of our Service into the next century.

## Meeting the Challenge of Transformation

The key to transforming our air force into a leaner, meaner Service that retains its reputation as "the world's most respected air and space force" lies in the hands of blue-suit leaders across the ranks and at all levels.[3] Officers and non-commissioned officers alike must exhibit tremendous leadership as they implement fundamental change throughout the air force and seek to take care of our cherished asset—quality people. As we charge ahead in restructuring our Service, undertaking "Quality Air Force" initiatives,

We gratefully acknowledge the permission of the author to reproduce this article which was first published in *Airpower Journal,* Fall 1993.

creating composite wings, implementing two-level maintenance, revamping training and education programmes, and assessing equipping requirements, we must never forget the critical importance of the human factor to organisational success.[4]

Far-reaching change inevitably creates enormous anxiety and tension among the people who make up an organisation. This natural development is further aggravated in today's air force by the uncertainty and turmoil associated with defence budget cuts, force drawdowns, base closures, selective early retirement boards (SERB), and reductions in force (RIF). Leaders across the air force must carefully manage the transformation of our Service with due concern for people as well as for the mission. Otherwise, we run the serious risk of producing a well-armed, yet hollow, force lacking in morale, esprit, and cohesion. The current situation places a premium on involved leaders who set the example, insist on quality performance, maintain a consistent focus on the mission, and, above all else, take care of their people.

Involved leadership is all the more critical given the likelihood that the air force will be the force of choice when the nation responds to fast-rising regional crises. No other Service can go directly from the US to the fight in a matter of hours and apply overwhelming firepower with the precision and lethality that we can. Regrettably, we still live in a troubled world racked by age-old animosities, proliferating arms, and unyielding instability.[5] All these pose a potential threat to US security interests around the globe. Thus, the air force must be prepared to safeguard those interests through the assured capability to project highly agile, extremely flexible, and decidedly lethal aerospace power to any hot spot in the world. But there can be no global reach or global power without involved leadership and quality people.

Fortunately, we have a tremendous heritage to draw upon as we take on this challenge. The brief history of the air force is replete with visionary leaders—Benjamin D. Foulois, William ("Billy") Mitchell, Frank M. Andrews, Henry H. ("Hap") Arnold, Claire L. Chennault, Carl A. ("Tooey") Spaatz, Ira C. Eaker, Hoyt S. Vandenberg, Elwood R. ("Pete") Quesada, Curis E. LeMay—who shepherded the air arm though good times and bad, then wielded this most flexible of military instruments to win our nation's

THE LEADERSHIP IMPERATIVE IN A TRANSFORMING AIR FORCE 153

conflicts. Selfless airmen served in the front lines during the Cold War, providing awesome nuclear and conventional capabilities that deterred Soviet aggression, defended Western democracies, and assured the ultimate victory of Western liberal values over a bankrupt Communist ideology. Clearly, the realisation of a Europe whole and free in the early Nineties was due in no small measure to more than 45 years of sacrifice and commitment on the part of US airmen.

More recently, the adroit application of aerospace power assured the triumph of Coalition efforts to turn back blatant Iraqi aggression against Kuwait in the Persian Gulf region. It is indisputable that the fierce 1,000-hour air campaign against Iraq and its forces in the Kuwaiti theatre of operations made possible the brief 100-hour ground war that culminated in a decisive victory for the coalition. This impressive feat resulted from the extraordinary leadership and devotion to duty of blue suiters at all echelons—from the Air Staff and major commands to US Air Forces, Central Command (CENTAF) Forward all the way down to the units.

These remarkable military professionals projected enormous combat power halfway around the world to halt further aggression, created an expeditionary air force in the sands of the Arabian Peninsula, developed a comprehensive war plan orchestrating hundreds of air assets, and launched a massive air campaign that demolished Iraq's war-fighting capability. Their extraordinary performance provided compelling evidence of Guilio Douhet's assertion that "aerial warfare will be the most important element in future wars."[6]

We must now capitalise on the same energy, skill, enthusiasm, and dedication that produced a decisive victory in the Gulf War to successfully transform our Service into the premier air and space force of the 21st century. That endeavour will require a personal commitment on the part of officers and non-commissioned officers (NCO) throughout the air force to get involved with their people, to address subordinate concerns over organisational change and personnel turmoil, and to instill a keen sense of pride in being part of a unique military organisation that takes care of its own.

This kind of involved leadership is essential if we are to provide the comprehensive air and space power necessary to defend our nation and its global interests against a vast array of threats in the austere fiscal times that lie ahead.[7] While there is no textbook answer on how best to provide the requisite leadership during this challenging period, the following discussion highlights some important considerations for those who would lead the way in our transforming air force.

## Top Priority: Integrity

The most important characteristic that an air force leader must possess is personal integrity. Webster's *Third New International Dictionary* defines integrity as an "uncompromising adherence to moral and ethical principles" It is that and much more in a professional military organisation such as ours. Integrity constitutes the essential ingredient for sound, effective leadership. An officer or NCO who lacks integrity is worthless to the Service and highly destructive of its ethical standing with the public. Such an individual neither earns nor deserves the trust of superiors or subordinates. And no one can lead effectively without such trust.

If you expect your people to give 110 per cent day in and day out and to willingly undergo the rigours of combat, then you must exhibit unquestioned honesty, be forthright in what you expect of your troops, and behave in an ethical manner in all that you do. If you would have others follow you, then cultivate a well-deserved reputation as a solid military professional who possesses the highest personal standards and demonstrates unerring ethical behavior. Take responsibility for your actions and those of your people. Never try to avoid blame by pointing the finger at someone else. Rather than wasting time in an unethical effort to shift the blame, strive to identify the cause of the problem and take immediate action to resolve it. Superiors do not expect you and your people to be perfect, but they do expect you to recognise genuine mistakes and to correct them.

Moreover, the leader with true integrity has the courage of his or her convictions and the will to take action on those convictions. That characteristic is crucial in a self-monitoring profession such as ours wherein we must make tough ethical calls as to the propriety of individual action. A few years ago, a wing commander furnished his office and quarters in an extravagant fashion that was blatantly wasteful of air force resources. He had behaved similarly as a vice-commander of another wing, but no one had called him on it there. No one had the guts to do the right thing and report him to his superiors or go through inspector general channels. Consequently, he continued his profligate ways when he became a wing commander until a junior member in his unit had the courage to file a fraud, waste, and abuse complaint against him. Unfortunately, his eventual removal from command threw an entire wing into turmoil and tarnished the image of the air force due to the commander's lack of integrity and the failure of other air force people to do the right thing earlier.

A leader's personal life must always be above reproach. Set the example of self-discipline and moral rectitude for your people to follow. Take prompt corrective action in the event of sexual harassment or other inappropriate behaviour. Realise that the American public closely scrutinises your behaviour and that of your subordinates as a direct reflection of the United States Air Force. We cannot afford nor can we tolerate any "Tailhook" affairs in our Service. Perhaps Gen Arnold said it best:

> Personal integrity also means moral integrity. Regardless of what appear
> to be some superficial ideas of present day conduct, fundamentally—
> today as always—the man who is genuinely respected is the man who
> keeps his moral integrity sound, who is trustworthy in every respect.[8]

## Loyalty Cuts Both Ways

Loyalty is an essential ingredient of involved leadership. Loyalty up the chain entails not only the staunch support of one's superior but also the courage to disagree with him or her and the will to provide honest feedback on issues within your purview—all in private. Few senior officers like yes-men (or yes-women) who do not think for themselves but instead try to get ahead through ingratiating behaviour. Once your boss has made a decision, however, loyalty requires your unflinching support for that decision, especially in front of the troops. It matters little whether you personally agree or disagree with the decision or how you expect your subordinates to respond to it. You must give it your wholehearted support as long as it is not immoral, illegal, or contrary to regulations. Never attempt to pacify your people by joining them in criticising your superiors.

Loyalty also entails taking care of the needs of your people and supporting them in the face of adversity. Gen George S. Patton once observed, "There is a great deal of talk about loyalty from the bottom to the top. Loyalty from the top down is even more necessary and much less prevalent."[9] Thus, put the health and welfare of your troops first. See that their needs are adequately taken care of. Then be prepared to stand behind your subordinates when they are in the right, and beside them when they are in the wrong. There can be no more dispiriting, morale-busting development than to have a superior not support you in the face of adversity. However, the involved leader who has the courage to take up for subordinates in both good times and bad will be repaid manifold by troops who deeply appreciate such unselfish loyalty.

In 1943, then-Col. LeMay came to the aid of an Eighth Air Force pilot during a mission critique when it became apparent that he was being made the scapegoat for a bomb run to Bremen that had gone bad. Although most of the other officers conducting the critique were his senior, LeMay stood up, stopped the inquisition, and made it clear that his superiors had completely lost their perspective in seeking to pin the blame on someone for what in essence had been an honest mistake. Interestingly enough, LeMay had gone to bat for a pilot who was not even in his bomb group because he was so incensed at the injustice being done to a brave airman who was doing his best in the war-torn skies over Europe.[10]

## Strength of Character Will Carry the Day

It won't always be easy to do what is right in the confusing and uncertain days that lie ahead for our air force. But it will be absolutely essential for the future of our Service and the nation that we stick by our principles, defend our people, and stand our ethical ground on the difficult issues that confront us. Strength of character will be pivotal in this regard. We can learn much from our air force forebears who have risked it all for what they believed in.

Gen Arnold exhibited tremendous character in promoting air power and the widely shared vision of an Air Service that would be independent of the US Army during the inter-War years. As an air power advocate, then-Lt Col Arnold testified in favour of Col Billy Mitchell at his court martial in 1925, despite strong warnings from senior officers that such action would endanger his career. Arnold steadfastly supported Mitchell and continued to fight for a separate Air Service because of his firm conviction that it was the right thing to do for the defence of the nation. As a result, he was publicly admonished by the chief of the Air Service and exiled to Fort Riley, Kansas. Not one to be dissuaded by a little adversity, Arnold persevered in his beliefs, excelled in his career, and eventually became chief of the army air forces. From that position, he directed the development of, and influenced the employment of, the massive air armada that pummeled the Axis powers during World War II. Moreover, he laid the foundation for the creation of an independent United States Air Force in 1947.[11]

In a similar manner, Gen Benjamin O. Davis, Jr., demonstrated extraordinary character in fighting the destructive bigotry that pervaded the Air Service. In World War II, he led the all-black 99th Pursuit Squadron and 332d Fighter Group to great honour and distinction in the Mediterranean theatre of operations. He stood for exceptional professionalism, rigid discipline, and equal opportunity for black aviators to fly and fight. He attacked racial segregation ruthlessly in a 1945 testimony before a general officer panel evaluating how best to employ blacks in the military. Thereafter, he spoke out against segregation to military and civilian audiences as well as the Press. All that took tremendous courage since segregation was War Department policy at the time. Ultimately, this activism, combined with the impressive performance of Davis and the Tuskegee airmen he led, provided compelling evidence of the propriety of integrated air units. In the light of all that, Gen Vandenberg, chief of staff of the air force, approved the order to integrate the professional standard in a variety of senior command and staff billets while combating racism wherever it raised its ugly head.[12]

## "People Are the Essence of Our Business"[13]

Our greatest strength as a Service lies in our high-quality people. We are extremely fortunate to have the best people we've ever put in uniform as we draw down the air force. They are well educated, highly trained, and committed to excellence—literally the best and brightest our nation has to offer. Their exceptional quality is recognised worldwide. Former Warsaw Pact military leaders have been astonished at the authority and responsibility we entrust to our young officers and NCOs. Many have been so impressed that they are now professionalising their military based on the American model, often with American assistance. While the current drawdown in force is regrettable in many respects, in the end it will produce a core of experienced aerospace professionals who possess the expertise, the energy, and the commitment to keep our air force number one in the world.

As we implement extensive changes and fundamental restructuring in a fiscally austere environment, air force leaders must capitalise on the talent and skill of these top-notch people. Continue to push authority and responsibility down to the lowest levels possible. Implement quality initiatives that are tailored to the unique requirements of your organisation, then strive for constant improvement of the process. Nurture and cultivate the creativity and ingenuity of your troops. Strive to empower those people working on the cutting edge who best know how to get the job done efficiently and effectively. Ensure that the right procedures are in place to make it tough to say no to good ideas and encourage anyone with a good idea to surface it via those procedures.

While Eighth Air Force commander in the late Eighties, Gen James P. McCarthy capitalised on the bright, young officers and NCOs in his command by having them participate on numbered air force (NAF) working groups that addressed the hot issues of the day. In this manner, he focussed the creativity and ingenuity of his young leaders on such initiatives as enhancing unit conventional capabilities, improving pilot retention, increasing bombing accuracy, and streamlining alert changeover procedures. The NAF working groups developed comprehensive proposals for action that were reviewed and approved by the commander, then submitted to the commander-in-chief, Strategic Air Command (CINCSAC). Ultimately, many elements of these proposals were approved by CINCSAC for implementation throughout the command. In a similar vein, Gen McCarthy unleashed an air refuelling wing to rewrite the book on daily tanker operations. Unencumbered by regulations or headquarters oversight in virtually every area except safety, the wing developed a number of innovative procedures that were eventually adopted throughout the command to optimise tanker operations.[14]

In this era of growing regional threats to US interests, we must concentrate on squeezing the most combat power possible out of shrinking aerospace assets. Urge your troops to apply their brain power and their ingenuity to the vital task of exploiting the enormous combat potential of air force weapon systems. Gen George Kenney was a master at developing innovative ways to generate the most combat capability possible from rather limited air assets under his command in the southwest Pacific during World War II. As Gen Douglas MacArthur's air component commander, he (1) employed bombers as airborne artillery in support of struggling ground forces; (2) delivered troops and equipment by air into the heart of battle; (3) devastated enemy shipping and closed down sea lanes by employing "skip-bombing" techniques; (4) converted bombers into heavily armed interdiction platforms; (5) deceived the Japanese into making futile air strikes on mock airfields and established expeditionary airfields nearby; (6) launched mass surprise attacks against major Japanese airfields to gut the combat effectiveness of their air forces; and (7) dropped parachute fragmentation bombs (his own invention) to demolish enemy aerodromes.[15]

Gen Kenney was a true master at ingeniously exploiting the vast potential of air assets to seize control of the air, devastate enemy forces, and provide tremendous support for ground and naval operations in the southwest Pacific. We would do well to follow his lead in the lean years ahead when we inevitably will be called upon to use limited aerospace assets in innovative ways to deal with regional crises that erupt.

## Do the "Impossible"

Too often in the past, we have allowed bureaucratic inertia or conventional wisdom to stymie good ideas and novel approaches to doing our business better. We can no longer afford this tyranny of the status quo. Today, air force leaders must create an atmosphere that encourages people to take on the daunting challenges that confront us with innovative solutions, then support those solutions up the chain despite the odds against them. Inspire your people to do great things by convincing them that they can truly do what others write off as impossible. Don't allow innovation to be blocked by a negative, excuse-seeking mentality that blames the system. Instead, embolden your troops by implementing their good ideas when possible and staunchly supporting others by recasting and resubmitting those that must be approved by higher authority. Never accept as a final answer the oft-repeated lines "It's never been done that way before" or "The boss will never approve that." Continually buck the conventional wisdom and strive to convince your people that they can indeed "make it happen." Build their confidence, reward their initiatives, and support their good ideas. In turn, the results of their efforts will greatly impress your superiors.

When he took over as Eighth Air Force commander in 1987, Gen McCarthy immediately sought to develop realistic conventional deployment exercises for his bombardment wings. However, he encountered stiff resistance from Headquarters SAC, the NAF staff, and his wing commanders. Nevertheless, he persevered in developing an exercise that would have bomb wings deploy seven-bomber packages to relatively austere airfields to fly two weeks of conventional training sorties in Red Flag or similar exercises. This would be a tall order for bomb wings that had gotten used to operating almost solely from home station. Through force of personality, Gen McCarthy convinced his staff and wing commanders it could be done, then overcame the objections of higher headquarters to deploy the first unit (the 97th Bombardment Wing) to Clinton-Sherman Industrial Air Park, Oklahoma, in less than three months' time. The resulting Mighty Force exercise programme saw Eighth Air Force bomb wings deploy to a variety of continental US (CONUS) and overseas locations, set up tent cities, feed the troops from mobile kitchens, conduct bladder refuelling, use mobile communications systems, respond to mission-type orders, and keep aircraft flying for two weeks of intense conventional operations.[16]

Subsequently, under the direction of Lt Gen E.G. Shuler, Jr., Eighth Air Force bomb wings performed evermore demanding and realistic deployments that pushed units further up the conventional learning curve. He too fought an uphill battle against non-believers to conduct two highly successful NAF-wide exercises (Mighty Warrior 88 and 89) that entailed deploying all Eighth Air Force bomber and tanker wings as well as some command elements to austere operating locations in the CONUS and Europe. These deployed units conducted a combined command post and field training exercise that spanned a two-week period of rigorous flying operations at war-time sortie rates.[17] The dedicated efforts of all those who strived to bring off these realistic conventional exercises, despite the naysayers, paid off in the unprecedented capability of SAC bomb wings to deploy and fight during the Persian Gulf War.

## Maintain an Unwavering Focus on the Mission

In these increasingly austere and uncertain times, it is vitally important that we keep our mission of defending the United States through control and exploitation of air and space in the forefront of the minds of our people.[18] Convince your troops of the significance of what we are about in the air force and the vital importance of their contribution to this mission. Inform them about the vital role that aerospace power plays in implementing a regionally focussed defence strategy that relies largely upon global reach and power to safeguard America's vital interests. Educate them on air force doctrine and the evolution of our Service during this century. Emphasise our great leaders and impressive accomplishments in two World Wars, Korea, Vietnam, the Cold War, the Gulf War, and innumerable crises. Stress their place in the continuous and proud line of dedicated American airmen who have given their all to fight and win their nation's wars. Remind them of Gen Douglas MacArthur's admonition: "Yours is the profession of arms…You stand as the nation's war guardian, as its lifeguard from the raging tides of international conflicts, as its gladiator in the arena of battle."[19]

Seek to build a cohesive team of committed aerospace professionals who are capable of generating the maximum combat power possible from shrinking resources. Concentrate on those fundamental activities that underwrite unit readiness to perform our mission and that give us an unquestioned capability to deploy and fight. Meanwhile, avoid the diversion of time, energy, and resources to less significant activities that contribute to neither. Work the substance hard and the image will take care of itself.

Lead the way for your troops by giving 10 per cent in dedicated duty performance on a daily basis. Set the professional standard for them to emulate. Inculcate an unrelenting drive for excellence. Moreover, utilise an enlightened leadership approach that insists on quality performance but does not shoot them in the face every time your people make a mistake. Be firm but fair. Never accept mediocre performance. When people don't measure up, insist on taking the necessary corrective action, whether that consists of remedial training, removal from flying status, reassignment, administrative counselling, non-judicial punishment, or even court martial. We cannot afford incompetence, disregard for standards, or dereliction of duty in any unit, most especially in those where lives may be on the line.

A few years ago, a KC-135 tanker mishap occurred in which several air crew members died. The aircraft commander made too steep a descent in attempting to land the aircraft, bounced it off the runway, attempted to go around, but failed and drove the doomed tanker into the ground next to the runway. The aircraft broke up and the crew compartment became engulfed in flames. It turned out that this aircraft commander had a track record of serious problems in landing the airplane—problems that had never been adequately addressed through retraining or administrative action. He was a dedicated officer who was well liked by his peers and his superiors and appeared to be headed for a successful air force career. Thus, no one wanted to hurt his prospects by taking the tough remedial action dictated by his poor landing skills. Consequently, the unit mission and safety considerations were compromised by an overwhelming concern for an individual's career. The result was a tragic mishap that quite possibly could have been avoided. Obviously, much worse things can happen to an aviator than busting a check ride, going through additional training, or even coming off of flying status. Air force leaders must have the courage, the strength of character, and the wisdom to make the tough decisions when the circumstances warrant.

## Realistic Training is *de Rigueur*

The post-Cold War era of come-as-you-are crises makes it imperative that we keep air force units honed to a razor-sharp edge. Achieving that goal requires that we engage our troops in the most demanding, realistic training possible in peace-time. It also necessitates taking the initiative to evolve tactics, techniques, and procedures to stay abreast of the diverse threats and situations we may encounter around the globe. Seek to capitalise on the enormous talent and brain power of your people to further your unit's war-fighting capabilities. Moreover, seek to exploit the inherent capabilities of assigned weapon systems to contribute to the fight. Don't allow your people to become complacent or your unit to stagnate.

While he commanded 3rd Bombardment Division in England during World War II, Gen LeMay insisted on just this kind of rigorous training and mental ingenuity to prepare his crews for combat and to continually refine their war-fighting skills. LeMay evolved various formations to concentrate the defensive firepower of his bombers and enhance their survivability. He developed new procedures to enable air crews to take off in foul weather and improved procedures to form up hundreds of bombers over Britain for massive attacks on the continent. When his people weren't flying missions, they were attending ground school, firing live rounds at the target range, performing intensive target study, learning foul weather takeoff procedures, honing formation flying skills, or refining bombing techniques. Air crews were not overly enamoured with their commander's demanding approach to business and soon began referring to him as "Old Iron Ass." But Gen LeMay took their criticism in stride and said, "I don't mind being called tough, since I find in this racket it's the tough guys who lead the survivors."[20] Ultimately, LeMay's emphasis on training and preparation paid off when his bomber groups achieved an impressive record of putting bombs squarely on target and returning to base with minimal losses.

In a similar manner, Eighth Air Force began training selected bomb wings to perform long-range strikes from the CONUS in 1987 in anticipation of future crises that might necessitate such missions. Under Gen McCarthy's direction, the NAF staff worked out the details of these round-robin sorties with affected bomb wings, Headquarters SAC and other agencies. It then tasked wings to fly Mighty Strike exercise sorties into the Mediterranean and other regions of the world to prove the concept and refine mission procedures. Continuation of this realistic exercise programme under Gen Shuler had Eighth Air Force primed and ready to launch long-range B-52 strikes from Barksdale AFB, Louisiana, against vital power and communications facilities within Iraq at the initiation of the Desert Storm air war. Seven bomber crews flew halfway around the world, dispatched their deadly ordnance of conventional cruise missiles from outside Iraq's borders, then returned home after a record-setting 35-hour combat mission.[21] That operation put potential aggressors on notice that the United States can reach out and touch them unexpectedly with devastating strikes flown from the CONUS.

If we are to remain the world's most respected air and space force, we must have the vision to anticipate future crises and develop the appropriate aerospace capabilities to handle them through realistic training and rigorous exercises. However, no amount of preparation can prevent our units from becoming hollow due to uncertainty and fear over the future. Only involved leadership that keeps the mission in the forefront while providing a stable, secure, and reassuring environment can do that.

## Take Care of Your People

During these trying times of force drawdowns, base closures, SERBs, and RIFs, it is imperative that we take care of our most valuable resource—air force people. We must not be a cold, uncaring institution but a professional outfit that takes care of its own by assisting those transitioning to civilian life while continuing to provide a decent quality of life for those who remain with us. Our dedicated airmen are the backbone of the air force's combat effectiveness. We must continue to do right by them (and their families) if we are to maintain the enthusiasm, esprit, and commitment that binds our people into a coherent war-fighting team.

Therefore, place a high priority on the quality of life for your troops and their families. Ensure they have a decent environment in which to live and work. Demonstrate an evident concern for the welfare of your troops. Be creative and persistent in addressing their needs. After taking charge of SAC, Gen LeMay sought innovative ways to take care of his people. He utilised spot promotions to reward standout performers. He prevailed upon the Army Corps of Engineers to replace open-bay barracks with semi-private dorms for enlisted troops. He worked with Senator Kenneth S. Wherry of Nebraska (R-Nebr.) to secure funding to build new married quarters at SAC installations. He even went so far as to establish hobby shops at all his bases to provide his troops an enjoyable outlet for their mechanical talents. Gen LeMay firmly believed that he could demand the utmost in performance and commitment from his people if he took good care of them, and they proved him right.[22]

Similarly, you should strive to provide a quality work environment for your people. Use self-help where feasible to upgrade work areas. Involve your people in planning and effecting upgrades, then take part in the work yourself. Your people will work hard to fix up their own work areas, take pride in the result, and welcome your participation as an indication of your concern. Even modest improvements can help inspire troops because they know the boss cares.

Structure your outfit to encourage innovation and reward performance. Look out for the best interests of your people. Seek any and all opportunities to recognise your exceptional performers. Capitalise on the awards and decorations programmes, speciality awards, and awards whenever possible at the NAF, major command (MAJCOM), and air force levels. Create your own unit awards and spread the wealth to deserving people. Be sure to recognise your top people in public forums such as commander's calls or award ceremonies. Written and verbal pats-on-the-back are always in order.

Take a sincere interest in furthering the careers of your troops. Put in the time and effort to do performance reports, promotion recommendations, and decoration nominations right. Encourage your people to improve themselves through professional military education, specialty courses, and college or advance-degree programmes. Support the efforts of individuals to get good follow-on assignments. A well-placed phone call or endorsement letter can greatly enhance prospects for individuals to land a desired job. Never hesitate to go to bat for a deserving subordinate. In the end, your people will respond to your concern for their welfare with dedicated service above and beyond the call.

## Maintain a Visible Presence

Effective air force leaders must get out of their offices and become immersed in all aspects of their unit's operations. Maintain a visible presence throughout your outfit—observing, directing, encouraging, critiquing, or praising as appropriate. Get out and put your footprints on the organisation. Infuse the unit with your spirit, enthusiasm, commitment, and high standards. Energise your people to excel. Solicit their concerns on frequent visits to the flight line, maintenance shops, launch control facilities, guard posts, or wherever your people work—day and night, in good weather and bad. Hold periodic commander's calls or similar gatherings to keep your people informed and to enable them to express their concerns directly to you.

When he was commander of Twelfth Air Force in North Africa during World War II, Gen James H. Doolittle saw it as his job to visit every unit under his command, engage his troops, discover any problems, and begin to work the solutions. To facilitate this process, he often arrived at a unit and announced that he was going to fly a combat mission with them aboard one of their aircraft (B-17, B-25, or B-26) as an observer or co-pilot. He "was convinced that nothing gives your men the confidence in you and in themselves that having you go with them does." He tried to pick the tough missions so he could get a good understanding of the challenges that confronted his bomber crews in combat. Moreover, he wanted everyone in his command to know that the "old man" would fly the dangerous sorties and that he was knowledgeable about bombing tactics, formation flying, and the methods to evade flak and fighters.[23] Doolittle's actions reflected a common approach to combat leadership in World War II that saw group, wing, division, and NAF commanders risking their lives to gather first-hand knowledge about the progress of the air war and to bolster the confidence of their troops.

As a military leader, you must be present and visible when the critical is happening in your unit. Never hesitate to take charge during an emergency or crisis. Your troops will want to see you in the thick of things, and that is where you need to be if you are to lead effectively. Your presence will bolster the confidence of your people and allay their fears. By all means, let the experts do their jobs, but be present and on the scene to provide overarching guidance and continuity. Then, take responsibility for the outcome.

In 1987, one of the best examples of on-the-scene leadership in peacetime occurred at Barksdale when a KC-10 exploded on the ramp shortly after Gen John T. Chain, Jr., CINCSAC, arrived on station to speak at an NCO Academy graduation. Despite the stress of this ill-timed and deadly mishap, the wing commander remained calm, cool, collected, and in charge.

His professional demeanour was contagious. His people performed superbly under dangerous conditions in response to his crisp directions. They quickly moved to control the mishap area, taxied endangered airframes out of harm's way, extinguished the fuel-led inferno, attempted to rescue a maintenance person from the airframe, and minimised injuries incurred. That evening, the commander appeared on local newscasts to calm the fears of the local civilian and military communities and to lay at rest rumours about a terrorist incident at the base. His confident performance was especially reassuring to those living on or near an SAC installation that kept bombers on alert. Undoubtedly, the superb performance of then-Col Brett M. Dula during this pressure-filled emergency contributed to his subsequent selection to become a general officer.[24]

## Exploit the Full Measure of Your Authority

While deputy commander-in-chief of US European Command, Gen McCarthy stressed the need for leaders to use the full measure of the authority entrusted to them by their superiors. Too often, individuals are reluctant to do so because they incorrectly believe that their boss wants to be in on every decision. So they buck all substantive decisions up the chain and shy away from taking the initiative in fear of jeopardising their careers. In most instances, air force superiors expect subordinate leaders to decide upon all matters within their purview as long as they keep the boss informed. Superiors have enough to do without having to make a subordinate's decisions for him or her. Thus, they prefer to make only those extraordinary decisions that lie beyond the authority of their subordinate leaders. Moreover, they readily expect those leaders to be self-starters who can get a good read on the boss' agenda, then undertake initiatives to further that agenda.[25]

The key to this approach lies in fully understanding the goals and operating philosophy of your superior, as well as his or her expectations for you and your unit. Armed with this knowledge, you can move out smartly to exploit your authority in performing the unit mission and implementing appropriate initiatives, all the while keeping your boss informed. If you operate in this manner, you will gain greater latitude from your superior, greater satisfaction in your job, and greater success in your career. As a boss yourself, you must be willing to allow your subordinates to behave in a similar manner. Groom them for positions of increased responsibility by encouraging them to exercise the full measure of their authority while always keeping their superior in the loop. For your part, strive to get involved only in those decisions that cannot be handled at a lower level and that require your action or that of your superior.[26]

If you do so, then you will be travelling in good company. During World War II, Gen Spaatz was especially adept at assigning responsibilities to subordinate air commanders, empowering them with the necessary authority to carry out those responsibilities, then getting out of the way while they discharged them. His willingness to repose confidence in his commanders inspired them to great heights in accomplishing the mission for "Tooey."[27]

## Involved Leadership: The Ultimate Key to Success

As we transition to a new, streamlined air force that focusses on power projection and employs the latest in management techniques, we must continue to provide the involved leadership that is essential to the successful transformation of our Service. Ours is a particularly human endeavour. We ask our dedicated people to undergo risks, to withstand hardships, and to make sacrifices in defending the United States and its global security interests. We owe them the very best we can provide in the way of quality leadership at all times, but most especially during this era of enormous change and uncertainty.

Gen George C. Marshall's advice to his commanders in World War II applies equally well to those who would lead in today's air force:

The truly great leader overcomes all difficulties…The lack of equipment, the lack of food, the lack of this or that are only excuses; the real leader displays his quality in his triumphs over adversity, however great it may be.[28]

If the United States Air Force is to remain the world's premier air and space force, we must triumph over the adversity that confronts us as we transform our Service into a leaner, meaner combat organisation capable of meeting the challenges of the future. We dare do no less if we are to meet the security needs of our great nation and keep faith with our illustrious air force forebears.

## Notes

1. See details of this framework in Donald B. Rice, *Global Reach—Global Power: The Air Force and US National Security,* White Paper (Washington, D.C.: Department of the Air Force, June 1990); and Idem, "Reshaping for the Future," testimony before the House Armed Services Committee, February 20, 1992, in *Vital Speeches* 58, no. 12, April 1, 1992, pp. 354-261.

2. See organisational initiatives in *Air Force Restructure*, White Paper (Washington, D.C.: Department of the Air Force, September 1991); and General Merrill A. McPeak, "Restructuring the Air Force: Organise, Train and Equip," address to the Air Force Association Convention, September 18, 1991, in *Vital Speeches* 58, no. 3, November 15, 1991, pp. 69-74.

3. From the USAF vision statement in "State of the Air Force," *Airman*, December 1992, p. A3.

4. See full panoply of endeavours identified in "Reshaping the Force" section in Ibid., pp. A4-18.

5. See *National Military Strategy* (Washington, D.C.: Joint Staff, January 1992) for discussion of regionally focussed defence strategy (p. 1), the strategic landscape, US interests and threats to same (pp. 1-4), the need for an unquestioned capacity to respond to regional crises (pp. 7 and 11-12), and the strategic principles of readiness, aerospace superiority, strategic agility, power projection, decisive force, and technological superiority (pp. 9-10). The attributes of aerospace power make the air force particularly well suited to implement the defence strategy articulated herein.

6. Giulio Douhet, *The Command of the Air* (1942; reprint, Washington, D.C.: Office of Air Force History, 1983), p. 91.

7. For an intriguing discussion of the unique nature of our "comprehensive" air force that seeks to provide the full range of air and space capabilities, see Gen Merrill A. McPeak, "Does the Air Force Have a Mission?" address at Maxwell AFB, Ala. Text of the address is in "McPeak: No Clear Mission Statement Until Now," *Air Force Times*, no. 52, August 3, 1992, pp. 4-5.

8. Gen H.H. Arnold to Lt Col Leroy L. Stefen, letter, November 5, 1946, January

7, 1947, p. 2.

9. Gen George S. Patton, Jr., *War as I Knew It* (New York: Bantam Books, Inc., 1981), p. 346. Also see p. 390 for guidance on proper care of troops.

10. Edgar F. Puryear, Jr., *Stars in Flight: A Study in Air Force Character and Leadership* (Novato, Calif.: Presidio Press, 1981), pp. 232-233.

11. Ibid., pp. 17-19; and H.H. Arnold, *Global Mission* (New York: Harper & Row, 1949), pp. 120-122.

12. John L. Frisbee, ed., *Makers of the United States Air Force* (Washington, D.C.: Office of Air Force History, 1987), pp. 229-255. For a first hand account of the challenges General Davis confronted, see Benjamin O. Davis, Jr., *Benjamin O. Davis, Jr., American: An Autobiography* (Washington, D.C.: Smithsonian Institute Press, 1991).

13. Favoured expression of Gen James P. McCarthy (Retd.), when discussing the importance of people to the air force mission. Used at USAFE colonel's orientation, December 2, 1991, Ramstein Air Base, Germany.

14. Gen James P. McCarthy, "SAC: The Command for the Future," *Combat Crew* 38, no. 3, March 1988, pp. 3-4.

15. For details, see Gen George C. Kenney, *General Kenney Reports* (1949; reprint, Washington, D.C.: Office of Air Force History, 1987); and Frisbee, pp. 127-150.

16. Gen James P. McCarthy, "The Conventional Challenge," *Combat Crew* 37, no. 9, September 1987, p. 2; and Jeffrey P. Rhodes, "SAC Extends Its Wings," *Air Force Magazine* 71, no. 8, August 1988, pp. 44-50.

17. Lt Gen E.G. Shuler, Jr., "Mighty Warrior 88: Training as We Intend to Fight," *Combat Crew* 38, no. 10, October 1988, pp. 3, 6-7; and "Mighty Warrior 89," *Combat Crew* 39, no. 11, November 1989, pp. 3, 9.

18. McPeak, n. 2, p. 5.

19. Gen Douglas MacArthur, "Duty, Honor, Country," *American Legion Magazine*, November 1986, p. 50.

20. Thomas M. Coffey, Iron Eagle: *The Turbulent Life of General Curtis LeMay* (New York: Crown Publishers, Inc., 1986), pp. 56-59.

21. James P. Coyne, *Airpower in the Gulf* (Arlington, Va.: Air Force Association Aerospace Education Foundation, 1992), p. 4.

22. Coffey, n. 20, pp. 294-298.

23. Gen James H. Doolittle and Carroll V. Glines, *I Could Never Be So Lucky Again: The Memoirs of General James H. "Jimmy" Doolittle* (New York: Bantam Books, 1992), p. 306

24. Maj Gen Brett M. Dula is currently commander, Second Air Force, Beale AFB, California.

25. Gen James P. McCarthy, "Commanding Joint and Coalition Operations," *Naval War College Review,* 46, no. 1, Winter 1993, p. 11.

26. Ibid., p. 12.

27. Puryear, n. 10, pp. 89-91.

28. Quoted in Lt Col Charles M. Westenhoff, *Military Air Power: The CADRE Digest of Air Power Opinions and Thoughts* (Maxwell AFB, Ala.: Air University Press, October 1990), p. 149.

# 10
# Ethics and Values in Military Leadership

*Arjun Subramaniam*

In our relentless quest for success, recognition and even fame in an increasingly consumerist competitive world, the military also seems to have become obsessed with "Doing a Thing Right" rather than "Doing the Right Thing." Intense competition to climb the 'pyramid', numerous environmental compulsions, and the desire for quick results in the face of complex pressures have possibly resulted in ethics, values and principles falling by the wayside. Media reports of stage-managed encounters and killing of terrorists and senior leaders looking toward civil courts for resolving promotion issues in India, human rights violations of prisoners by US military leaders, the tail-hook scandal, etc. are but indications of the broader decline from the proverbial tradition of an officer being a gentleman first who would lay down his life for a cause and principle.

Over the last decade or more, we have been reading extensively about ethics and values in corporate governance (Infosys and Tatas are now household names!) rather than about military honour and integrity. We need to clearly reestablish our lead not only in good governance, but, more important, in ethics-based leadership in the armed forces. During the earlier days of the Indian Air Force, nobody really talked about values and ethics because it was ingrained in almost every action that was done or every word that was written or spoken, from the very beginning. Today, the time has come to start laying the foundation of ethical and value-based leadership once again or we run the danger of having the very structure of our house destroyed. Before proceeding further, we need to ask ourselves two basic questions and answer them as honestly as we can.

- Are we facing a crisis of leadership, not in terms of performance and results, but in terms of ethics and values?
- If we are genuinely concerned, what is the way forward? Is there a need to widely institutionalise the teaching of values and ethics in military institutions of learning?

The bottom line, of course, is to first recognise the need for ethical and value-based military leadership and to reaffirm its importance in projecting the armed forces as an instrument of credible national power. Only then can we shake off the cocooned feeling that all is right and start reflecting at all levels on what needs to be done to restore the pride, elan and impeccable pedigree of the armed forces.

## Core Definition of Ethics and Values

There is no better place to start than at the core definition of ethics and values. Ethics as defined by the *Concise Oxford Dictionary* is "the science of morals," "moral principles" and "rules of conduct." It relates to what is honourable or morally correct or the study of both right and wrong. Some questions that immediately spring up when one looks at the bare definition are: Where do these morals come from? What is their pedigree and can we use them as a template for both our professional and personal conduct at all times? Only when these questions are answered convincingly will a military leader apply them to all facets of his leadership, be it during peace or war. The word ethics owes its origin to the great Greek philosophers, Plato, Socrates and Aristotle, and is a literal translation of the word ethos that means habitual or customary conduct. To Aristotle[1] ethics meant the study of excellence in the virtues of character. Closer home, the *Bhagvad Gita* propounded the concept of *Dharma* or 'righteousness' or doing one's duty, be it in peace or on the battlefield.[2] With the advent of Christianity, the moral aspects of what the Church considered right or wrong crept into military ethics. The Chinese have also contributed in full measure in the area of what military leaders should and should not do through the teachings of Confucius and Sun Tzu. From all these philosophical musings and moral codes laid down by new and established religions and philosophers emerged a set of rules of conduct that were honourable. If one looks at the two phrases emphasised, in ancient times these were applicable only in two main activities viz. sports and warfare. These Rules of Conduct and Honour Code have stood the test of time and have formed the foundation for the emergence of a number of value systems. Truth, justice, equality, integrity and courage are amongst key examples of military ethics.

What then are values? Falling back again on the *Concise Oxford Dictionary*, it means one's principles or standards; one's judgment of what is valuable or important in life. It relates to attaching significance or regarding highly. If one looks at the definition, what emerges clearly is the fact that values are personal benchmarks that are greatly influenced by parents, teachers, mentors, peers, superiors and, of course, the 'environment.' Mark the word environment because today, the environment, more than anything else, has become the scapegoat for decaying values. If one were to explain very simply to young military officers and men, one could say that ethics are a broad, strong and inviolable framework that comprises a few rules of military and personal conduct in which you fit in values that are need and situation-based, as spelt out from time to time by the top leadership. Integrity comes from a Latin word that means entire and whole. In relation to professional conduct, we define integrity as "uncompromised values," i.e. professionalism is behaviour aligned with uncompromised values. To be consistently professionally effective requires balancing passion, vision, and action with integrity and aligning these elements at each step along the way. Integrity, according to many purists, is the only way out and encompasses all known ingredients of leadership. In short, integrity is uncompromising and dictated neither by environmental, nor by organisational compulsions.

## Historical Evolution and Decay of Military Ethics and Values

Images of the great warrior Arjun being given a treatise on morals, ethics and values on the battlefield by Lord Krishna are vivid in every Indian mind. Should he decimate the revered teachers who had taught him every skill they knew, or the warrior cousins he had grown up with? That was when Lord Krishna stepped in with his Divine justification of *Dharma Yudha* or Righteous War: a war he urged Arjun to fight with a clear conscience because it was the right thing to do.[3] Homer's heroes from the *Illiad* and the *Odyssey* fought each other at Troy over a moral violation of ethics. Battlefield ethics of fighting equals and returning the bodies of slain warriors indicated the existence of an honour code.[4] The Roman Empire fell because of a progressive decay in morals and ethics that blinded successive emperors from differentiating between what was right and wrong. They ordered the military to plunder, destroy and rape; and the military blindly obeyed till the rage of the common man pulled the empire down. Renewed multiple pressures on medieval military leadership led to subjugation of classical military ethics and universal values like honour, integrity, courage and honesty to the spread of religion. The Industrial Revolution and its fallout of colonisation did have its share of unscrupulous and unethical conquests of natives, but, at the same time, it laid the foundation for the emergence of a worldwide similarity in military leadership as practised by the British and the French. Ethics and values are practised by British stalwarts like the Duke of Wellington who once said, "The battle of Waterloo was won on the playing field of Eton," indicated that good military leadership could not be acquired in a matter of days or weeks but accrued from years of value-based grooming and learning.

While military ethics have remained almost static for thousands of years, military values have undergone many transformations. Historically, military leaders have always struggled to cope with political or nationalist directives and modern military values owe their origin to the emergence of the nation state and the rapid proliferation of military technology. World War II saw the success of generals like Rommel and Slim who occupied the moral and ethical high ground and yet won. Rommel always struggled to come to terms with Nazi Germany and yet managed to carve out an exemplary niche for himself amidst the moral degradation that was to ultimately cause the collapse of Nazi Germany. It also saw the emergence of politically savvy generals like Eisenhower who were operationally sound and yet malleable and flexible. Then came Korea and Vietnam wherein a nation's military leadership had to succumb to political manipulation.

The aftermath of the Vietnam War saw a complete reappraisal of military leadership in the US armed forces. A grassroots drive was initiated to restore the faith of a nation in its military leadership and of the men in uniform in their leaders. Closer home, Gen Thimayya's resistance to the "forward policy" and Defence Minister Krishna Menon's highhanded treatment of senior military officers was based on the need to preserve the honour of the armed forces. It is another matter, however, that the ill-fated Menon policy was ultimately implemented, leading to the 1962 China debacle which brought into focus the need to reinforce ethics and values in the Indian Army that were severely compromised during the conflict. Field Marshal Manekshaw, Air Chief Marshal P.C. Lal and others epitomised all that was best in military ethics. To a large extent, the success of the Coalition forces during "Operation Desert Storm" was due to focussed, ethical and value-based military leadership as displayed by both Gen Shwarzkopf and Gen Horner. The same cannot be said of the recent war in Iraq where the media has exposed the blatant aberrations in military values and ethics by the US and British officers and soldiers in the absence of any strong value-based leadership.[5] History is replete with examples of both upholding what are the best in military ethics and values and what are the worst. It is for practitioners of this profession to dig into history and make a choice.

## Pressure on Military Leadership

The changing nature of warfare, rapid socio-economic changes and expansion of national interests well beyond geographical boundaries have placed fresh challenges on military leadership. Terrorism, insurgencies and ethnic warfare have seen the most brutal and horrifying excesses in Bosnia, Chechnya and Rwanda. The proliferation of democracy has also placed fresh demands on military leadership in terms of compliance and taking orders from political masters. Materialism and economic progress have exerted their own pressures on the moderately paid practitioners of the military profession. Intense media scrutiny has also resulted in many leadership aberrations being made public, forcing the military leadership to increasingly look inwards and focus on ethics and values. The pyramidical structure in the armed forces has always existed; competition has always been intense and soldiers in the past have retired or exited from service gracefully and with minimum fuss. This was mainly due to two reasons.

Firstly, there was very little transparency in the assessment and promotion system; and, secondly, the Honour Code was so strongly ingrained in officers that aberrations were kept in-house to preserve the *Izzat* of the defence Services and not wash dirty linen in public. Today, things are completely different. Military leaders do not want to retire young because of economic and resettlement uncertainties. There is, at times, an intense desire in many leaders, whose ambition far exceeds their ability, to rise in rank by 'hook or by crook.' In this race up the ladder, ethics, values and principles are the first casualties. Increasing transparency now comes into play and leaders who feel they have been denied a rightful place in the sun have started taking the legal route to redress their grievances, bringing issues of fairplay, ethics and values into the public limelight. Equally troublesome and perplexing questions are faced by commanders in anti-terrorist internal security (IS) and counter-insurgency (CI) duties where the divide between right and wrong is wafer thin. How does one adhere to the principles of *Jus ad Bellum*, that lays down what constitutes a just cause for a decision to wage war, and *Jus in Bello,* that decides who should be immune from direct and intentional attacks in war? When targeting enemy military forces, how should officers and soldiers weigh force protection against civilian casualties?[6] How do you teach your men and officers to retain their sense of balance in the face of brutal, unscrupulous and fanatic insurgents and terrorists who exploit the land and local people to their advantage, even using them as human shields? With rapidly changing social norms and increasing permissiveness in society, marital discord and extra-marital liaisons amongst men and women in uniform are on the increase. How do military leaders cope with such changes? AIDS is another challenge in our search for a new set of ethics and values for the military. How do we as military leaders cope with these problems and instil in our officers and men a set of ethics that are constant and values that combine progressive thought and conservative tradition with the aim of making the military leader stand out in comparison to business and political leaders as guardians of a free and progressive democracy?

## Different Perspectives on Values and Ethics

The aftermath of the Vietnam War and the public outcry against declining morals, values and ethics forced the US armed forces to look inward and institutionalise the ethics and values that were expected of men and women in uniform. In the mid-Nineties, the US Army formally listed its seven values[7] as:

- Loyalty.
- Duty.
- Respect.
- Selfless Service.
- Honour.
- Integrity.
- Personal Courage.
- Character.

The US Air Force (USAF) concised it to just three core values,[8] viz.
- Integrity First.
- Service Before Self.
- Excellence in All We Do.

Some of the issues that merit close attention and are universally relevant are discussed below. These traits have been particularly singled out as they are perceived to be important in the context of the Indian armed forces too.
- **Loyalty.** Loyalty should not be confused with blind obedience to illegal or unethical orders. Leaders must follow their conscience when giving orders and subordinates must exercise their judgment when the orders are unethical and violate the laid down values. As long as leaders and subordinates understand that loyalty is first to the organisation, its values and principles, and not to the individual, the dividing line between loyalty and sycophancy would be clearly defined.
- **Respect.** A good leader must always respect individuals, whether senior or junior. He must honour their status, value their opinions and accept inputs humbly for whatever they are worth. Individuality and self-esteem must be respected, as that will foster mutual respect, something that is imperative for value-based teamwork. It is common to confuse between respect and subservience. While respect is an affirmation of

mutual or one-sided affirmation of professional capability or personal standards, subservience is 'blind respect' that is based on fear, greed and ambition.

- **Integrity**. Integrity of thought and action is central to good military leadership. A person of integrity does not change moral principles when they become unpopular or inconvenient. Broadly speaking, it means adherence to moral and ethical standards. Integrity is all encompassing and includes both moral and physical courage, honesty, propriety, accountability and justice. A look at the USAF values indicates that excellence is important but it is at number three on the list. What can be deducted from it? It is realisation that if one concentrates on the means and the methods, keeping the good of the organisation or the immediate environment in mind, the excellence will automatically follow. The Honour Code is said to have been very evident in a recent exercise with the USAF, especially during debriefs where violations were admitted honestly by USAF pilots right in the beginning without waiting for others to point them out.

The basic worry in the United States today relates to how they can retain their global supremacy without undermining their moral foundations. In her review of Martin L. Cook's book *The Moral Warriors: Ethics and Service in the US Military,* Shanon E. French zeroes in on the issue of military advice to political leaders/policy-makers and advocates non-partisan advice based on ethics and sound judgment. An interesting aspect though is the author's opinion of what a military leader should do if he disagrees with the execution order of a military mission that has specific political clearance. The right option considered is resignation and not defiance or disobedience as it would reflect 'maturity of judgment' and this was exactly what Gen Thimayya almost did when faced with unpalatable higher directives.

## Chinese Model

The simplest articulation of ethics and values for the military can be traced back to the early day of Mao and the Long March. In its early days, the People's Liberation Army (PLA) formulated its three Main Rules of

Discipline and Eight Points for Attention that laid down ethical rules of conduct for its personnel.[9] It reflected a grassroots approach and has stood the test of time. Some of the prominent ones are:

- Do not take a single piece of thread from the masses.
- Speak politely.
- Pay fairly for what you buy.
- Return everything you borrow.
- Pay for anything you damage.
- Do not hit or swear at people.
- Do not damage crops.

## Erosion of Ethics and Values

While we have a tradition of customs of the Service, and the attributes of leadership do focus on values, ethics and value systems in the Indian armed forces have never been institutionalised. We have rather relied on tradition and hand-me-downs to inculcate ethics and values in our officers and troops. The armed forces have lived and operated in isolation all these years, admired from a distance by both the common people and the political establishment. Ethical misdemeanours were more often than not viewed as mere aberrations and not systemic faults, and swept under the carpet after symbolic courts of enquiries or even court martials. Institutional concern was not very apparent as the overall quality of military leadership was considered to be very high and comparable to the best in the world. Things started changing in the Nineties because of both geo-political and environmental changes. The major factors that have accelerated the erosion of ethics and values in the Indian armed forces are:

- Rapid economic growth and growing disparity in incomes between the military and other professions.
- Increased involvement of the armed forces in internal security duties without adequate institutionalised sensitisation.
- Increased involvement in anti-terrorist operations and the associated dilemmas of force protection vs non-combatant immunity, collateral damage and civilian casualties.
- Enhanced civil-military-paramilitary liaison and increase in the exposure

of men in uniform to various forms of corruption.

- Poor resettlement opportunities for officers and men who superannuate early in life.
- Changed priorities of the younger generation and absence of enough 'role models,' coupled with reluctance on the part of senior officers to assume serious mentoring roles.
- Lack of any serious institutionalised training in ethics and value-based leadership for officers and men.
- Intense media scrutiny of matters relating to the military.
- Closed assessment system and absence of a fair in-house redressal system that forces military personnel to go to court and tarnish the self-image of the armed forces.
- Changing morality of personal relationships in society.

## The Way Forward

The only way forward is to first recognise the fact that ethics and values in the armed forces in general are being routinely compromised. The feeling of "if you get away with it" then it does not matter if it was right or wrong and it "pays to be a winner" is widely prevalent and accepted. The next step is to adopt a bottoms-up approach in inculcating ethics and values in both officers and other ranks. Presently, there is no institutionalised sensitisation to the importance of ethics and values in good military leadership. Along with military history, why cannot we introduce ethics and values in the curriculum at the National Defence Academy (NDA) and the Air Force Academy as part of a character building and training programme? Why can't we include the study of ethics and values from an even younger age at our Sainik schools and institutions like Rashtriya Indian Military College (RIMC)? We have also seen a top-down approach in which senior officers articulate their views and concerns on values, ethics and leadership and expect the younger generation to accept them without understanding or being convinced about the 'payoffs' of ethical and value-based leadership. Instead, why don't we start at the very bottom of the pyramid? Do we really think that a few leadership capsules conducted by institutions like the College of Defence Management and the CLABS (Centre for Leadership and Behavioural Studies) at the College of Air Warfare are likely to inculcate good leadership skills? Indeed, it is a good beginning, but it should be accompanied by a grassroots drive to inculcate the ability to differentiate right from wrong.

A clear data bank of ethical misdemeanours over the years must be created and shared periodically along with the action taken by the three Services so that the point is driven home that no compromise is acceptable as far as ethics and values are concerned. A reduction in the involvement of the armed forces in internal security duties is an inescapable imperative. This would make it easier to adhere to core values and ethics of the military profession and insulate the various rungs of military leadership from the risks, temptations and pressures associated with internal security duties. Resettlement and parallel absorption in the public and private sectors of retired officers and men, or veterans as they are now called, is vital in keeping relatively young military leaders secure about their future. Compromising ethics and moral values in order to secure an uncertain future is one troubling issue that needs to be addressed on priority. Mentoring in the armed forces is becoming a lost art that has to be revived if we are to pass on ethics, values and traditions to the younger generation. Many middle ranking and senior officers are, at times, so busy furthering their own careers that they see little value in investing time and intellect on the younger generation, who in turn are getting used to 'quick fix' solutions and increasingly reluctant to take the difficult path of doing the 'right thing'.

Sceptics may say that there is no use for study of ethics and values as they carry little meaning in the 'heat of combat operations'. Nothing can be farther from the truth as it is only when you continuously reflect on good ethics and values, will you arrive at the correct decision in battle or under pressure. **So, the *Mantra* should be to catch them young and inculcate in them the ability to quickly differentiate between right and wrong so that when the going gets tough, a military leader seldom takes the easy way out.**

## Values for the Modern Military Leader

Moral values and ethics can be enforced by law or ensured by creating an environment of fear, the likes of which existed behind the Iron Curtain.

Sadly, these methods have never stood the test of time and crumble in the face of adversity or 'when no one is looking.' Personal conviction[10] is the only way to ensure the sustenance of any framework that exists for ethical conduct in the armed forces. As alluded to earlier, it is important to clearly establish an ethical framework for our men and officers that helps them distinguish right from wrong from a very early stage of their military careers. These can be termed as Core Ethics and could include inviolable attributes like Integrity, Honesty, Responsibility, Accountability, Justice, Trust and Courage. It is not enough to articulate these in a document or doctrine or a White Paper, but actually to go down to the nurseries of military education and teach our young cadets and officers, with examples from history and relate these to their present lives. Having established a basic framework, it is for the leadership to spell out the values that fit into the framework, and these values would form the building blocks of a strong and enduring organisation. Leadership has three components, viz, technical expertise, institutional authority, and moral authority. Technical expertise is the ability, skill and knowledge necessary to do what must be done to accomplish the desired objective. Institutional authority is derived from the position in the organisation occupied by the individual. Moral authority is knowledge of, and concern for, what is best for the institution and those who follow you. Some of the values that may be considered are age old ones, and some have emerged as a result of our changing times. A sample of these attributes is given below. These values should be able to guide and motivate our military leaders to realise both organisational and personal goals.

- Professional Excellence.
- Self-Confidence.
- Flexibility of Thought and Action.
- Decision-Making Ability.
- Technology Orientation.
- Intellectual Ability.
- Multi-skilling Ability.

## Ethical and Value Imperatives for Senior Military Leadership

To avoid unnecessary clutter, it is also important to lay down certain imperatives for the senior military leadership as the consequences of their actions can be far-reaching. The additional burden of command makes senior military leaders the cynosure of not only the eyes of the men they lead, but the eyes of millions of their countrymen, thanks to the increasingly transparent and even prying media. Let us acknowledge that the pressures on them are tremendous. Apart from diverse, invisible and often unscrupulous opponents in battle, they also have to cope with the chronic stress of modern day living that permeates from their own personal lives to the lives of the men under their command as well as their families. The highly regimented, rule bound, fast moving and competitive work environment may lead to feelings of alienation, inadequacy, powerlessness and worry about basic survival in the rat race. In such a situation, unless a leader is equipped with all the basic core values and ethics and reinforced with years of experience and wisdom, the chances of taking unethical or wrong decisions are very high. This was clearly evident in the recent cases of prisoner abuse at Guantanamo Bay and Abu Ghraib where senior Coalition leaders are said to have tacitly approved of the debasing torture of legitimate prisoners of war (POWs).[11] Therefore, other than the core values and ethics, what are the imperatives for the senior military leadership?

- **Credibility and Trust**. Credibility and trust go hand in hand. Spell out to your subordinates clearly what you expect of them. Share your vision with them and live your values as you preach them.[12] Do that and you will win their trust and their efforts. The maxim of practise what you preach and only preach what you can practise is so very important to win the trust and loyalty of increasingly discerning, aware and intelligent subordinates.

- **Control of the Environment**. Control of the environment is important to do the right thing. Let the environment control you and you will fall prey to the pressure it exerts on you. This is only possible if a military leader is professionally sound, politically aware and environmentally sensitive. This would ensure a proactive approach towards ensuring a harmonious politico-military relationship and ensuring that the prestige and honour of the armed forces is maintained at a time when the bureaucracy, police and para-military forces are increasingly growing assertive.

- **Risk vs Ethics and Duty as Conscience Dilemmas**. Understanding the Risk vs Ethics and Duty vs Conscience Dilemmas is very important for military leaders at all levels. Service in the armed forces is risky. Risk takers are more prone to making mistakes and getting into trouble. If you crucify honest mistakes, it will lead to a loss of values like initiative and courage. So you need to institute measures to educate these risk takers on the moral and ethical dimensions of their actions so that an element of caution creeps into the risk, making it a trifle more balanced. It is a tough call and has to be honestly addressed. History is again replete with generals having to go into battle with a 'sinking feeling' that the higher decision, though not the morally right one, was probably the only decision left in the overall national interest. Operation Bluestar and Operation Pawan in Sri Lanka are two classic examples wherein the Indian armed forces placed duty above everything else, suffered heavy casualties, but came out with their heads held high because of stable and focussed leadership. More recently, this issue has assumed fresh significance with a number of retired US generals, included Gen Anthony Zinni and Gen Shinseki, coming out with scathing attacks against Donald Rumsfeld for riding roughshod over sane professional military advice and going into Iraq in 'cowboy style' with inadequate troops for peace-enforcement and peace-keeping. The outburst, it appears, is a long pent up conflict between duty and conscience, something that gets extremely difficult for senior military leaders to resolve in such situations. In the final analysis, it will be inner strength that is bolstered by strong ethics and values that will show the way.
- Developing your subordinates for tough and varied combat conditions is another aspect of today's fluid battlefield environment. Training them for instinctive decision-making under pressure (so crucial in the air force) will only happen if they are capable of independent thought and action, of doing the right thing at the right time.
- Senior military leaders like winners, but they must realise that all winners don't do the right thing. Right values are neither safe, easy nor advantageous. Practitioners of right ethics and values often lose, but they still go ahead and lose because they defend the values that have been ingrained in them.[13]

- Complex decision-making at senior levels also involves the dilemma of Right vs Right. How do you resolve an issue that pits Truth vs Loyalty or the Individual vs the Team or Short-Term Gains vs Long-Term Ones? Do you stick to a rule-based solution or a 'care'-based one, or do you decide where the greatest good for maximum people is achieved?

- **Transformational Leadership**: Transformational leaders are those who seek, by means of moral example, to persuade their followers to adopt a goal that is in the best interest of the Service. Example is not the main thing—it is the only thing. The transformational leader, therefore, is neither morally nor intellectually arrogant because his success does not depend upon merely reaching a certain objective, but rather upon convincing his followers that the goal is worthwhile. It is the goal of the transformational military leader to create a morally courageous, physically tough and technically proficient force that will continue to realise its objectives in the future even when the present leader is no longer present.[14] "We" and not "I" is the hallmark of such leadership.

- **Humanity**. Combat, peace-keeping and peace-enforcement operations run the risk of failure despite all the training, contingency planning and tactical brilliance, and, at times, the only intangible element that propels the final push that transforms defeat into victory is a leader's ability to call on hidden reserves of endurance and will power in the men he commands. This, invariably, is possible only if a leader is humane, leads from the front and has a genuine 'feel' for the troops he commands.

- **Professional and Personal Ethics**. Unlike the ongoing debate that is raging in 'civvy' street and the corporate sector on the need to separate professional ethics and conduct from personal conduct and ethics, military leaders have no such choice. Their lives are so entwined with those of their subordinates that every action of theirs is a mirror for others to emulate, and, therefore, the crying need for consistent ethical and moral standards, both at work and at home.[15]

## A Case Study

In June 2005, Col Ted Westhusing, a 44-year-old leading military Ethicist, scholar and a full professor at West Point was found dead in Baghdad with a single gunshot wound to the head. The army concluded that he had committed suicide with his Service pistol. He was, at that time, the highest-ranking Service officer to die in Iraq. A note found in his trailer seemed to offer some clues as it read, HOW IS HONOUR POSSIBLE IN A WAR LIKE IRAQ! Col Westhusing had volunteered to serve in Iraq because he was upset with reports of unethical practices in Iraq and wanted to try and help in stemming the rot. It was only a matter of time before he is reported to have received a complaint that a private security company had cheated the government and committed human rights violations. He reportedly confronted the contractor and conveyed his concerns to superiors who launched an investigation. In e-mails to his family, he seemed very upset that traditional military values such as honour, duty and country had been replaced by profit motives where the military had come to rely on contractors for jobs once done by the military. His family will never know whether Col Westhusing actually committed suicide because he was depressed or was done in by the contractors.[16]

## Conclusion

Stephen Covey in his book *The Seven Habits of Highly Effective People* clearly mentions that managers are trained to do a thing right, and leaders to do the right thing. The military needs leaders because good leaders almost always turn out to be good managers, whatever their style may be. As far as the Indian armed forces are concerned, it would augur well to see the signs emerging from Iraq and the conduct of the occupying Coalition forces. The saying that forewarned is forearmed rings true in the case for enhanced awareness of the need for ethical and value-based military leadership. Education and awareness programmes are vital for integrating these values in doctrine and training plans. Ethics are never dispensable. They are an integral part of human survival. But in the 21st century, such survival will be more complicated and precarious than ever before, and the ethics required of us must be correspondingly sophisticated. Finally, ethics are absolutely necessary to tackle the pressure of truth, occupy the moral high ground and reinforce the position of the military as the vanguard of a nation's leadership.

*If it is not right, do not do it.*
*If it is not true, do not say it.*

— General Marcus Aurelius
Roman General

## Notes

1. Aristotle, *Nichomachean Ethics* (Indianapolis: Bobbs-Merril, 1985).
2. Gen (Retd) Shankar Roy Chowdhury, *Culture and Military Ethics* (Ramakrishna Math-Vedanta Kesari).
3. Ibid.
4. Aristotle, n. 1.
5. Human Rights Watch Report 2004, "The Road to Abu Ghraib."
6. Dr. David L. Perry, *Strategic Leadership* Course (US Army War College, 2005).
7. *Seven Army Values-US Army Field Manual* 22-100.
8. USAF, *Little Blue Book*.
9. Chinese White Paper on Defence, People's Republic of China (PRC) State Council Information Office, December 2004.
10. Maj Gen Jerry E. White, "Personal Ethics vs Professional Ethics," *Air Power Journal*, Summer 1996, pp. 30-34.
11. n. 5.
12. Jack Ward Thomas, Chief USDA Forest Service, Society of American Forests Convention, Portland Maine, November 1995.
13. Norman Shwarzkopf, "Ethical Leadership in the 21st Century," talk at the Institute for National Leadership, February 2004.
14. Thomas, n. 12.
15. n. 5.
16. Who Killed Cod Tel Westhusing, Blogs at www.moreaples@hotmail.com

# 11
# On Command and Leadership

*Jasjit Singh*

*National safety would be endangered by an Air Force whose doctrines and techniques are tied solely on the equipment and process of the moment. Present equipment is but a stop in progress, and any Air Force which does not keep its doctrine ahead of its equipment, and its vision far into the future, can only delude the nation into a false sense of security.*

— Gen Henry H. "Hap" Arnold, USAF

The terms command and leadership in military institutions are mostly employed synonymously. On the face of it, this appears logical; but a closer scrutiny reveals a degree of distinctness that is often lost in the assumptions of synonymy. At its simplest and crudest level, one could assume that a military person could be a leader even if he does not hold command authority: his authority emerges from his leadership acumen and ability. On the other hand, a person may be in command but not able to exercise leadership whether due to limitations of his personal traits (especially will power and or professional competence) and/or shortcomings, due to numerous other reasons. However, there is no doubt that command and leadership in military forces are deeply interlinked elements.

To be able to grasp the intricacies of military leadership, we will need to explore the issues related to command. Very often, a commander is seen to be giving orders in the execution of which he may not be personally involved or be a party, while a leader would have to be involved, at least conceptually if not physically, with the execution of a mission that he leads. The successful commander would, naturally, know when to command and when to lead. But the leader would have to lead and exercise influence every time if he has to play the role of a successful leader, and possess the skill to create conditions for organisational success to accomplish the missions effectively.

In ancient times, the distinction between command and leadership was much more diffused compared to modern militaries. Military commanders also had to be leaders if they were to succeed in battlefields. Alexander stands out as clear example. But with the complexities of modern warfare increasing exponentially, especially during the past two centuries due to industrialisation of warfare, the two terms imply somewhat different attributes even though each subsumes the other. One of the simplistic ways of differentiating command and leadership in modern military systems emerges from the relative location of the person on the battlefield: leaders would be found at the front, while commanders would be somewhere at the back. And this is most visible in air forces where the leaders at the head of combat missions (or captains of transport aircraft and helicopters) are normally also fairly young though they carry an enormous burden of responsibility for national defence. A very small number of the total force actually engages in combat situations while the overwhelming proportion supports their missions in myriad ways. And the very nature of air forces ensures that the number of leaders of combat missions remains very small, often less than the number of commanders up the chain. For example, a mere 35 squadron commanders led the Indian Air Force (IAF) in actual combat in 1971; and the number, as during the Kargil War, may well be much smaller in future. This is what led Winston Churchill to say after the Battle of Britain, "Never before in the history of human conflict has so much been owed by so many to so few."

In view of the above, it is important to understand the difference between the operational environment as it normally exists at the frontline and in the rear echelons. Some of these may be summarised as follows:

| At the Frontline in Contact with Enemy | At Command HQs and Above |
|---|---|
| Demands courage, stamina and strength, personal example in leading from the front and the confidence of those being led for tactical effect. | Demands vision, conceptual ability to deal with complex multiple current and future systems/tasks for strategic effect. |

| | |
|---|---|
| Emotionally highly stressful, fear and immediacy of threat. | Emotionally complex but less stressful, remoteness of threat. |
| Leadership direct, influencing a few, and three-dimensional orientation (individual, technical, and tactical). | Leadership direct over a few, but indirect over many formations, subordinate commanders and leaders, orientation mostly operational and strategic which would still encompass the three-dimensional orientation. |
| Far removed from political influence and potential restraint. | Directly in contact with political leadership, direction and restraint, subject to constant review and, hence, changes in plans. |

Note: Adapted from Charles F. Hawkins "Toward a Theory of Military Leadership."

It is obvious that the senior commanders would normally have gone through the earlier stages of leadership at tactical and operational levels. But if the time gap between the early periods of direct leadership and indirect command at a later stage is large (as would happen in militaries which have long periods of engagement and service, with retirement ages high), the disjunction between strategy and tactical action could widen. This would be further influenced by the effects of rapid changes in technology. This is one reason why military forces try to keep the force (including leadership at the top) profile younger. Pakistan, for example, almost routinely picks its air chief from the lower end of an already younger panel of potential leaders in the early to mid-50s (compared to ours who mostly get around two years or so at the head of the Service before retirement at 62 years). China has recently laid down the upper age limit for command leadership of combat formations all the way up and the average age of People's Liberaton Army (PLA) commanders has already come down for officers from the late 70s to late 50s and will come down further in the coming years as the policy announced in the 2004 Defence White Paper takes full effect.

At the same time, in order to meet these and diverse other requirements of leadership, command and management of the military force, the senior leadership of tomorrow would have to be fully conversant with the realities of the transformation of war and armed conflict, on one side, and the nature of the evolving international order, on the other. The latter may appear far removed from the profession of fighting. But the fact is that the nature of inter-state relations has a profound impact on the nature of war itself. The presence of nuclear weapons with some countries, for example, which define their power equations with other nuclear and non-nuclear nations, would naturally affect the extent and scope of any war that the country may get engaged in. In fact, Pakistan's acquisition of nuclear weapons has fundamentally altered the nature of war in the subcontinent over the past two decades, providing its strategy of covert war much greater confidence of India being restrained from employing its much stronger conventional military for punitive responses by the risk of nuclear escalation and consequent holocaust.

In essence, it is clear that while leadership at the frontline may or may not include command responsibilities, the command responsibilities at the higher operational and strategic levels would inevitably include the dominant need to exercise leadership. Command is a full-time responsibility that subsumes leadership duties. At the same time, leadership is a full-time duty that is influenced by command decisions and directives. Leadership has to be synergised with command functions and goals to achieve the requisite effect on military operations. Unlike command at junior levels, the senior leader is watched by an increasingly wider community even beyond the military to the society at large. Hence, his conduct, character and personal integrity is subject to a much larger observation than that of a junior leader whose actions would normally affect a smaller and, hopefully, well-knit military unit where individuals have a common tactical role directly under the commander. This also raises the issue of integrity at the junior level as well as at the senior leadership level. There may be a view that personal integrity would be of greater importance at the junior level because of the direct influencing role could be affected by it, and by similar logic, the professional integrity of the senior leadership becomes more critical since it would affect the performance of the military force at large. But in reality it may not be possible or even desirable to dissect integrity in this manner. The truth is that integrity is the essence of both leadership and command as an integral element where personal and professional integrity are deeply enmeshed.

Fighting and winning a war is the central purpose for which states keep military forces. Therefore, this is the cornerstone of the existence of military power. The military leadership is the only professional institution that is expected to win wars, but this is subject to the caveat of having to be in tune with the political and strategic objectives set by the national leadership. In fact, contrary to general belief which focusses on an absolutist approach to military victory (mostly measured in terms of its kinetic effect on the enemy),[1] these political objectives define the military and political contours of "victory" and defeat. And when we see the fundamental nature of democratic governance and leadership, it becomes clear that this definition itself would contain many elements of compromise and constraints. For example, restraining the IAF in 1965 from attacking the Pakistan Air Force in East Pakistan was a political decision based on questionable grounds which led to a large number of IAF aircraft being destroyed by Pakistan Air Force strikes, forcing the IAF into a dubious defensive strategy. Even in the west, the IAF was not permitted to attack Peshawar air base (from which the Pakistan Air Force launched its first strike on Pathankot on 6 September, 1965) till the September 13. But besides the constraints and ambiguities of political goals, what the military leadership of today and tomorrow would also be faced with is the changing dynamics of modern warfare. At its simplest is the differences between "low intensity warfare" often also called "asymmetric warfare" or "4th Generation" warfare and a full-fledged "conventional warfare" which is further made more complex by the presence of nuclear weapons and the divergent doctrine and strategy for their employment by the contesting states.

At the root of the issues involved is that military power serves as the instrument of the political aims in achieving the nation's national interests that require the use of force. Clausewitz had gone even further to say that war is a continuation of politics by other means, thus, defining the supremacy of politics and political aims in the employment of military power. Hence, it is important that the military leadership, especially in a highly professional fighting force, should never lose sight of the political goals rather than getting carried away by military objectives which at times may lead to contrary, or at least, divergence from, political aims set for the employment of military forces. The only exception would be that political aims are also subject to change, often by the nature of responses of the international community, or from domestic political pressures or even as a consequence of reassessment of the political interests in the context of a significant changed/changing military situation on the battlefield or international politico-diplomatic responses which could escalate to a military threat (like that by China in 1965) or even intervention. The example of the 1971 War is symptomatic where the original aim was far more limited than what emerged as the military operations progressed.[2]

Military leadership and commanders at all levels need to imbibe the reality that the nature of war has changed in fundamental ways even, in the case of a full-fledged conventional war, as a consequence of technological changes in the past few decades. As noted earlier, far more firepower is now in the hands of the junior leadership than at any time before in human history. That itself demands at least an understanding of strategy and strategic effect at all level of leadership that could result from tactical action, leave alone operational art. Introduction of tactical nuclear weapons of even small yield at the tactical leave would inevitably escalate, leading to its being more strategic rather than remaining, as often believed, a mere battlefield weapon.[3] A regular dialogue between the political and military leadership on strategy-making is critical; and this has to be undertaken as a peace-time activity specifically examining possible situations and options so that responses during crises would be more realistic and conducive to our national interests. Unfortunately, there is much greater attention to "political directives" for war rather than the value of regular peace-time dialogue between the political and military leadership (especially in a Defence Committee of the Cabinet headed by the prime minister) and Chiefs of Staff Committee (the way it happened in 1947-48 Kashmir War) for clearer, mutually understood limits and capabilities of military power and its employment in war under varying circumstances. Such a process would create a common understanding between the two types of leadership, with the bureaucracy sitting in to ensure that procedures and processes are in tune with the thinking of the politico-military leadership and adjusted for the inevitably changing conditions in war.

Unfortunately, dismantling of institutions like the Defence Committee of the Cabinet and non-establishment of suitable alternative mechanisms have led to a serious deficit in Indian planning its military power for future wars which requires urgent attention. Classical examples stand out from our own experiences. For example, P.V.R. Rao, one of our finest civil servants wrote to the Chief of Army Staff on August 25, 1965 (when Pakistan's covert war in Kashmir was at its peak) conveying the prime minister's authorisation that the armed forces were free to choose their time and place for a counter-attack on Pakistan. But he failed to convey the same to the Chief of the Air Staff (who learnt about the authority a good ten days after the war had started and Pakistan was well on its way to defeat) and the Chief of the Naval Staff; and nor did he address the letter to the Chairman, Chiefs of Staff Committee so that this would then be disseminated to all three chiefs. The failure of the defence secretary no doubt resulted in one of the major handicaps to the lack of joint planning and synergy for the counter-attack on September 6 by Indian Army which would have led to an earlier collapse of Pakistan's military.

The obvious effect is a disjunction (which cannot be filled by the civil bureaucracy in principle and practice) between the political and military leadership's thinking and understanding of the major issues and factors which go into planning the employment of military power for political ends. At the same time, the lack of an institutional Defence Committee of the Cabinet coupled with the prime minister holding the portfolio of Defence Minister for prolonged periods for nearly two decades (1980-1998) further exacerbated the disjunction between the political and military leadership and command, leaving the civil bureaucracy, with limited professional expertise in modern military and warfare, to become the arbiter of military power of the state. One of the major negative trends has been the employment of the army increasingly for the constabulary role for and law and order management (for which large police force and civil service exist but are not made accountable or capable). One effect was the misreading by Pakistan about the Indian military's weakness resulting from prolonged police duties, which tempted its leadership to engage in the Kargil adventure in 1998-99.

The more recent example of the December 13, 2001 attack on the Parliament (when India mobilised its full military power to threaten war but was unwilling to do so) and the more candid discussions among the political leaders and the armed forces chiefs after the November 26, 2008 terrorist mayhem in Mumbai which did not lead to any military action or mobilisation are typical examples of trying to evolve a strategy in the middle of a crisis, with little mutual understanding of even the vocabulary that the two types of leaders use! This is not to suggest that we should have necessarily employed our military power in response to those attacks which themselves came after nearly a quarter century of sponsored terrorism in India by our neighbour, but to emphasise that terrorist attacks have clearly been escalating in sophistication even if the numbers have reduced and our national deterrence with punitive force against such attacks has lost credibility.

Technology inevitably has a strong influence on the decisions military leaders and commanders make at all levels. There is no doubt that rapid advances (of which the end is not in sight as yet) in military technology has a key role in shaping military power and its employment. This, in turn, gets related to the size of the forces – or "mass" – involved. But empirical studies have established over time that it is not technology or mass that leads to military victory, but "force employment" that really constitutes the roots of success. This is a reality that professional military leaders enamoured by technology often ignore. Hence, the caution that Gen Arnold places on it to emphasise the value of leadership vision. But even common sense would tell us that synergy between technology and mass is what would generates the requisite combat power for dominance over the enemy. And this synergising has to go back to the process and purpose of force planning itself and if all the elements of such synergy were not built into future force planning, the efforts to do so during crises and on the field so to say could hardly hold out promise of success. This synergy is the direct function of leadership involved in planning rather than direct command.

Once the requisite assets are created, the commander generates the combat potential from available assets – the "force in being" – and it is the job of for leadership to apply combat power to succeed in the mission. This no doubt tends to give us a somewhat diffused and even confused picture of leadership and command functions. But in reality there is no clear division between the two except, as stated earlier, the way it is exercised at various levels. It is here that the differences in leadership and command begin to make a difference.

It is in this context that we come to the conclusion that one of the most critical attributes required for leadership at all levels is vision – a leader at whatever level he may be can lead effectively only if he has the vision to lead his force to the end of the tunnel and beyond. Leadership vision is not solely the domain of the senior commander, but a vital requisite for a senior commander and a necessary asset for a junior commander as a leader. The only difference is that the nature and relevance of that vision would be somewhat different though integrated in a broader sense to the common vision of military power of the state with the political and strategic vision of the national leadership. There are no predetermined formulations for such vision in wars. As Clausewitz wrote:[4]

> During an operation, decisions have usually to be made at once: there may
> be no time to review the situation or even think it through ...... If the mind
> is to emerge unscathed from this relentless struggle with the unforeseen,
> two qualities are indispensable: first, an intellect that, even in the darkest
> hour, retains some glimmerings of the inner light which leads to truth; and
> second, the courage to follow this faint light wherever it may lead.

In other words, military command and leadership require a very high level of conceptual strength and acumen to rapidly deal with an ever changing situation where issues of life and death are at stake. It may be useful to note the difference between military training and education since the two have different roles at different levels of military command and leadership. Training is required to deal with definitive situations at the tactical/battlefield levels. But the strategic level inevitably implies uncertainties and ambiguity. At such levels, even the concept of "actionable intelligence" can be grossly misleading because rarely would the leadership get exact and timely information. What is critical for success, therefore, is a broad-based education (especially in social sciences and humanities that include history, culture, international relations, psychology, etc.) that provides the leader with the requisite acumen to successfully apply his judgement to deal with (and even preempt) uncertainties that constantly impact on warfare. At the same time, the higher leadership would have to possess the intelligence and discipline to accept the constraints and directions laid down by the constitutional political authority of the state after it has clearly enunciated the advantages and disadvantages of the planned courses of action to the political leadership. Here again, the issue of integrity at every step comes to mind. For example, Colin Powell, by all accounts an outstanding leader, appears to have faltered in not articulating his advice to President Bush that he was not in favour of pursuing a war against Iraq in 1991; though a later public acknowledgement appears to have mitigated the error somewhat. Most successful military leaders would tell you that bold action and conceptual courage can turn even defeat into victory. But the challenges of command and leadership in the military profession do not end here. There are issues of transformation of military power, transmutation of armed conflict, the role of the international geopolitical environment and domestic legitimacy besides a myriad other ambiguities and uncertainties that impinge on the military profession where nuclear weapons by themselves add numerous uncertainties.

Here we may go back to an important aspect that military leaders must be conscious of even if they may have limited role to play in it but would be deeply affected by its variables; and that is the issue of legitimacy (especially domestic legitimacy) of the use of military force for war (or, for that matter, for internal armed conflict). To begin with, we must record that legitimacy of use of force is an illusive concept that is heavily subject to manipulation also. A victory in war normally bestows legitimacy; and failure of actual outcomes to justify the cause for war undermines it, besides making it far more difficult to bring the war to a successful closure, as indeed the US invasion of Iraq on the grounds of its nuclear weapons programme undermined both internal as well international legitimacy of the US decision to go to war and prolonged the conflict, further complicating US policies and success. The politicians, the media and the government's public information strategy and organisation all play a big role in this process. Internal legitimacy derived from internal debate may appear to be divisive, but in reality that debate makes it stronger in the end. Obviously then, it is easier for an authoritarian system or a dictator to generate and stimulate legitimacy than the representative government system. In the face of an isolationist Congress and an impending presidential election, President Roosevelt had to hold back his preference to enter World War II when Britain was at its weakest point in 1940. It was finally nearly a year later that Pearl Harbour provided the trigger for a sudden spurt in internal legitimacy to go to war and every possible resource was invested after that in winning it.

This was due to the fact that unlike authoritarian systems, legitimacy in a democratic government can provide very strong support to military action once it receives society's collective preference in its support. Here we need to note another important aspect much debated in India mostly by the educated civil and military elites: that of laying every issue at the door of "political will" and/or its absence. At a fundamental level, we need to note that in a democratic set-up, the political will should – and barring the aberrations of individual leaders, mostly is – in tune with the national will. And national will in a liberal society takes time to make its impact on the political leadership though once it does so, it also ties down the leadership to a certain course of action in keeping with the collective preference of the society. For example, over the years, even the uneducated Indians became strongly antagonistic to the Nuclear Non-Proliferation Treaty (NPT) basically since they could identify themselves with the idea of haves and have-nots. No elected government, even if it was disposed to make some compromise in this respect, could go against the legitimacy of denial of the NPT as a choice for the country. The shape, strength and direction of political will then become a crucial issue for us in India.

The example of the 1971 War provides us with some understanding of political legitimacy and the issue of a just cause to support it. The government and the media focussed on the genocide by the Pakistan Army (not the most acceptable model of professional armies) and the 10 million refugees who took shelter in India. This was sufficient to not only support the war effort to rectify the situation, but was one of the shining examples of a just war waged by India in support of suppressed people in spite of the fact

202 MILITARY LEADERSHIP FOR TOMORROW

that our interests and policies have sought to discourage ethnic separatism of states and, hence, 1,200 officers and men died fighting for Sri Lanka's unity in 1987-90, threatened by a hardline regime in Colombo on one side and, on the other, a radical militant group (the Liberation Tigers of Tamil Eelam (LTTE)) seeking a separate Tamil state. On the other hand, there are reportedly over 15 million Bangladeshis (with their numbers continually increasing, including when there was a military dictatorship in Dhaka) in India looking for a better life, straining India's efforts to ensure a better quality of life for its own people, but any talk of military intervention to push this illegal population influx would hardly find any support in the country today.

In conclusion, one may say that legitimacy, especially internal legitimacy, is crucial to requisite support to the employment of military force. While military leaders by themselves cannot build such legitimacy, they need to remain the trends in the growth or decline in such legitimacy. At the same time, they must internalise the key elements of such legitimacy – normally built on the national interests and security of the country – while paying serious attention to this process not being divorced from moral considerations. Morality and the military leadership contain complex processes around many psychological and cultural-historical sets of issues. This adds to the logic of ensuring opportunities and sensitive attention to continuing and expanding broad-based education to military leaders as they move up the command and staff chain in the hierarchy.

In the final analysis, the factor of culture (particularly what goes under the nomenclature of strategic culture) impinges heavily on the military leadership and even command and, hence, should be included in any discussion of leadership. At the national level, every country displays the key elements of its strategic culture shaped by history, geography, religious beliefs, etc. through different ways. But one problem that we all face is how to determine which institution of any state may be identified with the determination (and its sustainers) of strategic culture. At best, we can state that at the national level, strategic culture reflects the values regarding the use of force. Colin Gray, writing in the context of American strategic culture explains strategic culture as being:[5]

That culture referring to modes of thought and action with respect to force derived from perceptions of the national historical experience, aspiration for self-characterisation .... And from all of the many distinctively American experiences (of geography, political philosophy), of civic culture, and 'way of life' that characterise an American citizen.

In Indian ancient political thought and value which has clearly survived the centuries of its civilisation, the use of force is considered to be an instrument of last resort. This also implies that most leaders, especially political and civil bureaucratic leaders, are more likely to be guided by this cultural correlate than the military leadership. In a way, we trace it, then, to even today's nuclear doctrine of "no first use" and rely for nuclear defence on a counter-strike strategy in case of a nuclear attack on the country or its forces. This can be seen in our experiences since independence in the preference of most non-military leadership for use of force only as an instrument of last resort. This poses additional challenges for the military leaders and commanders in that they would almost inevitably be forced to use force in a reactive strategy, losing the value of initiative and surprise, the two important factors in military victory and defeat. On the other hand, the military leaders of tomorrow must be well versed in the understanding of Indian culture, value system and the myriad elements of history and the strategic personalities of civil and military leaders.

But closer to the challenges ahead for the military leader is the issue of "military strategic culture." This must take into account two apparently far apart factors: one at the grassroots where loyalty to the unit, regiment and even a particular leader shapes the attitudes of commanders, and at another, the whole gamut of high technology and firepower-based war. US studies indicated in a survey of 1,900 officers undergoing professional military education in institutions in 2000 that "most officers believed that technology, doctrine, and organisation would make it easier for the United States to use force and achieve decisive battlefield victories."[6] But, as noted earlier, technology alone is no substitute for strategic thinking and superior force employment by the military leadership at various levels. The Pakistan

Air Force was unquestionably superior in technological terms (including the absorption of that capability through realistic training over the previous eight years) during the 1965 War with India when the two air forces were nearly equally matched in numbers on the western front. But very rapidly, the force employment and tactical skills of the Indian Air Force pushed it rapidly onto the defensive, and defeat.

However, as one of the leading professional fighting forces in the world, the Indian military is also enamoured by technology and even its jargon. And yet it tended to ignore key capabilities that enhance operational force employment choices. For example, the lack of interest in aerial refuelling which would have allowed the Jaguar strike aircraft to be deployed well beyond the enemy's aircraft combat radius in 1979-80, and the dismissal of the operational importance of the airborne early warning system in favour of low level radars in the mid-1980s[7] indicate inadequate appreciation of the technological changes taking place well after the value of airborne early warning was dramatically demonstrated by the Israeli Beqa'a Valley operations in 1982. And yet, a decade later, the Indian Air Force was so sold on the technological "force multipliers" that it failed to press adequately to take steps against the unplanned 24 per cent drop in combat force level!

The challenge for our military leaders in future would be to identify the technologies that would serve our military objectives, correctly assess when and in what shape they would mature sufficiently to be employed operationally, and work out the procedures and tactics for then optimum utilisation. All these normally take a long time; and have to be situated in the reality that the likely enemy is also working on the basis of access to the same or similar technologies and could be well ahead of us at certain times. Above all the military leadership must recognise and remember that technology is a poor substitute for strategic thinking which should form the base for force employment.

A vital characteristic of military organisations and institutions is the culture of a particular Service that shapes the future leader and his/her deeper values. Each Service has its own unique culture, shaped by its history, organisation, roles and missions, doctrine and theory of war that all go to shape the leader's behaviour. It is not surprising, therefore, that a leader's affiliations and loyalties remain the most important determinants of his views, more than rank, age or combat experience. This is much more visible in the Indian Army leadership, which rightfully takes great pride in the traditions of their regiments going back nearly three centuries in their present form. An officer's branch identity and regimental loyalty is visible on the army uniform whereas the navy and air force subscribe much more to their identification with the Service itself and, hence, able to maintain a more accommodating perspective in joint operations. In the past centuries, the land forces were perceived as the primary repository of a nation's military power, except for maritime powers like Great Britain which created and ruled history's largest empire by its domination of the seas (and, hence, the Royal Navy was treated as the senior Service). The fact that the army in India is the oldest Service and the largest in size adds to the belief that it deserves (as a right) to have a dominant role in the higher echelons of military leadership and direction of war.

This, of course has strong implications for joint planning and operations since the army seeks a dominant leadership and command role in every aspect of joint operations. On the other hand, there is enough evidence today that well after two decades since the passage of the Goldwater-Nichols Act which sought to further promote jointness in the US military, well accustomed to jointness over the previous century and the experience of two World Wars besides many other long and bitter wars, a military leader's Service (and even regimental) affiliation remains the determinant of his attitudes and actions.[8] It is pertinent to note that one of our finest soldiers and army commander in 1965 War, (and the colonel commandant of the Sikh Regiment) virtually sacrificed a Sikh infantry battalion in his desire for it to go into an offensive against the well-entrenched Pakistan Army immediately after it had won a victory fighting bitterly for two days to add to the laurels of an earlier victory on the same date, though decades earlier, and celebrated by the regiment as the Saragarhi Day.

## Notes

1. This is even more noticeable in the case of air and naval warfare. In fact, the focus narrows to the more dramatic air combat segment of air warfare rather

206 MILITARY LEADERSHIP FOR TOMORROW

than the total effect of the employment of air power in its numerous roles by the contestants.

2. Maj. Gen. D.K. Palit, *War in the High Himalayas: The Indian Army in Crisis 1962* (New Delhi: Lancer International, 1991)

3. We need to note that the atomic bombs dropped on Hiroshima and Nagasaki in August 1945 had on unquestionably strategic impact that continues till today, and yet such bombs dropped by aircraft later on were classified as "tactical weapons!"

4. Karl Von Clausewitz, *On War* (New York: Random House, 1943), translation by O.J. Mathijs Jolles.

5. Colin S. Gray, "National Style in Strategy: The American Example," *International Security*, vol 6, no. 2, (Fall 1981) p. 22.

6. Thomas G. Mahnken and James R. FitzSimonds, "The Limits of Transformation: Officer Attitudes Toward the Revolution in Military Affairs," *Newport Paper 17* (Newport: Naval War College Press, 2003), Chapter 3. The officers believed that advanced technology would also allow the United States to engage in high intensity short duration wars with fewer casualties. The assumptions in the Indian military with the new "Cold Start" doctrine are not very different.

7. Author's discussions with the VCAS in June 1986. The government, based on the advice of the military leadership in fact told US Secretary of Defence Casper Weinburger in October 1986 that India would have no problem if the US provided airborne early warning systems to Pakistan!

8. Mahnken and FitzSimonds, n. 6, p . 108.

# Index